The Value of Astrology

from ancient knowledge to today's reality

André Barbault

L'Astrologie Certifiée
Connaissances, Statistiques & Prévisions
(Knowledge, Statistics, Forecasting)
Translated by Kate Johnston

The Astrological Association

Original French language edition published 2006
Under the title *L'Astrologie Certifiée*
© Éditions du Seuil, September 2006
www.seuil.com

This English language edition first published 2014
with kind permission of
Éditions du Seuil
under the title *The Value of Astrology*
by The Astrological Association CIO,
BCM 450, London WC1N 3XX.
© The Astrological Association CIO 2014

Translation by Kate Johnston
French editor: Didier Castille
English editor and layout: Roy Gillett
Cover design: Catherine Keane

A catalogue record for this book is available from the British Library
ISBN 978-0-9502658-8-9

Printed and bound by Lightning Source

Translator's Preface

This is the first time that a book by the eminent French astrologer André Barbault has been translated into English. Of the 40 books that he has written over a lifetime dedicated to astrology, André Barbault regards this one as his testament and we are happy and proud to have made this impressive work available to the English-speaking world.

The inimitable elevated literary style and his extensive knowledge of the French language have made the work of translating this book very demanding. With André's approval we have not tried to imitate his style but have focused on accurately conveying the meaning of what he has to say.

The translation of André Barbault's work is long overdue. He is a challenging astrologer with an incisive critical mind and he is a rationalist who applies the rigour of science to astrological research in order to establish its core truths. His extensive knowledge of symbolism, great interest in psychology, psychoanalysis, ancient history, European culture and worldwide events all come into play in this book which is fascinating to read.

This has been a hugely interesting and enjoyable exercise. It is impossible to read this book without being enthused, educated and enlightened.

Kate Johnston (Translator); Didier Castille (French Editor)

Editorial notes:

André's romance style loses depth and insight when translated into strict English syntax. So this translation keeps the English as close to the French words and their order as possible. We hope this brings readers closer to the originality of André's unique insights.

The English meanings of the French book titles are given in the roman text inside the round brackets after the title. Where an English edition is known, the English title is given in italics.

Acknowledgements

André Barbault's insightful astrology writings have filled numerous books and periodicals and been acclaimed throughout the French speaking world for 80 years. Until now, however, not one of his books has been available in English.

The Value of Astrology offers captivating insights into the origins, classical tradition and modern uses of astrology. As well as André's pioneering and rigorous understanding of mundane astrology, for which he is famous, this book delves beautifully into astrology's relationship with psychology and painting, while also clearly summarising attempts to assess it statistically.

Great credit for making André's wisdom available to the English-speaking world in his unique style is due to the devoted translation work of Kate Johnston, and André's close associate Didier Castille. Both have approached the task as a painstaking labour of love.

The Astrological Association is proud to have been able to sponsor this eminent project. We would like to thank Dr Dorian Greenbaum for her advice and agreement for us to use her translations of Ptolemy's *Tetrabiblos* in Chapter 3.

The Association is also grateful to: Jane Struthers for her meticulous proof reading of the draft copy; Catherine Keane for her beautiful cover design; Frank Clifford of Flare Publications; Wendy Stacey and the Association Board of Trustees for their advice and support throughout the project; Dr. Nichols Campion, Lynn Bell and Monica Domino for reading and commenting on the pre-publication text; and to Trudie Charles for her indispensable endeavours at the end to find those final errors!

Roy Gillett (English Editor)

Contents

Robert Fludd, *Utriusque Cosmi*, tome I, Oppenheim 1617
This reproduction from the Hermetic Museum symbolises
the anthropo-cosmological principle, the unit of the
astrological world where the celestial macrocosm (here
represented by the Sun) merges with the human
microcosm, each human nature living like a vital central
focus in an infinite diffusion. The cosmos is in us just as
we are in it, where an anthropomorphic universe and astral
humanisation meet.

Author's introduction to the 2013 English Edition

It is an honour for this book to be published in the language of Shakespeare and especially so as it was unexpected at this stage of my eighty year long passion for astrology. I am indebted to Roy Gillett for his esteem. Since we met at the Chateau de Rambures Conference which was organised by Charles Ridoux in 2002, and also at the Paris Conference, he has paid me the tribute of dedicating the 2005 Carter Memorial Conference to my work together with a film made by Danielle de Diesbach.

This brings me even closer to the dynamic Astrological Association and to the eminent British astrologers, with whom I have already had the benefit of rubbing shoulders through my rich association with Charles Harvey and Charles E.O. Carter, both of whom spoke French.

It is with great thanks that I would like to wish my English readers a wonderful time as they immerse themselves in the world of Urania.

André Barbault – October 2013

Author's Introduction to the 2006 French Edition

In 1975 the book *Connaissance de l'astrologie*, now out of print, was published by the Éditions du Seuil. The present work is an updated version, with new input that is so enlightening that it justifies some changes.

However, this reprint in itself answers an editorial need. There is no work of this genre in the bookshops, that's to say no books by astrologers that present a complete overview of astrology. Certainly, there is no shortage of books on this subject, but their authors stick to the areas that inspire them, however large their input. This book, from the outset, plunges deep into the heart of the subject and encompasses the whole world of astrology: astrology's fabulous history, its magnificent philosophy as well as the prodigious psychology which it shows itself to carry are all addressed with regard to a general debate of the issue, of a confrontation of the faith it elicits and a real reason to doubt it; it also deals with the problems it poses, the statistical debates, exemplary applications (some unpublished), all of which lead to the epistemological renewal of an informed knowledge.

It's not only the makings of a 'de-occulted' astrology that we can see in this book. Another reason for republication is that, a quarter of a century later, the evidence in support of the art of Urania is more complete. In fact, since that time, a huge amount of new documentation has been added to the statistically verified records, this time at the highest level, on a demographic scale and the results are of such importance that this not-accepted knowledge is now at a decisive turning point in its history and on the way, at last, to being recognised.

What's more, a completely new chapter, 'Astrological Forecasting; the Facts' shows a perfect example of theory and practice coming together. There are the results of a long experiment by the author, in which a determined planetary configuration was systematically tested for over half a century, by his repeated forecasting of the coming of the same historical climate at each of its annual reappearances. It was the same with the testing of a long-ranging planetary great cycle which allowed him, over many decades, to make precise historic forecasts and then time the outcome of one of the greatest events of the 20th century; a living illustration of an art that thanks the book of nature for offering up its most beautiful fruits.

Could astrology be in the process of becoming adult now such knowledge is established?

André Barbault - 2006

Chapter 1 - The Art of Urania

For thousands of years, perhaps even since the dawn of time, humanity has interrogated the stars seeking to decipher the enigma of its being and its destiny on Earth. Our first existential anxieties provided a channel for our spiritual energy. By ceaselessly questioning, under the awesome vault of the starry sky, mankind took part in the work of nature, spreading the mystery of what it is to be human across the globe and up to the enveloping sky.

Very early in our history mortals were giving fervent homage to the stars. From the Chaldeans, stationed on their pyramidal towers, to the Incas up on their cyclopean terraces, all ancient peoples worshiped the Sun and, in the silence of night and infinite space, made a cult of the celestial torches. In the beginning the study of the sky combined religion, science and poetry. Indistinguishable from one another, astrology and astronomy were intimately linked to mythology and associated with star worship. It was against this background of paleontological human thought that astrology was founded and that its long history began.

So, has training a questioning eye on the firmament always been absurd? Take the Sun which launches its storms and fantastic eruptions for all to see; with each palpitation at its heart, this planetary body, more than one million times vaster than our globe, causes disruption in a variety of ways - we know the effect of sunspots – and this little Earth is nearly 150 million km away!

What appalling conceit sometimes prompts those who pride themselves on being 'scientific' to believe that when these early peoples applied themselves to the observation of celestial phenomena, they had to have fallen into illusion, error and superstition? Combining their intelligence and their faith to probe the universe and themselves they built a palace of Urania, its dimensions reflecting the size of their spiritual venture. Situated squarely between Earth and sky, *ars regia*, they seem to have wished it to be the crowning realisation of their collective knowledge. When we look back we can see that it is cosmic thought which determines what it is to be a human being. It is not just a matter of heredity, of geographical location, of economic status, or of the civilisation to which we belong: man is also, and even primarily, placed in a celestial setting. Astrology is deeply rooted in our earthly constitution, which is also cosmic, and our globe, being a star among stars, is inseparable from the rest of the world.

Like a ruin smothered by undergrowth, this construct has practically disappeared with the passage of time, so that even the concept of astrology has faded like a distant echo that sends back a message which is not only distorted but unformed. Because this legacy is so distant and uncertain, all interpretations are possible. We can only salvage what we can from the museum that houses this unknown astrology. We grasp ideas, some good some not, but we can only make poor copies; we alter meanings to bring them down to our level and this causes the substance to be lost and denatured. It is best to be aware of this.

It is not surprising then that conflicting simplistic ideas prevail today. On the one hand we have the rationalists who, crossing out at a stroke two millennia of practised, well-studied and well-received ideas, decide (without proof) that astrology is either a false science or a fallacious art. On the other hand we have popular belief, incurably fond of the fanciful and passionate about pointy hats and star-studded robes, according to which we merely have to decipher the commands of the stars to know everything about the mysterious destiny of human beings. This leads us to detach ourselves from the sheep-like behaviour of both sides. Where the former only see a 'daughter of ignorance', the latter only imagine a goddess adorned with the prestige of her amazing antiquity and noble descent. The error is in having only a fraction of the picture. To find the truth we must gather all the pieces of the puzzle.

'To predict the future using a horoscope', that is the only purpose that we ascribe to this royal art. It is certainly understood that this was one of the notable aims of horoscopy, the art of forecast being an early achievement, but to reduce astrology to an exercise in prediction is to have a poor grasp of its meaning. We mustn't forget that, originally, it was the conception and expression of cosmological order, the first step towards the recognition of, and of a personal relationship with, a logos, animating the universe; moreover it is in this role that it has actually shaped societies and life on Earth.

Just as we, along with everything and us, move with the Earth, a movement we cannot feel and which we have only become aware of by observing the stars which are not moving with us, it is also natural for us to be awake during the day and to sleep at night, to have a more interior life in the cold months and an exterior life when it is hot. Yet astrology is ahead of us because the very principles of human biology, which rest on the movement of the Earth in relation to the Sun, are empirically integrated in its vision of things. Moreover, the measurement of and division of time which regulate our life are founded on the relationship of our globe with the luminaries: the solar rhythm of the year and its seasons, the lunar rhythm of the month and the week (in addition to the patronage of the days of the week by the planets).

In human societies the order of the cosmos solemnises natural phenomena. It establishes the layout of sites, the orientation of temples, the regulation of religious festivals and public events, the aim invariably being the smooth running of the world by matching earthly life to the pulse beat of the universe.

At the next stage we see astrological practice used to predict the weather and regulate the lifecycles of plants and animals. It determined propitious times for sowing and planting, for cutting and gathering, for reproduction, shearing and the slaughter of animals.

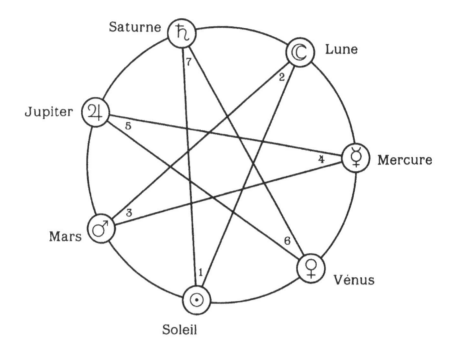

Saturday is Saturn (Saturne), Sunday is Sun (Soleil), Monday is Moon (Lune) and so on.

Astrology is part of our everyday lives, with each day taking its name from the planet that rules it[1]. This diagram, with the planets positioned in the order of their distance and speed, shows that their daily sequence follows a precise rhythm. The yearly solar calendar and monthly lunar one remind us that our measured time is astral.

At a later stage we move seamlessly from natural astrology, applying itself to general phenomena, to the realm of genethliacal astrology which addresses itself to a particular individual. As it descended to popular expression we can see a gradual degradation of its use at the service of the trivial interests of everyday life. We started to research the best time to purge ourselves, to bathe, to cut our hair, beard or nails. Is it any better today when the astrological columns in the press bring the beliefs of pre-Christian Babylon and ancient Rome right in to the heart of modern life, and distribute day in, day out to the natives of each thirty degrees of the zodiac, their ration of predictions about their health, career and love life?

Nothing is greater, though, than the idea that gave birth to astrology. Nothing nobler than the mind that animated it if only by the simple elevation of thought, inherent in the fixed gaze towards the heavenly heights, which inevitably meant that life on Earth was grasped at its highest level.

But before seeking to encounter the face of this stranger or to remove her various masks, we have to overcome an obstacle: the trap of preconceived ideas. We already have the psycho-sociological reality of its history: given the kind of reaction that it generates, it is no longer possible to subject this field of study to criticism, because there is an immediate, automatic furore, and there is nothing more blind than intellectual passion.

It is true that we still have today, as we have always had, devotees of unshakeable conviction who believe in the ideology of a perfect astrology, revealed by an ancient gnosis and conveyed by beams of light and wisdom, shrewd experts in the sidereal way resting on hundreds of thousands of years of observations. On the other side of the coin we have something no less extraordinary. Judge for yourself: ' […] this pitiful stupidity which duped men for so long' (Lalande); ' […] ludicrous chimera [….] such contemptible error [….] this universal folly which has infected the human species for so long ' (Voltaire); '[….] the longest illness which has afflicted human reason' (Bailly); ' […] absurd and shameful facts recorded in the annals of astrology ' (Arago); ' […] one of the weaknesses which has most dishonoured the human mind' (Letronne).

In antiquity, Favorinus amused himself by asking for the horoscopes of frogs and midges and Sextus Empiricus laughed at the embarrassment of a supposed astrologer presented with a donkey and a man born at the same moment, the one destined for the mill and the other for the life of a human being.

In 1968, a new Sextus rejoiced in a tasty farce: using a computer he drew up a horoscope for the serial killer Dr Petiot. He then, in the name of experimentation and research, placed small advertisements in the popular press, offering to everyone, free of charge, a personal computer-generated horoscope. In order to obtain the reactions of people to their horoscopes, he let it be known that he would send a follow-up still free of charge, with a more precise reading (you couldn't lure them in a better way). In the guise of a 'personal' analysis each person received the same document: the shortened text of Dr Petiot's horoscope.[2] The conclusion of this 'sociological' project: the majority of people recognised themselves in the portrait of this well-known criminal. What an amazing victory!

At the end of the 1950s when I was in the company of Françoise Dolto, Jacques Lacan and RP Bruno, at whose house we were preparing a convention on symbolism, Marcel Griaule told us how he had brought to André Danjon of the Institute, then director of the Paris Observatory, several boxes of documentation, evidence of the prodigious and unknown cosmology of the Dogons, a tribe of Egyptian descent in Mali. He had collected them and had them sent straight from the Sudan, where he had spent thirty years of his life studying their lives. Assuming the manner of a magnificent lord delighting in his gift, he believed he had brought the greatest present in the world to the high place of French astronomy. He was extremely surprised and saddened - he couldn't get over it – when he heard this 'big shot' declare, there and then, that the documents in question were not of any interest to him. Danjon had immediately turned on his heel and walked away, saying to him, by way of consolation, 'But do come and see my new telescope!' This noteworthy incident is a perfect illustration of indifference, a coming down of shutters, as if there was an impossible gulf between sky and man, when the reality is that life is primarily a cosmic phenomenon.

In 1980 we were treated to the 'high-ups' in the Rationalist Union conversing publicly about astrology ('It is a closed system', 'It has an answer for everything'), so that is that... Here we are again at the point where, in certain circles, just the word 'astrology' produces a defiant attitude which is enough to call a halt to all impartial examinations of the facts. This is what Rémy Chauvin has to say about his colleagues in rationalist universities:

> Let's pass on the problem of God. It has been accepted for at least two centuries that he does not exist. That is a relief. But there are still a lot of weeds in the fields of the rationalists. Take, for example, the planets. We mustn't talk about the planets; anyone who mentions the planets is suspected of being an astrologer especially if he implies that they can have any influence on whatever that may be. But, you say to me, what about the Moon and the tides? No doubt a rationalist will admit somewhat grudgingly that perhaps the Moon is not completely useless when it comes to explaining the tides. But hold it there; it would be unhealthy to wonder if, because it moves the sea, it couldn't also move the feet of a fly (Brown thought he could detect a definite influence of the phases of the Moon on the behaviour of a variety of insects): but this would mean allowing that stars have an influence on the biological world and therefore allowing astrology. This is no joke; I work in this area and I can assure you that should a young person venture to do a thesis on the influence of the Moon on vegetation and animals he would set everybody against him, and the work would have to be devilishly good to be admitted and even then I'm not sure the thesis would be accepted. So, planetary influences are excluded. That leaves the Sun. It is not a planet but all the same it has a loaded past on the astrological side. It isn't devoid of all influence over the Earth that is

undeniable, it is too big. But please, no unhealthy research on the influence of the Sun in biology! What about sunspots and their variations? Yes, maybe, at last, we can admit that they 'do something' to the Earth. But work on it is only moderately recommended. There are so many attractive things we could be doing, say the rationalists, why just get excited about that? Could it be because you happen to have repressed mystical and frankly astrological tendencies hidden in your subconscious?[3]

Here is another illustration of the same problem: a particularly adventurous astronomer, J. Allen Hynek, head of the Astronomy Department at Northwestern University in the United States who deigned to preface Michel Gauquelin's *Le Dossier des influences cosmiques* says in his introduction that he has done some astrological research with negative results: 'By the way, I was an associate then and the director of the observatory refused permission for me to even publish these negative results for fear that people would think that astronomers could be thought to be spending even the smallest fraction of their time in the study of such a subject!' As if it was frivolous... 'For an astronomer', he added, 'to have any business, however remote, with astrology seems to exclude him from the scientific community.'

But behind this bit of bravura, his superego is still guarded when it comes to the mention of Michel Gauquelin's statistical records (studied later). Our astronomer finds nothing better to say than that they 'cannot in any way justify the practice of casting horoscopes': they only refute and defeat 'astrological humbug'. That is to say that we come now, purely and simply, to 'scientific piracy' in embellishing 'new science' with the plumage of the old knowledge. Urania, who we could have thought of as a sort of Sleeping Beauty waiting for Prince Charming, sees herself changed into a witch, a kind of shameful disease of the human mind...And this same snuffing out of knowledge is repeated with this declaration by the astrophysicist Jean-Claude Pecker, in the magazine *50 millions de consommateurs* (January 1993): 'Astrology is a joke... let's call it entertainment with no scientific value.'

In fact it is clear that when this subject comes up in an authoritative setting, the risk of being ridiculed restricts freedom of thought or the courage to state one's opinions; it is as if it were more important never to look ridiculous than to advance the truth. So we can see what barriers have to be broken down just in order that astrology can be accepted as a simple subject of research. We have to recognise that this has resulted in a lamentable dereliction, and that we need to leave this shameful arena. We must open our minds to reality and re-establish neutral ground, free of superstition and fear. These are the only possible conditions for real research.

It is not that astrology is historically unworthy of this luxury. Remember that until the 17th century, the most illustrious geniuses of humanity had the 'failing' of practising or defending astrology: astronomers, from Hipparchus to Newton including Ptolemy, Copernicus, Tycho Brahe, Kepler and Galileo, philosophers such as Pythagoras, Plato, Aristotle, Plotinus, Seneca or Maimonides, doctors like Hippocrates, Galen, Avicenna and Averroes, theologians like Origen, Albert the Great and Thomas Aquinas, poets like Homer, Virgil, Dante, Ronsard or Goethe... to mention only the more well known.

This reminder presents us with a huge contradiction: the fact that so many of the most prestigious human minds could support something which could only have been a contemptible and stupid superstition... That our greatest men could be mistaken, and in such great number, this makes the human mind very interesting, and at the very least, makes us question the validity of prevailing thought. We know, as the history of science shows, that the role of the scientist is to carry out interrogation on interrogation and then to brand the truth that he professed yesterday as the error that he is proud to demonstrate tomorrow...But what could we be demonstrating tomorrow rather than just intoning something that makes us feel comfortable?

It could well be that the truth – understanding by this term the truth at the core of astrology – will be found quite simply by getting past the discrepancies between the half-errors on one side and the half-truths on the other. This is the first key that we will use in order to enter the entrance hall of Urania's palace.

Chapter 2 - Very Early Sources

Despite rich sources of information provided by archaeology, ethnology, anthropology and psychoanalysis, it is not easy to imagine the sentient thoughts of people from a distant time when faced with the universe. In addition to the access and the perspectives provided by these disciplines, we would, somehow, have to return to the womb of the *alma mater*.

The mind set which is dominant in our modern world gives rise to schizoid tendencies. This mental disposition is marked by a loss of emotional contact with reality, a lack of sensitivity towards the life on this planet. Having become a tipsy king of the Earth, man believes himself to be a creature apart, liberated from nature and having left the path where the things of this world are interlinked, to the point where we human beings are becoming the outlaws of the cosmos.

Early human beings were very different. Attached by necessity to their earthly condition, they respected the laws that connected them to plants and animals, to the elements and to the soil. Their souls were part of the fabric of 'magical participation' stretched between them and the things around them. These people really belonged in the workings of the world. They were at one with the universe; they were even the centrepiece. The conditions were perfect for them to read in Earth's shadows, as in the stars, the signs by which the divine spoke to these people of nature's temple.

Thus, at the most distant time in our history, there sprang up a system of ideas, inspired by the movement of the stars and the growth of plants. These ideas, by combining the life force with the laws of mathematics, connected human life and the systems which regulate it to nature itself and to the laws of the universe. Between the Neolithic era and the age of modern European science this way of thought was the prevalent one. This was especially so in Asia, where it originated and where it played a determining role in the rise of religions, embryonic science, social philosophies, morals and metaphysics. The widespread long-lasting nature of these ideas gave them a truly civilising character.

This 'astro-biology'[4] is the ancestor of astrology, its first precursor. It started to develop, many thousands of years before the Christian era, on the plains of Mesopotamia where the genesis of these ideas was integral to the development of a high culture from an agricultural society, just as the rise of experimental science in modern times is connected to great industries. In fact, by making the vital connection between stars and plants, the relationship between the growth of the wheat in their fields and the movement of the Sun in their sky, Chaldean observers discovered one of the first elements of science.

In the Chaldean civilisation, the harmony of the skies transmitted itself to Earth and to terrestrial beings in a unitary vision of nature, mankind and the universe. They applied the idea of numerical relationship, established by the measurement and calculation of celestial phenomena, to the sequence of events on Earth. We see them relating the impersonal mathematical laws of recurring astronomical cycles to the rhythms of vegetal life in the concept of a general unity of life, nature and the law.

There was a definite step in the direction of astrology after the emergence of the idea of a unity, or an interchange between the lives of celestial bodies and those of terrestrial bodies; and if the lives of human beings are also involved, it is because we are not fundamentally different from vegetal life or from nature, a construct resulting from the notion that human law and cosmic order are one and the same.

Every town in Mesopotamia had its temple-observatory in the shape of a tower or a tiered pyramid with the angles orientated to the four cardinal points. This 'sky hill' or ziggurat, which housed the doctors of the priesthood, was intended to link the Earth with the sky and had at its summit the sanctuary of a god.

The Chaldean astrology practised here was based on a pre-existing scientific astronomy founded on methodical observations, calculated in order to predict the evolution of time. Already it had become an 'astronomy based on place', and in particular it is an astronomy which looks at angular movements. The forecasts and predictions drawn from it were concerned with the fate of the sovereign and the state, and this allowed the establishment of an agricultural calendar and a calendar of religious ceremonies. All the important acts of public life were subjected to astral interpretation; for example, everywhere on any temple or palace are numerous inscriptions of the type: 'I, so-and-so, king of Assur and of Chaldea, I built this temple in honour of my lord, at a propitious time...' The documents relating to these ancient times go back to four thousand years B.C.E, but the first epigraphic attestation featured the celebrated prediction of Sargon of Akkad (2400 B.C.E.): this was a forecast based on an observation of Venus and it refers to the founder of the dynasty of Akkad. A tablet of baked clay, in a perfect state of conservation, which concerns a portent based on a lunar eclipse:

> The King of Akkad dies and his subjects are safe.
> The power of the King of Akkad will weaken.
> His subjects prosper.

This eclipse occurred on 11 of May (Julian calendar) 2259 years B.C.E and coincided with the death of Naram-Sin, the grandson of Sargon. There are thousands of tablets, conserved in the British Museum, which came from the library of Assurbanipal at Nineveh, and another fifty thousand tablets that were found in the library of the temple of Nippur, south east of Babylon, containing documents spanning the years between 3000 and 500 B.C.E.

The predictions concern the community via their royal representative, but they gradually switch from the king to the individual. Here are some predictions that wouldn't surprise the modern astrologer:

- If a child is born when Venus is rising, his life will be calm, voluptuous; wherever he goes, he will be loved; his days will be long.

• If a child is born when Venus is rising and when Jupiter is setting, later, his wife will be stronger than him.

• If a child is born when Jupiter is rising and when Mars is setting, he will have happiness and will see his enemies brought down.

The passage of a planet across the horizon...These first drops of milk of personal astrology drawn from the breast of Urania (effectively our first historical documents on the subject) form the basis of horoscopy, and we will see the respect due to them from the results of the calculation of probabilities.

It is natural that Chaldean astrology-astronomy was ordered within a generalised, animist and vitalist vision of the world... In ancient writings using the cuneiform script of the Sumerian language - the oldest language known to man - there is an ideogram which shows God in the shape of a star, and what is more, in a number of languages. The word 'God' is derived from a common Sanskrit root *div*, which means 'to light' or 'to shine'. We cast ourselves in this ancient tradition when we invoke the prayer 'Our Father who art in heaven'.

The divine call was first directed at the sky, towards the stars moving high above in another universe, and it is increasingly accepted that a belief in the stars was an essential phase in the general evolution of religions, which were gradually lifted out of animism and fetishism into superior types of worship. The heavens 'tell the glory of God', says the psalmist, and the celestial vault is the gateway to the divine city.

In the resulting spiritual system, the stars are imbued with vegetal energy; at the same time that God is defined as being 'bio-astral'. In the oldest documents, the Sumerian gods are in direct contact with trees and plants. Sin, the lunar god, is associated (as is Osiris in Egypt) with the life force which makes plants grow. The stars are living, animated and divine; the planets are identified with great gods; their movements express the activity of the gods incarnated in them, divine regulators of natural life, vegetable, animal or human. These nomadic stars which move in their sky become the 'interpreters' of the spiritual powers with which they are assimilated.

The official religion of Babylon is a religion of destiny imposed by the gods.[5] The rule of destiny, with its qualification of time, is established by the link with the divine, with history and with the world. Above all, it is divine will, the gods being the true kings of the universe, from whom, by delegation, the earthly kings take their power. The world of the gods, represented in human form, is only a superior and exemplary representation of the human world. Human beings are objects of fate; to live in a time laden with destiny is to participate in destiny. Stones and plants appear to function as objects of destiny and consequently temples, statues, towns and edifices also have a destiny. Thus we can understand the meaning of foundation stone ceremonies and the dedication of a building at a given time when the king or the priest acts for the deity, in a procedure designed to 'fix destiny'. Destiny can be seen as a pronouncement emanating from a transcendental power, which invests in mankind a purpose or a mission to fulfil; it is a form of determinism which overwhelms us and incorporates us in the cycles of the world. It is not, however, a complete misfortune because we can see ourselves as players in an organic vision of life.

In the Babylonian pantheon, the rule of destiny is administered by a hierarchical community of great gods. While each god has their own task or separate domain, the members of the divine assembly are united by a strong bond and exercise their power collectively. At the head of Sumerian society is the king-priest, the leader of a divine patrimony. He, too, carries an inner destiny (grace, predestination, talents....) and he serves and brings to fruition the actions of the gods as priest and head of society. Mr. David states that this Babylonian notion of destiny constitutes 'the first complete system of civilisation on which we can reasonably hang a string of beliefs, ideas and doctrines which served us well until the dawn of modern times'.

From the plains of Mesopotamia, this nascent astrology spread in ever widening circles, disseminating itself in every direction: Persia, India, China, Arabia, Egypt, Greece.

Likewise in China we see the king-priest of a celestial religion serving as an intermediary between God and men. Again we have the union of astronomy, agriculture and law (the agricultural calendar), as well as the basis of social order. This is the imperial cult of the Sky, the emperor being charged with making the unchanging order of celestial motion apply to public life; he is the Son of the Sky. Through this cult human society connected itself astro-biologically to the celestial order. The fall of the first dynasty, that of the Hia, would have been caused by an astronomical error, the occurrence of an unforeseen eclipse of the Sun. Because the Sky had demonstrated by the ensuing chaos that it had turned away from this dynasty, they had to appeal to a new emperor to put right the unrest and re-establish the accord between the Earth and the Sky of which power must be the agent of essential virtue. At their geneses, Confucianism and Taoism were fed by this astro-biological thought. The Tao is the life force of the universe and of man: 'The Tao, which manifests itself in the Sun in the sky, also manifests itself in the heart of man.' If Taoism is directly related to astrology, Confucianism also models human nature on the nature of the universe and establishes a moral code based on the laws of the sky.

In India, the same basic thought forms the root or the framework of the principal philosophical pathways. It is evident in the bio-solar religion of the Veda, and the speculations of the Upanishad lead to the identity of the human soul and the soul of the world, while the techniques of yoga are related to a vitalist theory of the harmonious relationship between microcosm and macrocosm. For its part, Buddhist thought comprises a philosophy of nature combined with astronomy; it adopts the notion of an impersonal law which gives moral support. Being astro-biological philosophies, the Sankhya and the Vaisheshika are neighbours of Taoism, and Jainism carries strong traces of it; the appearance of the notion of universal love is historically linked to the affirmation of universal astronomical law.

Judaic and Islamic monotheism were both equally subject to astro-biological influence, because the idea of a single god emanates from the idea of the unity of the universe, coming from this concept in the same way that the solar god rapidly became the supreme god, the preponderant divinity in the polytheist pantheon.

Astrology came to Egypt much later. There, it took on a stellar character with the establishment of the triple connection between the start of the Nile flood, the solstice in Cancer (the scarab) and the heliacal rising of Sirius (Sothis). The civil calendar was founded on these phenomena: when this star, the brightest in the sky, rises in the east with the Sun, the great flood renews the fertility of the earth which fills the granaries of the country. The rising of Sirius was also used to forecast the state of the nation. The twelve signs of the zodiac appear on the ceiling of the Ptolemaic funerary vaults.

The Hellenic civilisation gave its own definitive structure to astrology. Its various philosophical systems made contributions which were always in keeping with astro-biological thought. Greek science or 'wisdom', as shown in the writings of physicians such as Thales, Anaximander and Anaximenes, affirms a belief in the essential and substantial unity of the world. The underlying dogma of astrology was created here: the unity of man and the universe, the interdependence of the part and the whole. With Pythagoras (the title 'mathematician', later held by astrologers, was invented in his school), this universal accord expresses itself in harmonic, rhythmic, numerical and geometric ways. The philosophers of the Eleatic school, Herakleides, Empedocles, Leucippus, Democritus and Anaxagoras, applied this connection between man and the world to the laws governing the elements. In the Socratic school, Plato makes a huge contribution with his propositions in the *Timaeus*, a book which will become the breviary of astrologers: the world is one, it is a living being, the stars are living gods, the creation of human beings on Earth is brought about by the cooperation of all the planetary gods; they are imitations of the world which is itself an imitation of God, a theme taken up later by Philon and others. Later, Aristotle helped to determine the basic rules of astrological interpretation with his theory which relates the four elements to the four elementary principles: hot, cold, dry and wet. But it was primarily the Stoics (Zeno, Chrysippus...) who contributed most to the elaboration of astrological theory when they based the influence of the stars on the notion of 'sympathy', expressing the epic nature of the myths in astronomical or cosmogonic allegories, and completing the idea of man-microcosm...In medicine, Hippocrates founded the principles of astro-biology in applying to the human body the measure of the rhythms that astronomers observe in the universal body (cycles of illness, critical days, etc.). This cosmological medicine gave birth to the astrological idea that there is a link between the four elements and the four Hippocratic temperaments, a correlation which continues to make a fortune for today's astrologers.

According to Pliny, the great astronomer Hipparchus steadfastly believed 'in the connection between the stars and man and that our souls are a part of the sky'. One of his astrological texts is the *Commentary on the Phenomena of Aratus* inspired by *The Treatise on Phenomena* of Eudoxus of Cnidus. It essentially fell to Ptolemy to make an appraisal of astrological tradition. The Hellenic civilisation opened itself permanently to astrology with the arrival of Berossus (around 280 B.C.E.), who came to Cos from his natal Mesopotamia to teach, as did his contemporary Conon of Samos, a friend of Archimedes. The Stoics were their first disciples and collaborators. They supplied them with their essential tools and introduced them to the sanctuary of philosophy; they were followed by the Neo-Pythagoreans and by the Neo-Platonists.

It is thus that natal astrology took shape in Greece. Freed from the primitive images of early peoples and from the imaginary shapes and myths of oriental astrology, the Hellenic astral religion gave birth to spiritual entities that were perfect and immortal. The mythology belonging to the Greek Pantheon had the effect of hiding the direct relationship between star and god behind the bio-cosmic transformation of divine will into the laws of nature, the Stoic Posidonius putting astrology in the same category as other general theories about the forces of nature. In this spiritual universe an elaborate cosmology is linked to a doctrine of correspondences (a doctrine of universal sympathy - astrological tenets being founded on the principle *similia similibus* – applied to the unity of the cosmos and the interdependence of all its constituents), again one of the constituents of the philosophical foundation of astrology.

This influence was openly recognised by a large sector of Hellenic civilisation. It fashioned the tragedies of Aeschylus, Sophocles and Euripides. It inspired the work of Homer: the Homeric hymns to Apollo and Aphrodite as well as the *Iliad*, which reflects the anthropocentric religion of the time. Hesiod also wrote about it in *Works and Days*. Architecture and sculpture express the same thought. The symbolic value of astrology is depicted behind temples and sanctuaries erected to the deities: Zeus, Poseidon, Diana; the most beautiful masterpieces of statuary that portray the astral divinities for all eras, the only lasting human prototypes. This is where the astro-mythic dream of our origins gave birth to the most prestigious creations of art and culture.

Rome continued along this path. Varro and Figulus made the scientific rules of the 'mathematicians' (previously called the 'Chaldeans') available to ordinary people. In his *Georgics*, a true astrological almanac before its time, Virgil put his poetry to the service of natural astrology. Manilius sang to the beauties of the sky in his *Astronomica* and celebrated astrology as a divine revelation reserved for noble souls. Seneca dedicated a part of his *Natural Questions* to him for initiating his belief in the influence of the stars; for Lucian, Horace, Persius, Quintilian, Tacitus and Macrobius it was the same. Cicero and Sextus Empiricus were major opponents of astrology. They witnessed the damaging spectacle of astrology in the hands of charlatans, something that was bound to accompany the moral degradation of a civilisation falling into decadence. But the great families and the emperors had their official astrologers: Octavius, Augustus (who stamped silver coins with his natal sign of Capricorn), Tiberius, Agrippa, Otho, Vespasian, Domitian, some of them having even become adherents or experts, like Titus, Marcus Aurelius, Septimus Severus and Alexander Severus...This was history rich in colourful anecdotes.

Looking at the world as a whole, we must not forget the astro-biological civilisation of America before Columbus, that of the Mayans and Aztecs. At the height of the Mayan civilisation, between 400 and 600 C.E., Copan was a city of priest-astronomers in their observatories. A rectangular temple stood at the top of a terraced pyramid, as in Babylon, and was orientated towards the four cardinal points, just like a Chaldean temple or a Chinese palace. Here maize was venerated in a cult which celebrated the periodic renewal of the life force that is associated with the sun-god, a role played by wheat in Chaldea or in the cults of Osiris or Demeter.

It should also be acknowledged that Christianity owes something to the influence of astro-biological thought. In the Gospel of St John, Christ is presented initially as being the true light and as having the quality of immortal life, and is thus incorporated into a bio-solar god that has been spiritualised by the philosophical influence of ancient Greece. In addition, the celebration of the Lord's nativity takes place at midnight on the winter solstice, the moment in the year when the Sun is at its lowest, a perfect symbol for the return of the light. For the passion and resurrection of Christ – the twelve apostles forming a zodiac for this Sun -

the Church set the date close to the spring equinox, on a Sunday, a day dedicated to the Sun. Moreover, the early Christians prayed facing east, towards the rising Sun. In addition the ethic of universal love comes from the belief in astro-biological solidarity, in a universal 'sympathy' between all living creatures; the ideal of one-ness which came from an astronomical source. Remember also that on the tympanum of the great doors of various cathedrals there is a cross surrounding Christ formed by the fixed signs of the zodiac: as we can see in Angoulême, Arles, Burgos, Canterbury, Chartres, Moissac, etc., the four signs have become evangelical symbols, the bull for St Luke, the lion for St Mark, the eagle for St John, as well as the angel of Aquarius for St Matthew. The cosmic nature of Christianity still endures with the resplendent rose windows of the cathedrals with their twelve zodiacal-apostolic branches. So the Church is enveloped in its cosmological atmosphere.

It does not seem excessive to recognise that life in ancient civilisations was, as a general rule, dominated by astrological ideas. On all continents the law of the sky presided over the order of terrestrial life. Empires were organised in harmony with the march of the stars, their social structures reflecting the cosmic order. Everywhere temples and altars were modelled on the cosmos. The pyramid with its seven planetary terraces orientated towards the cardinal points, from the top of which the priest-astrologer-astronomer observed the stars, can be found in such disparate places as Mexico, China, Chaldea and Angkor. The calendar is an astronomical programme, concerned with nature, politics and religion; social rites, as well as customs and beliefs, form part of the laws that the sky imposes on nature as a whole. Religions - principally Taoism, Manichaeism and Mazdaism, but also Buddhism, Confucianism and Christianity – have taken root in cosmic-biological thought. We could say that, up to a given point in time, symbolic astrological thought was intertwined with the religious esotericism of all the ancient civilisations at the same time as it was predominant as a way of thought.

Chapter 3 - Grandeur, Decadence and Renaissance

When astrology came to the west it embarked on a conquest of civilisation. It permeated medicine through the Salerno school, from Hippocrates to Arnaud de Villeneuve and Marsile Ficin by way of Celsus, Galen and Avicenna. Traditional medical astrology was disseminated by works such as the *Passionarius* by Gariopontus, the zodiacal poem *Flos medicinae* and *Regimen sanitatis Salernitanum*, the Salernitan Rule of health which gave rise to the *zodiac melothesia* which equates each sign with a part of the human body.

In the Middle Ages the movement was principally taken up by the Arabs. Albumasar wrote the *Flowers of Astrology* and the great Albategnius wrote his *Treatise on the Benefits of Astrology*, which established a system of separating the sphere surrounding the Earth into astrological divisions. Other astrologers such as Ibn Yunus, Al-Biruni, Ibn Esra, Haly and Almansor expounded the technical methods. The philosopher Alfarabius, only touched upon lightly by Averroes, was also inspired by this movement but went on to undermine astrology in a jumble of formulas, divination and superstition.

At this time, the Church was promulgating adherence and disapproval. Saint Dionysius the Areopagite, Saint Caesarius and Saint Jerome all demonstrated their acceptance of natural astrology. Saint Augustine first accepted Manichaeism and astrology, then rejected them both. After Johannes Scotus Erigena, Albert the Great took the subject up again and introduced astrology to Saint Thomas Aquinas who, in over two hundred pages of his *Summa*, lays out his acceptance of astrology and looks judiciously at both the possibilities and the limits of the determinism of the stars. Some popes such as Leo III, Silvester II, Honorius III and Urban V were the friends or protectors of astrologers, but, faced with a practice that knows no limits and undermines the existence of free will, the Council of Trent opposed astrological prediction without going as far as rejecting the essence of natural astrology.

The prosperity which led to the golden age of our knowledge started from the 11th century. It began with Dante whose *Divine Comedy* is a cosmological epic and is true to the art. Alfonso X of Castile, known as 'The Wise', studied alongside Alchabitius and established the Alfonsine tables, used for both astronomy and astrology. Charles V, the Wise, was himself also a practitioner (an exhibition at the National Library of France showing some works and manuscripts from his library has incidentally draw attention to his astrological pieces). Campanus gave his name to a theory about the astrological sphere and Cardinal Pierre d'Ailly considered himself a great astrologer in his time. It is impossible to mention all their contemporaries or those who came before or after, such as Roger Bacon, Stoeffler, de Novara, Schoener, Fernel, Agrippa…

Paracelsus deserves a special mention. He was a doctor as much as an astrologer and alchemist whose hermetic thought, in the tradition of Plotinus, made him a great theorist. His work was a great poem about man, nature and God.

The great astronomer Johannes Müller, better known as Regiomontanus, gave his name to a system for dividing the sky astrologically. Luca Gaurico, professor of mathematics at Ferrara, owes it to astrology that he became a bishop; he was the protégé of Popes Julius II, Leo X, Clement VII and Paul III. Catherine de Medici asked him to cast the horoscope of Henry II before she fastened on the famous Nostradamus. The part played by astrology in Nostradamus's prophesies is speculative as his quatrains are always deciphered *post eventum*, and not without a cacophony from those interpreting them.

Humanist thinkers took up and augmented the tradition of relating the great astronomical world to the small world of humans. Humanist philosophy took up the theory of 'man as microcosm' from the Middle Ages through Scotus Erigena, Alain de Lille, Bernard Silvestris, Bouelles, Agrippa of Nettesheim, Pico della Mirandola and

Hieronymus Cardanus who was a master at the game. Pico della Mirandola was one of the few deniers of the time and his virulence secured him the accurate prediction, by three astrologers, of the year of his death! After Jacques Pelletier du Mans introduced scientific poetry and initiatory speech to France, at the behest of Urania, the scientific poets of the time sang of the sky, the stars and their power over our world, astrological thought being the privileged subject of poetry. It is the same with Maurice Scève with his songs of the *Microcosm*, and the poets of the Pléiade: Du Bartas, Baïf, Rémi Belleau and in particular Ronsard who placed astrology at the centre of his spiritual universe. Montaigne, also, respected this tradition.

The celebration of the five hundredth anniversary of the birth of Nicolas Copernicus provided an opportunity to cite this passage from the great astronomer's *De revolutianibus orbium caelestium libri sex*: 'it is why, if the worthiness of the arts was evaluated according to the matters with which they dealt, that which some call astronomy, others astrology, still others among the ancients, the accomplishment of mathematics, would be the very highest.' Professor L.A. Birkenmejer, of the University of Krakow, established that Copernicus was in full accord with astrology all his life; he practised it as an enlightened amateur and his best friends were astrologers.

While Calvin was one of the fiercist denigrators, carrying Agrippa d'Aubigné in his wake when it came to scepticism, Melanchthon studied it with passion, translating and commenting on the works of Ptolemy. Among the notable names of this time there are numerous astrologers (Scaliger, Leovitius, Moestlin, Magini, Fludd, Wolf...), the prominent astrological works being by Cardanus, Oger Ferrier and Francesco Giuntini, who was a superior in the Carmelite order. Michael Servetus himself wrote *An apologetic discourse in favour of astrology*.

> Man contains in himself a much bigger influence than
> that of the stars; he will overcome the influences if he

lives in righteousness but if he follows his blind
inclinations, if he descends to the class of brutes and
animals by living like them, he no longer rules as the
king of nature, but is ruled by nature.

This declaration by Tycho Brahe establishes the deep
understanding that this great astronomer had of our
knowledge, a knowledge that he was constantly advocating
in his public lectures on astronomy in Copenhagen. Emperor
Rudolf II, who himself interpreted charts, called him to his
court and set him about calculating the *Rudolphine Tables.*

I can pride myself in having tested this truth: man, at
the moment of entering the world, when he can stay
no longer in the maternal womb but starts to live an
independent life, receives a mark, a reflection of all the
celestial constellations that is to say the marks of the
planetary influences, and he keeps this character until
the grave. [...] It does not cost me to boast about this
and with all sincerity because of my thirty years
personal experience.

These are the words of Johannes Kepler, one of the greatest
geniuses of humankind. Astrology had as great a place in his
life as astronomy. He was severe in regard to astrologers in
general and, after a long critical look, was strongly
convinced that the tradition needed cleansing. He left an
entire astrological oeuvre: (in many core works *De
fundamentis astrologiae certioribus*, *Tertius interveniens* and
Harmonices mundi [*Harmony of the World*], in which he states
his third great astronomical law, it is not uncommon to find
astrological references among his astronomical texts); divers
almanacs (his 1618 calendar for the month of May
announced a catastrophe which corresponded with the onset
of the Thirty Years War) as well as some horoscopes (his
birth chart for Wallenstein, a hero in this war, is a historic
document).
  All the zealous enemies of astrology can find to say

about the latter century is that Kepler did horoscopes because he needed to, Leonardo da Vinci by distrustful curiosity and Galileo for amusement. With regard to Galileo, the proof of his scientific interest in the question is as evident as it is for Kepler: the numerous chart interpretations that he wrote, particularly for his family; the particular care he took with the calculations; his recourse to the judgement of other astrologers when a case was delicate; the records he kept that provide proof of his orders for charts; the number of astrological works, carefully annotated in his own hand, contained in his library; the pure astrological research (notably concerning the satellites of Jupiter relative to the influence of this planet)... Moreover, the astrologer Francesco Frisoni, having found the drawing of Galileo's own birth chart carefully drawn up by himself (in two comparative versions, one for 4 p.m. and the other for 3.30 p.m.) was able to prove that the great Pisan was born on 15 February 1564 and not on the 18th or 19th as generally stated. In addition we mustn't forget the zodiacs of San Miniato and those of the chapel of San Lorenzo in Florence, nor the bas-reliefs of the Temple of Malatestiano at Rimini, the frescos of Schifanoia at Ferrara, or all the evidence of written works.

With regard to Isaac Newton, English scientists weren't able to ignore his letters and astro-alchemical writings when they commemorated the bicentenary of his death in London in 1927, and again at the tercentenary of his birth when he was celebrated as the 'last of the Magi'.

In the 17th century there was no longer any consensus and astrologers became more and more isolated figures; we can name D. Fabricius, Vanini, Boulliaud, Cunitz, Malvasia, Kircher, Bourdin, Morin and William Lilly. Gassendi set himself up as the greatest adversary of the age. Leibnitz thought astrology was a simple illusion, but tolerated it in his role of president of the Berlin Academy whose official almanac contained astrological forecasts and whose officials, working in the observatory, drew up birth charts for famous people.

It is the end. We still have Henri de Boulainvilliers who laboured under the sarcasm of Voltaire. Though Pingré, Euler and Bode carried on in an atmosphere of doubt and criticism and Goethe proclaimed loudly and exquisitely the truth he felt to be in astrology, as did Balzac a bit later on, the Zeitgeist is no more. A sign of the decline is the example of J. D. Cassini who, while supporting astrology in private, declared that only astronomy merited interest; from now on he will no longer examine a chart of the sky at birth in an observatory. What happened?

The condemnation and rejection of astrology merits an entire thesis because it is possible to get lost in a morass of conjectures. We believe, and it is commonly said, that the Copernican revolution in demolishing the concept of a geocentric universe effectively destroyed this knowledge, as if it rested on the presumption of a fixed Earth at the centre of the world but, as we have seen, the three scientists who brought about this scientific revolution were astrologers. Copernicus believed that the reality of the Earth turning round the Sun took nothing from the veracity of astrology; moreover he entrusted the manuscript of his *De revolutionibus orbium caelestianum libri sex* to his astrologer friend Rheticus who copied it, formatted it, obtained an authorisation from the King of Saxony to print it as well as give a donation, and gave it to the printers. It is also to an astrologer Practorius that we owe the first exposé of the new system, one that was strongly contested by the most reputable scientists of the day. In his *Tertius interveniens*, thesis 40, Kepler, who advocated the heliocentric system and played a big part in getting it accepted, gives the reasons for this configuration of the sky in relation to the Earth as a means of understanding the movements of the solar system as it appears from down below. Finally, we know that Galileo, who with his telescope provided ocular proof of the validity of this system, told his pupil Paolo Dini that the heliocentric theory 'could not undermine the basis of astrology'. We can round off the historical case by adding that in the second half of the 16 century, while Copernican theory was being rejected by the universities it was mainly astrologers who, paying no heed to the mockery of the scientific world or to the threat of excommunication by the theologians, courageously defended the new doctrine....

The historian A. Bouché-Leclercq declared in his celebrated academic *Greek Astrology*, 'Once the Earth is reduced to the status of a planet and launched into space, the foundation is undermined and the whole edifice immediately crumbles. The only system incompatible with astrology is the one proposed long ago by Aristarchus of Samos, taken up and demonstrated by Copernicus.' It is astonishing that this author has not pointed out that this system was also that of Pythagoras and Philolaos, who he knows are linked with astrological thought. He has also said nothing about the relationship that Copernicus, Kepler and Galileo had with astrology. One can criticise the historical inconsistencies of this historian but, that aside, we still have to ask in what way heliocentricity hampers astrology. No scientific demonstration has been given and we are still waiting.

Actually, the problem is only a simple question of the angle of observation, the principle being that all configuration is a function of its field of application: if we want to study a supposed influence of the cosmic environment on us, Earthlings, we have to by necessity configure the solar system in a geocentric way; in the same way that, *mutatis mutandis*, we would practise a selenocentric system if we live on the Moon, a chronocentric one if we were on Saturn. As for the argument, 'Having been a star, the Earth became a simple planet', it can be turned round against the critic: if the Earth had been the centre of the world, a gigantic star around which would have gravitated other stars obviously of less importance, it wouldn't be so much that the Earth would have been subjected to the influence of these stars than they that would have been subjected to the influence of the Earth. Conversely, being such a small thing in the solar system in which it participates, an aphid next to a mammoth Sun – and even more so in the case of humans who are like microscopic aphids on this globule! – the Earth must be all the more subject to the determinism of the surrounding universe to which it belongs.

Behind this lack of historical and astronomical criticism looms another of the psychological kind, which attacks human anthropocentrism. Montesquieu was the first to express this in *My Thoughts*: 'For astrology doggedness is a conceited luxury. We believe that our actions are so important that they are worthy of being written in the great book of the sky. Even the poorest artisan believes that the immense luminous bodies which move over his head were only made to tell the universe what time he will leave his shop.' The argument was taken up again by Laplace in his *The System of the World*: 'Man deceived by his senses into regarding himself as the centre of the universe, easily persuades himself that the stars influence his destiny and that it is possible to predict that destiny by observing their aspects at the moment of birth. This error, dear to his self-esteem and necessary for his troubled curiosity, is as ancient as astronomy.'

Since then, this argument has continued to make a mint: 'How flattering it is for the poor human individual, to believe that he has a 'destiny', and that this destiny is written in the stars' (Jean Rostand, *Le Figaro Littéraire* (The Literary Figaro, 19 January 1952). 'What immeasurable pride to believe that the destiny of a mammal born on a little planet could be related to the course of the heavenly bodies! Put in their place in the galaxy the Sun, the Earth, life and the human race, and these beliefs will seem futile.' (M. Dauvillier, professor of cosmic physics at the Collège de France). Has this criticism on the basis of psychology more grounds than the historical and astronomical criticism? What more do we know about the existence or the non-existence of phenomena after having cited the motivation of pride, self-esteem, the illusion of the senses, the flattery or futility of believing in this phenomenon? This is no more than a value judgement about something 'believed' while purporting to pass judgement on the reality of the thing itself. This judgement rests implicitly on the generalisation of a historical scientific observation that anthropocentricism is the main source of error, of blindness and darkness. But this generalisation has no scientific basis; it cannot constitute evidence in this case, especially as the proposition on which this critique rests is in danger of being completely upturned. In only basing itself on feelings and human behaviour, they just want to see it as egocentricity enlarged to an astronomical scale. They could see the physical reality of the human condition in its humblest state and the infinite smallness of man in the immensity of the cosmos just as well by looking at the situation objectively. How can these microscopic creatures, scattered in their billions over the Earth's crust and so delicate and sensitive to so many things, remain impervious to the tremendous movements of the gigantic planetary worlds which surround them?

Of course this counter-argument that the infinitely small is dependent on the infinitely large is no more evidence in favour of astrology than the other is evidence in its disfavour. Nevertheless, after these unscientific statements by scholars one is allowed to appreciate, as more conforming with reality, the good sense of Emmanuel Berl:

> I believe in astrology primarily because it seems natural to me that a phenomenon as important as the movement of the stars will extend their action as far as me. In the world I live in it is the opposite which appears supernatural. I also believe in it because as a historian I cannot be unaware of the considerable role astrology has played for mankind.[6]

Ultimately, the historical, astronomical and anthropological reasons used to justify the repudiation of astrology have clearly proved to be without merit. So why then are these false arguments, nevertheless, sufficient to knock it down? It is because we are witnessing a paradigm shift in sensibility and collective thought: the mind detaches itself from the subjective in order to attach itself to the objective, focusing its interest on the exuberant prospect of world conquest. The advent of the telescope diverted astronomers away from speculating on astrological matters in order to satisfy their curiosity about the sky now that its mysteries could be revealed by the objective enlargement: a new career in astronomy, a huge subject in itself, had opened up, spanning many centuries and dispensing with the study of the relationship between the sky and mankind. It was astronomy of the sky for the sky. Added to that, there are other things to do rather than spend time looking at a map of the sky at birth in order to follow the progress of a patient. We are in the time of Pascal, of Torricelli, of Malpighi and of Boerhaave, among others, who invite the stars to come down to the level of cells in order to perform pathology. The discovery of blood cells and of sperm and ova sheds new light on the mysteries of life: the mind now satisfies its need to explore by looking inside human beings in order to understand their internal affairs and not by following them in the macrocosm outside. We turn away from the sky in order to conquer the Earth, life below suddenly having so much to teach us, the mysteries to be revealed being right here... On this the philosophers are going to proclaim the liberty of man in the bosom of the world.

Circumstances in larger society also affected things. In France, in the affair of the poisonings by the Marquise of Brinvilliers, while astrologers were suspected and only just escaped the arrests of the burning court and the accusations of La Reynie, a lieutenant in the royal police, astrology itself fell because of the disreputable nature of the controversy. It was in this climate that the great blow was delivered, in 1660, when Colbert founded the Academy of Sciences; astrology (with theology and politics) was excluded from the list of admissible disciplines. The break up was officially completed without any scientific investigation. We will search in vain for the smallest historic snippet that is able to present any scientific justification whatever for such a ban.

At the very most we are at the heart of a current way of

thinking which has turned its back on ancient knowledge, its rejection being in reality only like a retreating wave on the ocean of thought that carries it. This intellectually dishonest attack created the malaise that goes with a bad conscience and, to over-compensate, the criticism escalated. The hostility of astronomers couldn't get any more virulent, leaving aside the towering reality that all their predecessors, from Hipparchus to Newton, were more or less astrologers! To be exact, the problem is that what has only been a condemnation of principle goes on, because of this real tradition of hostility that has closed the door on all objective research, to become an absolute and definitive condemnation without any supporting evidence. 'This purported science has not been refuted; it has fallen into disuse' (Pierre Thuillier); like a flame which has flickered but not gone out in the current climate of disaffection.

Ultimately the burial of astrology has taken place under the banner of scientific and philosophic Cartesianism. Descartes, above all, is the symbol of this setback. One day, as he was writing to Father Mersenne, the plausibility of astrology came to mind:

> I became so bold that I now dare to seek the cause of the position of each fixed star. Because, even though they appear very irregularly scattered here and there in the sky, yet I don't doubt that there is a natural order among them which is regular and determined. Knowledge of this order is the key to, and the foundation of, the highest and most perfect science that man can have regarding material things, all the more so as by this means we could know a priori all the different forms and essences of terrestrial bodies instead of being satisfied with having to guess them a posteriori and by their effects.[7]

Then years later after having decided to hide his date of birth because he said, 'I had an aversion for the makers of horoscopes, of the errors to which one seems to contribute when one publishes the birthday of someone', he expresses this radical condemnation in his *Discours de la méthode*: 'I think I already know enough about bad doctrines and what they are worth to not be deceived by them, neither by the promises of an alchemist, nor by the prophecies of an astrologer, nor by the masquerade of a magician or the bravado of any of them who make a profession out of knowing more that they know.' So finally the story ends with the judgement of a pessimistic observer (who also totally rejected Harvey's discovery regarding the circulation of blood).

The attack became widespread. La Fontaine ordered 'astrologers, charlatans, makers of horoscopes [to leave] the courts of princes and Europe', or have them fall into a well. Moliére takes on the 'tellers of horoscopes [who] by their false predictions profit from the vanity and ambition of credulous minds'. In the century of the Enlightenment we have extermination. Diderot sets the tone with the entry 'Chaldeans' in the Encyclopaedia, although he nuanced his thoughts on the word 'astrologer', combining the opening with an outdated closure in regard to the calculation of probabilities:

> When one concedes that because of the obvious connection between all the beings in the universe, it wouldn't be impossible that an effect related to happiness or unhappiness in human beings must absolutely coexist with some celestial phenomenon so that the one being given, the other happens or always inevitably follows – can we ever have a large enough number of observations to have certainty in such a case?

Voltaire is not so cautious; he's happy to juggle with light objections and amusing anecdotes, seeking, using his favourite procedure, to win his case by first making sure all the scoffers are on his side. Comte couldn't see the use of a constructive examination of the question, he only makes mention of the 'attractive chimeras of astrology'. But the main attack comes mostly from the astronomers, who conduct the burial, in the manner of Laplace: '[...] it was upheld until the end of the century before last, the time when the general spread of knowledge about the true system of the world destroyed it for ever.'[8]

We still need to face the facts: astrology isn't dead, and the disgraceful old lady has the indecency not to pass away. That is because she is not what the pundits of the last few centuries thought her to be: the vestiges of prehistoric thought, something like the remains of a primitive way of thinking living on borrowed time, a sort of medieval skin disease to scrub away, a parasite of the mind to get rid of. No, we still need to face the facts. It has its very own destiny, which eludes both the condemnation of its adversaries as well as the wishes of its supporters. This destiny is woven against a background of an evolving collective unconscious, understood to be like a deep feeling process obscurely fashioning minds to the way the world is going.

For the marriage of the sky and Earth are written in the hearts of mankind. It is thus that astrology takes root at the deepest level of our terrestrial state, which is also cosmic. It is ancient and universal, and its great age, its persistence as well as its proliferation are full testimony that it carries, within itself, the dynamic of a fundamental idea connected to the very powers of the human psyche. Like Anything contained in the primitive psyche, it is an undifferentiated force, as full of darkness as much as a conveyer of light, carrying a dung heap of superstitions on its breath, for the benefit of fairground fortune-tellers; it is also the noblest form of conjecture, rooted in ancient tradition which continues through successive civilisations, immortal despite changes in human intelligence, paving the way towards its ultimate revelation: an evolved knowledge, conscious of itself and restored to its full state of learning.

The cultural capital of our civilisation is rich in artistic iconography with astrology as its subject and with the

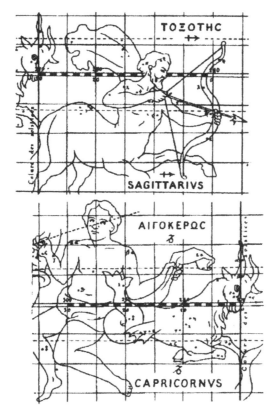

message conveyed by the evocative power of the image. Its 'uranographic' subject matter shows convincingly that its symbolism arises from within the collective unconscious. In particular we can see the practice of condensing, where two very different intrinsic principles are amalgamated or fused in a conjunction of original workmanship, a treatment which produces monstrous chimeras as if from a primitive mentality like fantasies with the creativity of dreams, the imagination, the emotions, of art. Some signs of the zodiac came directly from this such as Sagittarius which amalgamates horse and man in a marriage which represents the fabulous centaur, and Capricorn, Pan changed into a goat fused with a triton with a fish's tail.

The excavations in Egypt ordered by Bonaparte which led to the discovery of hieroglyphics and their deciphering by

Champollion and his successors, as well as the research that took place in the Orient in the middle of the nineteenth century (tablets from the library at Nineveh) were behind a renewal of interest in astrology. The flow had been blocked off for two centuries (except in England) and had been hardly visible, except in the degenerate form of almanacs (*La Maison rustique, Le Liégeois…*), a type of astrology related to the folklore about the influence of the Moon. It was only in the last decade of the nineteenth century that these texts began to be examined in the spirit of philological and historical enquiry. Some researchers discovered that the apparent obsolescence of the deciphered documents hid a distinctive vision of the universe which had a profound and extensive influence on the lives of ancient peoples, but the prevailing way of thought wasn't open to such research.

At this point astrology starts to go via the back stairs; its renaissance takes place in the general setting of a muddled revision of occultism with Urania appearing somewhat blighted in the company of the cabala, alchemy, chiromancy, orientalism, not unlike the practices of reading tea leaves and crystal balls. There are estimable researchers – in France, Paul Choisnard and Eugène Caslant, both graduates from Ecole Polytechnique as well as Henri Selva, and in Germany von Kloeckler — who, searching out obscure books on the back shelves of libraries, undertook an investigation of this astrological tradition that was covered in unanimous disapproval: it took some courage. Specialised books began to appear at the beginning of the last century, and over the years a real astrological library has built up. Apart from some solid works by serious people, this production is only too often appallingly mediocre, stuffed with extravagant fantasies and gross errors, the consequence of the unregulated enthusiasm of practitioners living in ivory towers and the fact that anyone can do it.[9]

Not only has the mummy started to move, but having been passed to the laboratory, the museum piece takes to the streets and astrology is just about everywhere today: in everyday conversations, in the press and in publishing, on the airwaves, on the Internet… It has become a bizarre phenomenon of our times. It goes without saying that this renaissance, as was the case with its eclipse, happened in a setting that was favourable to its arrival.

Its adversaries make great play of attributing the return of this ever-rising flood to the current psychopathological climate. This craze is part of a general return to the irrational, accompanied by a torrent of superstitions, inherent in the insecurity of the modern world in which we live. Traumatised by wars, revolutions, upheaval and the complexity of a society with the dual crises of over-population and the fear of extinction, people tend to feel more and more alienated from the values of objective reality and take refuge in the secret places of their imaginations, a marginalised world where their dreams and feelings can reign supreme. Thus they turn their backs on their critical senses, on logic and on reason, and develop a thirst for myths and the miraculous. If and when astrology presents itself to them like an art or science that is intended to predict or to foresee the future, it is the complete answer to the needs of their anguished souls.

However obvious this explanation it is also too short: it only explains the general craze, the scandal of the sidereal columnists and other star merchants. It does not explain the growth in disinterested research that has stimulated a true international 'astrological movement' carrying out real work: studying, verifying, educating, training, informing… some American universities are starting to open their doors to studying the subject, and opinion is more open in most advanced circles, to the point, now, that the problem of astrology really rests in our intellectual and cultural life. Beyond this propensity that anxious people have for morbid curiosity, we must look for a much larger, far-reaching and profound explanation.

In fact, the 'phenomenon of astrology' is a fact of life which is part of a general historical process, linked to the cultural and scientific revolution which began at the end of the 19th century. Now we are witnessing the exhumation of Urania and a new wind blows over the planet. Truly sensational new discoveries have taken place, which completely change the scope of science: cathode rays, X-rays, radiation, electric waves, wireless broadcasts, radioactivity, atoms and electrons, microbes and viruses, cosmic rays... While we discover and explore the infinitely small, giant telescopes reveal a universe of nebulas and galaxies. At the time when aviation was about to conquer the sky, the first submarine was exploring the depths of the oceans. In philosophy, Bergson puts the role of intuition at the heart of knowledge, and Freud delves into the depths of the mind. In the arts symbolism gives an initiatory character to the poetic experience, in linking poetry and metaphysics and in rediscovering traditional ideas at the source of philosophies and ancient religions. Then came quantum theory, relativity, wave mechanics, the expanding universe, the demonstration of the unity of matter (beloved of alchemists), transcendental phenomenology... We are a long way from the peaceful certainties of Lagrange, Laplace and Comte! Non-Euclidean geometry, non-Archimedean measurement, non-Newtonian mechanics, non-Maxwellian physics, non-Aristotelian logic, non-Cartesian epistemology... Everything is questioned in this new dimension of the universe.

It is not just chance that astrology makes another appearance in this explosion of human thought. It was two thousand years before man accepted the heliocentric world system conceived by the Greek thinkers. Here again in the history of science we see the errors of yesterday becoming the truths of tomorrow; we just have to be ready for this truth for which the ground is prepared. Astrology is knocking on the door again.

Chapter 4 - The Scholarly Tradition

What is covered by the word 'tradition'? What are the sources? To what great works should we refer? What value should we give them? Enough questions…

Every civilisation with enough interest in its past has its own mythology. For the Ancients, the gods were the ideal reference: divination by the stars, the foreseeing of the future allowing the schedule established by the sky to be annulled, could only have been taught to mankind through a divine channel. Therefore they were keen to involve gods, heroes, kings and ancestors of the people (Enoch, Abraham…). Their adversaries did likewise by invoking rebel angels, or dethroned gods to their side (Atlas, Prometheus, Chiron, Hercules…). Are myths any less popular today? In this astronautic era, there is the dawning of a hypothesis that celestial things could have been revealed to us by 'Galaxians' visiting us between two voyages in a flying saucer… According to the beliefs of 'traditionalists', it happened in a golden age when a sacred science of mankind, the heritage of a prestigious knowledge, would have reigned supreme. Today only the vestiges remain, the crumbs from a feast of the gods under the aspect of traditional hermeticism which links the sky, the Earth and mankind under the eyes of astrology, alchemy and magic.

In as much as we can invoke the astrology of long ago, the tradition appears, at least psychologically, to have been like a collective organisation of beings, bound to the god who sheltered them in a primitive unity. The cement that held this collective mystique together was the heartbeat of universal life, people feeling and thinking together, led by a faith maintained under a sheltering sky which was at one with the Earth. It was like a choir of a thousand voices: thousands of beings, unified in the same spiritual structure, cutting from the same living substance images of the same gods and moulding the same kinds of faces, the same spirit moving the same hearts and minds.

How was this collective structure transmitted to us and

in what form did we receive this heritage? Apart from inscriptions in the augural style of the baked brick tablets of the Chaldeans, the earliest written evidence which begins the testament of this tradition is from a relatively recent date. Of Berossus for the Chaldeans, and of Manetho, for Egypt, who, during the third century B.C.E oversaw the birth of Greek astrology, only second-hand reports remain. We also have the apocryphal work of Nechepso and Petosiris on which the reputation of Egyptian science is based, and the *Astronomicon*, a work from the first century, in which Manilius lifts up his voice in songs to the glory of the celestial alignments. Finally, we have the magnum opus dating from the second century C.E., the four books on the judgement of stars, collectively called the *Tetrabiblos* or the *Quadripartite* of Claude Ptolemy.

In the pantheon of world science, one system has a place of honour : 'Ptolemy's system' (which was the same as Hipparchus' system) that he sets out in his Almagest goes on to reign supreme over astronomy for almost one and a half thousand years, becoming the law right up to the Copernican revolution! He did the same for astrology with his Tetrabiblos, which held court up to the 20th century! This royal piece of tradition is well named: it is the astrological bible! An astrologer said of this 'astrological holy writ', 'It is as if Cardanus, Argole, Porphyry, Campanella, Naïbod and the orthodox Ptolemeens used to wash their hands in respect before writing the name of Ptolemy, like the rabbis do in writing the sainted name of Yahweh.' He who is called the 'prince of astrologers' gave us the first unique work of reference. We can leave behind the laconic expression of Chaldean augural evidence and the poetic art of Manilius; for the first time we find ourselves in the presence of a technical work, a teaching manual, let alone its connection to the greatest names (Porphyry, Proclus, Albategnius, Regiomontanus, Cardanus, Melanchthon, Camerarius...) who made various observations on, or translations of, this *Tetrabiblos*.

Beyond this is the realisation that it is all we have. In

fact, the works which follow across the centuries are just drops in the ocean, from *The Books of the Mathematics* of the Stars by Firmicus Maternus (4th century), via the arab astrologers (700-1400), to the astrologers of the Renaissance, whatever their contributions; it isn't until the 17th century that the thinking changes and a new wind liberates astrology from this ultimately tyrannical tutelage. It would be more judicious to state that these successors (especially Gauric, Cardanus, Ferrier, Junctin...) fully involved themselves in discussing, clarifying, developing and experimenting with the Ptolemaic data with all its implications without actually going beyond it. We have to wait for this definitive passage from Antoine de Villon, professor of philosophy at the University of Paris, whose work *L'Usage des éphémérides* (The Use of Ephemerides), 1624 ('[...] that which I have written in this book, and taught orally in public seven whole months in this famous university of Paris...'), constitutes one of the best documents of the tradition at its current state of development:

> Because in the first place you have to realise that Ptolemy, according to the opinions of all the astrologers, has not dealt extensively with everything belonging to this science, but only with its roots and principles, leaving the rest to the reasoning and good judgement of the prudent astrologer; who while keeping to the maxims of this great observer of the stars can, by hard work and long experience, find a lot of things which are not expressly stated in these maxims.

But prior to the alterations of the copyists and the errors of the exegetes, what is this kernel worth of itself? How does Ptolemy, a loyal conservative and authorised trustee of the tradition, open the testament up and even perfect the rules for what was known of genethliac astrology? What is behind the golden legend and what information does he give us about himself? Though, we have to shed light on the oracle, we must shake this idol to see what falls out of the entrails: gold or copper?

The salvaging of the tradition that this *Tetrabiblos* represents has not been subjected to really rigorous jurisprudence: what part of Ptolemy's teaching is drawn from Aratus, from Berossus, from Hipparchus, or from Posidonius? All we know is that these contributions are from Antiquity, mainly from Chaldean and Egyptian sources, with no references or statement about where they come from or their origins that he has attempted to consolidate, refine and restore in an appropriate order.

Furthermore, if all the masters feed from this prestigious breast, and each goes away to seek their own pittance, sometimes only having gorged on empty food, the resulting commentaries, not having clarified the original text, are often hopelessly obscure, not to say contradictory. This is the cause of the profound differences in interpretation that we find between the work of Cardanus, the most important Ptolemaic commentator, and Placidus de Titis, the disciple who was most attached to the 'prince of astrologers' whose system purports to have come from the same source. So we have to understand that the locks of tradition are jammed, no key can open the sanctuary of truth for us, and we must limit our hopes to getting near to snippets of the truth which often rub shoulders with falsehoods.

But let's not be overly pessimistic. This state of things is only disappointing for the idealistic traditionalist. Once shaken the idol coughs up some pieces of precious metal; a rich seam exists and that is what counts. Besides, our Ptolemaic forebears can be excused: the sap that flows from the trunk has become more complex since leaving the roots. They weren't looking at 'a tradition' but at 'traditions', and the presumption of the idea of a single superior tradition is mindlessly taken over by an astrology that has huge difficulty reaching back to its past. It seems more truthful to imagine Ptolemy identifying the contradictory currents in problematical historical material. With a sort of argumentative faith he tries to intellectualise, and even to rationalise, an approach to human knowledge which is intrinsically obscure. Because what happens over time is not the eradication of the gnosis of a perfect sacred science in a state of decline, but rather the slow and laborious development of a field of knowledge only just born.

But, as a starting point, and given the problems inherent in the subject, there is not much to say against the *Tetrabiblos*. As soon as he takes up his pen, Ptolemy gives us some clear definitions.

> [*Tetrabiblos* I, 1.1-2, trans. D. G. Greenbaum, ed. Hübner, pp. 3.31-4.45. Ptolemy, Claudius, Ἀποτελεσματικά, ed. Wolfgang Hübner, *Opera quae exstant omnia*, Vol. III 1, Stuttgart/Leipzig 1998] Of the preparations for the goal of prognostication through astronomy, O Syrus, two are the greatest and most authoritative. One is first in order and in power, by which we comprehend for every occasion the configurations of the movements of the Sun, Moon and stars which happen in relation to one another and to the Earth. The second is by which, through the natural particular quality of the configurations themselves, we investigate the changes in the surrounding environment which they bring about. The first, whose theory is comprehensible on its own terms, even though it may not achieve the result it would from joining with the second, has been systematically treated for you, in its own composition, as best we could by the method of demonstration. Regarding the second, even though it is not as self-sufficient as the first, we shall now produce a treatise which accords with philosophical principles.[10]

This opening discourse is striking and straightaway silences the prejudice in the confusion between astronomy and astrology: the science of astronomical certainty and the art of astrological conjecture shouldn't be confused, the first acting as a support for the second, as in the relationship between anatomy and physio-psychology. Ptolemy then immediately starts to define the various causes to which we are subject in order to take a position on free will by affirming the notion of relativity in astral determination.

> [Robbins, F. E., trans., *Ptolemy, Tetrabiblos*, Cambridge, MA 1940, repr. 1994 (Tetr. I, 3.6, trans. D. G. Greenbaum, ed. Hübner, pp. 15.259-16.263)] One should not believe that events inseparably connect to humans by a cause from above, just as if they had been ordained by law for each person from some indissoluble and divine command and result from necessity.[11]

Astrology shouldn't be a fatalistic doctrine, because celestial causes aren't everything; they manifest themselves alongside, and allowing for, all the factors that nature has given us, the most important being 'the diversity of the seed [which] provides the principle power in nature in the generation of each thing', the specificity of the seed comes into the determination of race, sex, country, mores, customs, foodstuffs.

> [*Tetr.* I, 2.8-9, Robbins p. 19 (= *Tetr.* I, 2.19, ed. Hübner, p. 12.200-207)]: Unless each one of these things is examined together with the causes that are derived from the ambient, although this latter be conceded to exercise the greatest influence (for the ambient is one of the causes for these things being what they are, while they in turn have no influence upon it), they can cause much difficulty for those who believe that in such cases everything can be understood, even things not wholly within its jurisdiction from the motion of the heavenly bodies alone.'
> [*Tetr.* I, 2.9, Robbins p. 19:]...and as we do not find fault with the physicians, when they examine a person, for speaking both about the sickness itself and

about the patient's idiosyncrasy, so too in this case we should not object to astrologers using as a basis for calculation nationality, country, and rearing, or any other already existing accidental qualities. [(*Tetr.* I, 2.20, ed. Hübner, p. 13.216-220)][12]

So, this relativist astrology is not a divinatory art, but a knowledge founded on observation and, logically, its goal is to make it lie.

But, I think, just as with prognostications, even if it be not entirely infallible, at least its possibilities have appeared worthy of the highest regard, so too in the case of defensive practice, even though it does not furnish a remedy for everything, its authority in some instances at least, however few or unimportant, should be welcomed and prized and regarded as profitable in no ordinary sense. [*Tetr.* I, 3.15, Robbins p. 31: (= *Tetr.* I, 3.17, ed. Hübner, p. 20.350-355)][13]

One can only weigh up the wisdom of interpreting projected results. Ptolemy sets about finding numerous images and analogies to persuade others that it is altogether natural, reasonable and necessary to use this practice: 'Do we reject the art of navigating ships because of the number of shipwrecks?'

This analytical process allows him to make some forecasts, in spite of the relative nature of the results, and authorises him to take a judicious role, the foreseen events happening according to 'the tendencies which originate in the sky', 'not bound by a fatalistic inevitability', able to be diverted or softened in their effect 'with the help of recognised natural remedies like having an effective contrary force'. He also shows the logic in the inevitability of things and the relativity of celestial causes:

[*Tetr.* I, 2.6, Robbins p. 13]: Why can he not, too, with respect to an individual man, perceive the general

quality of his temperament from the ambient at the
time of his birth, as for instance that he is such and
such in body and such and such in soul, and predict
occasional events, by use of the fact that such and such
an ambient is attuned to such and such a temperament
and is favourable to prosperity, while another is not so
attuned and conduces to injury? [= *Tetr.* I, 2.11, ed.
Hübner, p. 9.139-145][14]

There we have the well known psychological equation
'character is destiny' which when closely associated with
celestial causes, squarely founds astrology as astral
psychology.

To avoid suspicion of personal bias, I'd like to take
another quote from the critical historian Bouché-Leclercq's
scholarly study, *Greek Astrology*. In this he recognises that,
while distancing himself from the idea of predestination
held by some, Ptolemy 'simply says that our constitutional
mix or temperament is, for us, the first principle, and that
the first principle entails, if not every detail, at least the
generalities of existence [...]. The temperament of
individuals born under the influence of a particular planet
allows detailed study of the character of that planet'. Also he
sees in the descriptions of planetary factors (physical and
psychological traits, faculties, professional aptitudes...)
which punctuate the *Tetrabiblos* 'physical types or physical
forces planted by the Greek imagination'. Besides it is very
significant that this work ends with a final phrase which
marries mathematical cause to temperament: '[...] if one
knows how to judiciously link the mathematical cause to
what comes from temperament.'

Going back to sources is a good way to strip away the
prejudices that have been heaped on astrology by time. In
fact, it has always been considered, at least by superior
minds, to be like psychology (or even to be psychology) and
though purely empirical and 'intuitional', it was deeply felt
and lived and was the first human science of the ancients. It
is only for the vulgar that it has gradually been distorted to

become seen as the underdeveloped product of a divinatory practice. Nevertheless the proof of its psychological nature is there in the text.

Moreover, Ptolemy is more explicit, because he sees a direct relationship between heredity and 'astralities' (first principle and astral cause). According to him, conception and birth are linked in a profound way, the configurations of the one being related to the other. The embryo has all the potential, which allows the instantaneous strike of destiny and the future, to be held in its entirety, at the point of initiation which is the moment that life commences.

> [*Tetr.* III, 1.106, Robbins pp. 225, 227; p. 225] For the child at birth and his bodily form take on many additional attributes which he did not have before, when he was in the womb, those very ones indeed which belong to human nature alone; and even if it seems that the ambient at the time of birth contributes nothing toward his quality, at least his very coming forth into the light under the appropriate conformation of the heavens contributes, since nature, after the child is perfectly formed, gives the impulse to its birth under a configuration of similar type to that which governed the child's formation in detail in the first place. Accordingly one may with good reason believe that the position of the stars at the time of birth is significant of things of this sort, not however, for the reason that it is causative in the full sense, but that of necessity and by nature it has potentially very similar causative power. [= *Tetr.* III, 2.3-4, ed. Hübner, p. 169.75-88][15]

This is the first hypothesis which attempts to put astrology along with biology on the genetic map. At first glance this seems like madness: we will see that important statistical results support this theory.

On this basis, Ptolemy puts astrological phenomena in the same category as other commonly held theories about the forces of nature, with the implicit idea of the unity of life from which the universal essence of mankind emanates, connected to the surrounding world with all its various aspects: elemental, vegetable, mineral, animal. That mankind is at one with nature and human beings are made of nature is a fact of life. Hence the very astrological expression 'human nature'; nature kneaded, like clay, into the fabric of the world, qualified by its environment, in which its essence and its laws are assimilated into terrestrial reality.[16]

Thus, as a 'physicist' who invokes the natural temperament of the stars (the stars are anthropomorphised, in the same way that humans are 'astralised'), Ptolemy bases the characterology of human types (the first characterology to have existed) on the four fundamental natural principles which now relate as much, if not more, to psychical than to physical aspects of life: hot and cold, wet and dry. These qualities are soon put together in order to correspond to the four elements: fire (dry-hot), earth (dry-cold), air (wet-hot) and water (wet-cold). In the same way this quaternary is based on the rhythms of nature: the four seasons of the year, the four phases of the lunar cycle and the four diurnal-nocturnal times, sunrise, culmination, sunset and midnight. Apart from the quaternary, the ternary and binary are equally taken into consideration as factors in the unity of the circle. Ptolemy had a taste for geometric symmetry and he introduced polygonal aspects to the relationships between the planets, the living beings in the sky.

On this basis of interpretation an infinite chain of universal correspondences is deployed by the play of analogies, the perfect pattern being the relationship between the four elements and the four temperaments of Hippocrates (fire = bilious, earth = nervous, air = sanguine, water = lymphatic). Each planet is the symbol of which represents a special type of universe under divers aspects of life. Thus, Saturn is a star with a cold and dry tendency, and accordingly its characteristics are those of retraction, asceticism, severity, of serious events and hard situations, sterility, scarcity, isolation, old age, death; Jupiter, warm and wet, is the opposite, being associated with the blossoming of life's powers. Thus, planetary characterology becomes like an emblem for living creatures.

Other categories also come into it, in particular the masculine-feminine polarity. Above all, each planet is judged according to its affinity with the signs of the zodiac, its position relative to the Sun and Moon and its aspects to other planets. In some ways, Ptolemy gives us the rudiments of an astrological grammar with its rules of syntax.

In this consideration of the celestial configuration, special attention is given to the search for the planet which is more dominant than the others, the one which exerts the strongest influence on the subject. This has to do with topocentric movement determined by the place of birth; the planet that crosses the horizon or the meridian, in particular the one which rises (on the Ascendant) or which culminates (on the Midheaven):

> [*Tetr.* I, 24.52, Robbins p. 117] for they are most powerful when they are in Midheaven or approaching it, and second when they are exactly on the horizon... their power is ... less when they culminate beneath the Earth or are in some other aspect to the orient... [= *Tetr.* I, 24.4, ed. Hübner, p. 86.1259-1264][17]

> The stars prevail [...] when they are at the angles of the sky. But the principle places are the Ascendant and the Midheaven [The division of the doctrine of the nativities, *Tetrabiblos*]

Again quoting Bouché-Leclercq: these four angles of the sky, which he calls 'centres', have 'a specific energy of their own which they communicate to the signs and the planets with which they coincide. In all cases where the action of a planet is compared from the point of view of intensity, it is repeatedly said that you have to attribute greater value to a planet which is on or near a centre. The only competition, he said, was between the Ascendant and the Midheaven, the other centres (the Descendant and the IC) only being their opposites. Whereas Paul of Alexandria and Proclus gave the Ascendant priority, Ptolemy – and with him Manilius, Stephen of Alexandria and Dorotheus of Sidon – preferred the Midheaven, while Firmicus Maternus was undecided. Later on we will provide the overwhelming statistical evidence which demonstrates the real importance of this phenomenon of the angularity of stars.

Ptolemaic astrology is essentially planetary: the preponderant action is provided by the planets, the 'universal significators' which affect all areas of life. In chapter after chapter, Ptolemy draws up typological properties covering all the various manifestations of existence. Thus, Mars is supposed to signify success 'in the leading of armies', Saturn makes 'those that are serious and think deeply', and Jupiter those who are 'proper to govern others'.

By comparison, the space given to the zodiac is minor, its symbolism only being at a draft stage. It hardly calls to mind the zodiacal melothesis (the relationship of the signs to parts of the body of zodiacal man, popularised in the Middle Ages by the *Elucidarium* of Honorius of Autun and the numerous models taken from it) and the part played by the signs in interpretation is limited, whereas he puts more into the constellations, which were already considered as another register of values.

Ptolemy completes his work on genethliac astrology by creating a scholarly method of determining the stages of life, allowing the fixing of the dates of events (the system of primary directions), a text that has given scholiasts 'the sweats'. The second part of his work deals with universal apotelesmatic, or mundane astrology, a different subject which uses the interpretation of eclipses or cycles of the Moon, among other things, which are considered in the forecasting of world phenomena: weather, shortages or gluts, war or peace.

Beyond the spirit of the *Tetrabiblos*, if one stops at the

stage of applied interpretation, one goes from just about all to absolutely nothing, to the point where a colleague thought it useful to settle the question of the practical applications of Books III and IV by saying.[18]

> My approach, is just to put it all in the bin [...] What can you do with 'if Saturn sends a bad aspect to the Sun, it presages the death of the father by illnesses resulting from the accumulation of bad humours', or with this: 'When Saturn is in the signs of wild beasts, he makes these beasts tear people apart.'

At the very least, we have to interpret these interpretations! In any case, it accords with the mores and conditions of life in the society of that time and place.

What can be taken from this work is the importance of the setting up of a code of interpretation; the carving out of the principles of an astrological semiology, the establishment of the semantics of astral phenomena. Beyond that, at the practical level, even more at the level of a rigorous deciphering, we are moving in the mists of a naive astrology, which attaches itself to feeble physical justifications, invents pseudo-rational arguments, does not assign any limits and does not know where to stop on the slope of practical divination. Here, Ptolemy has lost command of a drifting boat in the form of an astrology that has no internal logic or consciousness of its real object.

But Ptolemaic astrology is, neither more nor less, the human knowledge that was relevant two thousand years ago: a primitive knowledge, at a stage that is embryonic and nebulous. We should question the belief that astrology would have been an exception to the rule of the historical evolution of general human knowledge, assuming that from its very antiquity it would hold the purity of an integrated and perfect knowledge. We have to unmask such naivety either as demanding the absurd or believing in the impossible.

With the little astrological revolution of the 17th

century the columns of the Ptolemaic temple were damaged
and undermined. The representative works of the century,
those of Antoine de Villon (1624), William Lilly (1647),
André Argole (1652) and Henri Rantzau (1657), among
others, were still faithful versions of the established tradition
but there was a new spirit abroad. Kepler is exemplary: he
sifted through everything, discussed, trimmed, threw out,
consolidated what had stood the test of experience and
enriched it with new factors. And then, three important
astrologers: Nicolas Bourdin, the Count of Pagan and Jean-
Baptiste Morin met in Paris; the kernel exploded.

Nicolas Bourdin, Marquis of Villennes, Secretary of
State and member of the Academy of the Abbot of Aubignac,
governor of Vitry-le-François, published *Urania*, an
annotated French translation of the *Tetrabiblos*, in Paris in
1640 and Ptolemy's *Centiloquium* in 1651, a commentated
translation of a piece that many claim to be a pseudo
epigraph, which pretended to be a summary of the
Tetrabiblos in one hundred sentences. This translator and
commentator chose to keep a low profile but count Blaise-
François de Pagan, marshal of Louis XIII and master of
Vauban, destroys his bridges with his *Astrologie naturelle*
(Natural Astrology) dated 1659. Here is a sample:

> We have already banned the triplicities or celestial
> trigones from our science, touching the regions of the
> Earth and its peoples. And now we must renounce
> Ptolemy's eclipses, Cardanus's conjunctions, and a
> great many novelties introduced by common
> astrology, touching on the consideration of universal
> causes. But what authority do we have for such a
> reform? Do we have the confidence to overturn the
> opinions of such celebrated authors, and can we reject
> so many thoughts and sentences without subjecting
> ourselves to criticism? Will we be obliged to write
> volumes in our defence, or have to keep for ever
> silent? [...] our design is not to keep following
> [Ptolemy] in this matter and not to spare even him.

The language was new, but the master stroke was given by Jean-Baptiste Morin de Villefranche (1583-1656), doctor and royal professor of mathematics at the *Collège de France*, and regarded as the greatest French astrologer. All the kings of France since Robert the Pious (whether Capetian or Valois dynasties) had their astrologers. Morin, the last in line of official astrologers, was adviser to Queen Mary of Medici and to certain ministers, such as Richelieu, for whom he made some remarkable political forecasts but with whom he went on to quarrel. On 5 September 1638, he positioned himself on the terrace of the château of Saint-Germain where Anne of Austria was about to give birth, to keep check on the Sun: it is through him that we know that the future Louis XIV made his first cry at 11.15 a.m. While Bourdin and Pagan sided with Copernicus whose system was not yet successful (the trial of Galileo being in 1633), Morin opted for the intermediate system of Tycho Brahe. He crossed swords (with his pen) with Gassendi, attacked Kepler and corresponded amicably with Descartes. His fame as a scholar is due to his important work on the determination of longitude. His astrological work was immense: apart from his *Remarques astrologiques sur le commentaire du Centiloque de Ptolémée mis en lumière par Messire Nicolas de Bourdin* (Astrological Observations on the Commentary of Ptolemy's Centiloquium Brought to Light by Messire Nicolas de Bourdin) (1657), he gave his whole life to his *Astrologia Gallica* in twenty-six books, published after his death (The Hague, 1661).

This is the revolution in thinking which explains Morin's transformation; it was the beginning of the extroverted era of western science; an irreversible trend, which expressed itself by supplanting inner and subjective values with exterior and objective ones. Everything which had a psychological character, the emotional or the subjective, was sacrificed for the benefit of external reality. We should mention the psychological dissociation which tore Kepler's sensibility and intelligence apart, placed as he was between the two stools of hermetic metaphysics and the experimental observation of astrology and astronomy. His was an uncomfortable but complete mind, unlike the Cartesians of his time who resolved the problem of dissociation by elimination, by shrinking the size of their inner being or, like Descartes, in searching for the solution to their anguish in a system. Morin resolved this conflict between the old and the new collective mentality differently with a form of elimination of astrology's past. He also enters into the spirit of method, analysis, order and clarification that he introduced to this knowledge. At the same time, in this reformulation, he ceases to commune with tradition: his rigid and rational methods cut astrology off from its vital core.

Against the distant background of a 'protoplasmic conscience', Ptolemaic astrology was (without knowing it) playing a syncretising role with its state of non-differentiation between subject and object, the self and the outside world, his day becoming confused with his night. Morin's astrology rejects his night and is based only on his day, the only reality, its object being less well founded. Morin states this profound and radical transformation of astrology in his twenty-first book: *De la Détermination active des corps célestes et passive des sublunaires*[19] (The Active Determinations of the Celestial Bodies and the Passive Determinations of the Sublunary World). Here he introduces the systematic use of the topocentric movement of the planets in the local sphere. This is cut into a dozen slices called 'Houses' (or sectors), that all the planets travel through in twenty-four hours: these are the various relationships between the planets and the Houses that take precedence in interpretation, Morin officially condemning, as the primary basis of this, the symbolic value of the planets as 'universal significators', the kingpin of the Ancients.

> This doctrine differs greatly from the truth [...] the Ancients have badly understood and still worse applied this universal order [...]. Thus the Sun, by itself, does not signify life more than it does the father,

nor the husband more than honours, nor conscience more than the leaders, etc. In interpreting the meaning of the Sun in the birth chart, one must not give preference to any of these analogies to the detriment of another. On the other hand, one must not attribute to the Sun all its meanings by possible analogies, considering it as the significator of the father, and of the husband, of life, and of honours, etc. at the same time, because one would inevitably find predictions of the same quality for all the categories at once, and the result would be completely absurd, and would be for ever invalidated by observation. For example, when a feminine subject sees her father die young and her husband live a long time.

From here, to overcome the inadequacies in the practice, he introduces a well founded, much improved interpretation technique, which, although limited in its possibilities and results, is aimed at particularising the way the planet manifests. Thus, life will apply more if the Sun is in House I (position prior to sunrise), the father if it is in House IV[20] (position prior to midnight), the husband if it is in House VII (position prior to sunset), and honours if it is in House X (position prior to culmination)…

So in the time between Ptolemy and Morin, a fundamental movement has taken place, a shift from the idea of essence to that of existence. The Ptolemaic Sun does not represent a particular man, in this instance the father or husband; it essentially symbolises masculine humanity from the angle of the life of the soul, a subjective representation of the paternal principle, the emotional experience of the father transferred, during his existence, on to all representation of masculine guidance, in particular the husband or the leader. Morin's Sun attaches itself exclusively to the physical person of the father or the husband.

Today the structure and content of the universal significator are intelligible to us because of our knowledge of the unconscious: the characters whose symbolism is linked to the same planet are those which have a common psychic resonance; by emotional transference, the individual moves, in turn, from father to husband, to boss, to chief. There is also a psychic link between the other expressions of solar symbolism: life, consciousness, morale, honours, society... That life arranges itself on the side of the father, the personification of the generative principle, is understandable because filiation is direct. If the connection between the father and a moral conscience or honours is not immediately apparent, psychoanalysis will show us the link: for the child the father is the first embodiment of moral duty; the father is 'introjected' by the infant, and it is in this identification with the father by the son that moral values are transmitted; the strength of this internalised paternal image creates a moralising authority, the 'voice of conscience' (the superego). From moral conscience we now move on to honour, for which the father, as the first example, serves as a model, and thereafter to honours (faced with public opinion) which are only ways in which this internal representation is objectified. The Sun equally symbolises the internalised social norms, society and the role of father, being to help the infant to make his way in the outside world. Specifically, the relationship between the State and the citizen is an exact copy of that first relationship between father and son: the State is a symbol of authority, and is an extension of the paternal superego if one accepts that public feeling is an extension of family feeling. So, at the level of the unconscious, there is a commonality between these different symbolic terms of the solar process, and that explains why it is possible to transfer from one term to another within the system of this planet.

Morin has actually ejected the centre of the symbol, emptying the universal significator of its substantive marrow. He never grasped this encapsulation of subjective reality confusingly conveyed by the Ancients. Having completely lost sight of the psychological aspects of real life, he only applied himself to the external theatre of life, that of events. Without knowing that in this way he could only get an indirect hold, a relative grasp, by discounting this inner life in his equation, Morin pulled the rug from under his own feet; furthermore, he contributed to the distancing of astrology from its state of astral psychology and brought it closer to being a divinatory art.

After him, we have to wait until our own time to see astrologers rethinking what they know about 'interpreting the interpretations', incorporating what is worth keeping of the Ptolemean and Morinean sediments into a way of thought that is of a higher level.[21]

Ultimately, this tattered starry robe that is astrological tradition is neither more nor less respectable or open to criticism than the art of Aesculapius, or the medicine of Hippocrates and his successors. It is the fledgling sum of a human knowledge, developed at length and with difficulty, both in truth and error, which must be subjected to the scrutiny of critical research, always keeping the thread of its internal logic so as to separate out the psychological truth that it keeps under its divinatory dross.

This is a work that involves appreciable complex judgements as expressed by Paul Choisnard when he spoke of 'a true astrology that we consider to be much more like a new science that has yet to be created than like an ancient science that has to be reconstituted.'[22]

Another astrologer, Karl Ernst Krafft, compares astrological traditions to superimposed geological layers, 'fossils […] of ideas and thoughts having lived in their time, but which no longer have life' and even goes as far as saying:

> Ancient astrology can be compared to a corpse which the soul has left a long time ago. Consequently all attempts to bring it back to life must seem as vain and misplaced as sightings of ghosts or exorcisms would be in the era of psychoanalysis […]. However well founded certain principles and certain practices of these traditions, their old-world formulations no longer correspond with today's mentality […]. That is

why even when impartial research justifies a number
of points imparted to us by astrological tradition, the
necessity of having a fundamentally new construction
in this domain cannot not be doubted.[23]

Whatever form Urania takes in the future, we cannot be
indifferent to the successive ways that she has appeared to
us in the past. Here as well, Choisnard makes the point
perfectly.

> But progress along a route is only real and stable
> in as far as it takes account of what has
> engendered and preceded it. If the study of
> ancient astrology, into the truth of it, boils down
> to very little, at least we should be in a position to
> prove it. In any case, it would still be very useful
> to dampen the misplaced ardour of both the
> neologists and the deniers.[24]

Claude Lévi-Strauss declares 'Astrology was a great system,
because for thousands of years it helped human beings to
think'.[25] There is no doubt that the spirit contained in this
tradition can continue to help us think, as one draws on the
past in order to create the future.

Chapter 5 - The Astrological Sky

We have already learned a little about the sky of the first astrologers. The essential astronomical components of their art were the celestial bodies which move across the starry vault, and in particular the wandering stars of our planetary system, the luminaries and planets. These heavenly powers are the principal players, physical entities in themselves as well as being the living components of the sky they inhabit. Without them the sky would just be a void, like a play in a theatre that has no actors. The astrological world is, primarily, a planetary world on which the whole of cosmic anthropology is founded.

But stars move in space and what counts is how they are configured against the celestial background, the horse cannot be separated from the race in which it runs, consideration of the one leading to the evaluation of the other. The circling of the stars in celestial space originated the notion of time, an astral time characterised by a succession of changing aspects in the sky; the framework on which they trace their arabesques is made of the cadences, rhythms and cycles linked to the astral configurations.

> Astral time, astral radiation and astral manna are synonymous terms describing the fluid medium which envelops the Earth and men, bathing them with its waves, hot or cool, light or dark and carrying terrestrial life in its sovereign flow. All variations in this astral fluid, this universal ether have an echo in our being, like the emanation of a breath or fire from the heavens. It is said that time is the material from which life is made. That is not just a simplistic metaphor, it literally means astral time. It was only gradually, due to the influence of measuring instruments, the hourglass, the water clock, the clock, that the concept of scientific time   perfectly homogenous, infinitely divisible, infinitely extendable, emerged from astral time.[26]

This is the way modern science made the economy of treating time like a specific value: a criterion for a 'scientific fact' is that it can be consistently reproduced; for modern science, time, an isotropic medium of homogeneous duration, is no more than a value that is empty of all reality. It is intrinsically without qualitative meaning, a pure ordinate of endlessly divisible measurement. Yet, this 'river of time' or celestial duration is the expression of the pulse beat of the universe.

> Astrology is a science that studies astral time rhythms and their influence on plants, animals and mankind. Terrestrial life, being directly dependent on astral life, will be supported or countered, depending on whether it adapts to the rhythms of the stars or neglects to do so. The aim of magical or religious - I could say astrological – festivals is to recreate this rhythmic adaptation, whether by encouraging terrestrial beings to be more disposed to celestial influences, or by activating the astral influence with liturgical acts, especially by dance and sacrifice. The calendar can be defined as: the order of the astrological rhythms and the rites by which man must strive to adapt both himself and his way of life. [...] In cults the purpose of the festivals is the renewal of life in nature and mankind, to make all who live here below participate in the renewal of the life of the stars, and for man, in particular, his immortal and divine life [...] Whichever gods they honoured or whatever ends they pursued, pagan festivals focused on matching the rhythms of terrestrial life to the movement of celestial life in such a way that terrestrial life was so imbued with celestial life that it received all its benefits and favours. [27]

The principle is that, as the upper governs the lower and like acts on like, every beginning or renewal in the sky engenders a beginning or a renewal on Earth....

Today it would be difficult to think in this way about this question of the relationship between mankind and the universe; even so, we must bravely overcome our scientistically[28] based prejudices in order to find the truths underlying this magical vision of the world. Besides, if the qualitative coordinate of time has not found a place in the scientific sphere, it is because of the minor nature, if not absence, of its manifestation in observed phenomena. This has led to a general disinterest in the question. Yet, without it, a whole dimension of human life is missing. An 'astrological event' is on the same plane as a 'psychological event', beyond the free exercise of the will we find a calendar which has been programmed by our roots in the animal world: the season of courtship, the season of conflict. Moreover, for fifty years, evidence came flooding in from all over the world, demonstrating the existence of time that had an astral quality - the discovery of the biological clock.

These stars—active agents, principles, signs; whatever label we give them—physically present in the celestial field were first noticed when travelling at their greatest speed, or rather at their apparent speed because of the phenomenon of terrestrial rotation: what is most immediate and striking for mankind is that they rise, pass overhead, set and disappear over the horizon to reappear on the opposite side, in the east. In addition there is the phenomenon of their respective relationships: these stars approached, met and moved away from each other in a series of phases and determined aspects. Finally, they were part of the general body of the starry vault, their courses followed in relation to the fixed stars, the constellations and the signs of the zodiac, along which they glide.

As we have seen, it was the passage of a star across the horizon which was noted first of all in the Chaldean inscriptions. The correlation established with this type of configuration produced an analogy that was manifestly bathed in magical thinking. It seems it was born from the idea that everyone has their own star in the sky, a guardian star, and that it is born with us and dies with us. In this assimilation of human life into the course of a star, birth is like the rise of a star, the fullness of existence is represented by its culmination and when it sets its extinction is like death. This line of reasoning explains why ancient astrologers searched the eastern horizon for a star, a planet or, failing those, a fixed star, which 'was born', so to speak, at the same time as the child; the star which was born, that is to say which rose in the east at the same time and place as the child, acts as a patron, like a ruler of the birth and thus oversees his or her destiny. This explains the importance of this favoured point in the sky - confirmed by Ptolemy and repeatedly emphasised by all the authors in the tradition – which, situated on the ecliptic at a longitudinal degree of the zodiac, is called the Ascendant (the place where at dawn the stars make their ascent into the sky); it has even engendered the name *Horoscope* ('I look at what's up'), a term that has come to designate the whole natal map of the sky.

It was later that a planet passing across the meridian and especially the upper meridian, the place of its culmination called the Midheaven, was also seen as important and a debate took place about which was more important, the Ascendant or the Midheaven.

Along the way, the analogical approach to interpreting the significance of the four angles of the sky became less naive; it went down the path of symbolising space, justifying Choisnard's view that astral psychology corresponds to celestial graphology. Origen considered astrology to be like 'reading natural characters', written characters, acting in his mind like the decoding of symbolic writing with the stars as the characters. This very modern definition corresponds well to the direct way that the position of mankind, faced with the celestial ensemble that surrounds and envelops him on all sides, can be interpreted.

The individual being born is placed at the centre of the map of the sky. The local sphere which surrounds him or her is first divided into two hemispheres by the plane of the horizon: what is above this plane is the visible theatre of the starry vault, and the other hemisphere, below, represents the part of the sky which, at that time, is hidden from us because it is under our feet. The axis of the meridian is placed perpendicularly from the highest point reached by the stars in their diurnal course to the lowest in their nocturnal course. The value of the self, of me, is placed at the position of the Ascendant: planets and signs rise there, this celestial emergence being similar, as we have seen, to a birth, but dawn is also the crossing of the invisible into the visible, of night into day, of sleep into waking. So the Ascendant represents the self as a phenomenon of consciousness, of action, autonomy, like the state of 'being ourselves', what we feel inside ourselves, through a feeling of me by being present to one's self. At the same time, can we say dialectically, the descendant, the place where the Sun sets, symbolises what is in front of you, the world that you project yourself on to where you meet your compliment or your opposition, whether to be a couple or to confront. The value of the Ascendant as the subject responds in aggregate to the value of the Descendant as the object (*objectum*, that which is thrown in front; *ob-jacet*, what I see in front of me, outside myself, what is distinct from me, that I am only able to see as separate from myself)… In the same way, the point of culmination, the Midheaven, symbolises the place where the being tends to rise, to establish their ambitions, to raise themselves to their highest level, to shape their future and at the opposite lowest point, at the IC, is their stock, family roots, earthly attachments and earthly ties. Following this the Ancients founded a whole table of correlations, allocating the different areas of existence to the divisions of the local sphere into twelve houses.

The consideration of the way the planets relate to each other, in the various ballet-like formations that they draw around us, has likewise given rise to a whole blueprint of interpretation. The division of these figures is performed geometrically in space with the circle being unity and its components being its division by two, three and four. These relationships between the planets are known as the 'aspects'. The prototype is the conjunction. When any two meet at the same degree of the zodiac, as with the Sun and the Moon at the time of the New Moon, these two bodies tend to merge, to unite, to make a single focus of both their participating tendencies. When placed in opposition, the two planets being 180 degrees apart, or opposite each other as the luminaries are at the Full Moon, we now get a tense astral formation, of confrontation, duality or division, analogous to a state of war between the tendencies represented by these planets. Between the conjunction and the opposition, are the sextile (60 degrees), the square (90 degrees) and the trine (120 degrees) phases that are just as meaningful, being sometimes harmonious, sometimes dissonant, characterising the way in which the interplanetary relationships and exchanges are regulated.

Moreover, the celestial spaces through which the stars move are not homogeneous; they have a quality their own which comes from the Sun. If one can speak of a 'day of human soul' linked to the daily variations of the solar circuit in the diurnal movement, one can no less speak of a 'seasonal life of the soul', linked to the annual revolution of the Sun round the zodiac. It is the symbolisation of nature, lived like the annual experience of the human soul, which can be seen here in the psychogenetic response of the psyche to cosmic stimulation. It is from this that we get, relatively recently, the characterisation of zodiacal types, that chime quite well with the imagination and that literature has increasingly popularised: the Aries type, initiated by the explosive entrance of spring, is hot, lively, impetuous, impulsive and ebullient, with a tendency to charge headlong, while the Capricorn type, modelled on nature at the beginning of winter, is reserved, concentrated, slow, calm, inhibited, patient. This classification of the character types has the range of a rich palette and there is no group of characterisations livelier, richer and more nuanced than this assembly of the twelve major human types with their silhouettes placed between sky and Earth, in the very world of universal correspondences. Naturally, the over-simplification of its use by popular astrology leads to deceit:

that there could be twelve individual categories catalogued by the zodiacal month of their birth would be too simple and too easy. Of course this simplistic classification can be used by way of an intellectual game, in the same way as one likes doing tests, as long as it is understood when you join in that one is using an arbitrarily isolated piece of the whole astrological operation and that with this approach, the result in a particular case will sometimes be successful and sometimes not. [29]

So astrology came to establish a code for deciphering the ensemble of celestial indices and their dependent respective relationships. The map of the sky at birth has the human being at the centre of a circle that represents the celestial sphere; the surrounding space is divided into houses and surrounded by the zodiac and dispersed in it are the Sun, the Moon and the eight planets in their positions of diurnal movement and their aspects. Each arrangement of the ensemble is practically unique, and will never be entirely repeated:[30] it is the mosaic of moving factors which are the ten planets and the twelve houses, together with hundreds of thousands of interactive permutations and millions of possible combinations, each configuration having its own internal logic that requires the wisdom of an interpreter.

In as much as astrology refers to a geocentric sky and even interprets the sky from the place of birth, it has been necessary to assume that the Earth is not moving and to make anthropocentrism its unacceptable way of thinking. What we have to understand, here, is that the seeker and the thing sought are related, the one depending on the other, as are the sign and the thing signified.

The reality is that astrology rests entirely on the motion of our planet (the diurnal rhythm, annual cycle...) and on celestial phenomena that have terrestrial expression, the star in question being in relation to us, Earthlings. The best proof that we have is that the first confirmatory results (to be seen shortly) use the topocentric movement of the rotation of the Earth in relation to the stars in the effect of angularity, that is to say when a planet rises and culminates at a given time and place on Earth. In the course of its rotation the radius vector for a given place meets all the entities in the sky; indeed in twenty-four hours, all the geographical points of our planet, by linear extension directly out into space, come successively in contact with each of the stars in the celestial sphere. With this effect of angularity we are able to exploit one of the most 'anthropocentric' astronomical phenomena! It is not only the movement of the Earth that is the issue; it is also the localised effect, which is both fleeting and singular, because it happens at a particular moment and in this place. What we have is an astral event, which affects a given person in a given place on the Earth's crust at the moment it occurs. As we have seen, the zodiac itself, since it is tropical, is founded entirely on the inclination of the Earth's axis. The astrological condition of human beings moves away from the mere Existentialist nature of astronomical phenomena, because astrology has a foothold in the sky, making it reflect mankind's Earth.

Thus, what we call astral determinism rests on the uranography of our planet with its dozens of movements; in particular the most rapid, rotation, translation, its own movement being relative to the movement of other stars in the solar system and, at the same time, to their respective movements. Mankind is on the Earth and Earth is a planet in space, they are of a piece; mankind is part of the Earth and the sky, intermingled with them, because such is the extent of astrology's cosmic anthropology. Its great philosophical insight extolling the unity of the world, the interdependence of its constituents and the connection of one to all has to imply a communal structure for atoms, for mankind and for the stars, all being fundamentally inseparable.

But, up to now, the rejection of astrology has always rested precisely on this wholly artificial notion of the separation of Earth and sky. Half a century ago, Paul Couderc, co-director of the Paris Observatory, on the basis of potted ideas and with only an elementary knowledge, described the planets as 'dead stars', too small and above all too far away (an argument already raised by Cicero) to exert anything but the most minute influence.

Yet in this day and age you could easily argue that the notion of distance is a highly relative value. Take the space between the Earth and the Sun: the Earth is at perihelion at the beginning of our continent's winter, and at aphelion at the start of the northern summer. In other words, the Earth is five million kilometres – which is more than twelve times the distance between the Earth and the Moon – nearer to the Sun, the source purveying heat and light, on the 1 of January than on the 1 of July. Yet it is right at the beginning of the year that, in our hemisphere, we feel very cold and have the lowest level of annual light... This is due to the fact that the Sun's rays are at the greatest angle to the Earth's crust, which proves that a factor like the inclination of the axis of our globe is more important than the astral distance of more than five million kilometres in the determination of our terrestrial life.

Ever since our spaceships reached the Moon in a fraction of time, this separatist mentality has taken a real knock. In the summer of 1995 it took barely half an hour for the signals emitted from Earth by radio waves to reach a space probe launched towards Jupiter, telling it to carry out a manoeuvre and penetrate Jupiter's atmosphere. The revolution in astronomical knowledge and also in astrophysics brought about by astronautics has led to the idea of interstellar emptiness – only recently an article of faith – being relegated to the stockpile of outdated ideas. Nothing had seemed more terrible to the contemplative mind than the impression given by the faint twinkling of these stars above our heads, with the indifference of a far off infinity separated from us by an immense and absolute void by an infinite distance, a total and definitive space between us and them. Well, this vertiginous pascalian anguish has now gone.

On the one hand, our planet is surrounded by an atmosphere made up of successive layers (troposphere, stratosphere, ionosphere and magnetosphere) which are an integral part of Planet Earth. On the other hand, the Sun itself has an atmosphere which reaches as far as us and in which we bathe, our magnetosphere being considered a simple extension of the solar corona. The interplanetary space of yesterday has now given way to the emissions of protons and electrons in the solar winds; distant echoes or magnetic tail ends of radio waves emitted by planets are all in the interplanetary field. Where we used to speak about an intersidereal vacuum – empty due to a lack of knowledge – we now perceive an immense cloud of matter and electrons in the shape of a pancake centred on the Sun in which the whole solar system bathes and which accounts for many known phenomena. We are now beginning to think that, in the cosmic environment, it is the interstellar matter itself which constitutes the fundamental material from which the universe is made. It is also thought that however thin the substance filling the space round the stars, in the balance of the cosmos, the mass of its molecular abundance is equivalent to that of the stars; also the interior of a star is constituted from the same matter as its surrounding exterior space. The communal interstitial matter of an Earth which continues out into the celestial and of a Sun which reaches right down to it could have its origin in the creation of our planet by the central star, the daughter being made of the same substance as the mother, their chemical composition being qualitatively identical.

On this same Earth the human species appeared as if created by the cosmic environment, human beings in the chain of the living effectively becoming an inseparable entity in the world because they are coextensive in this world. The submission of nature by mankind, which has increased enormously with technology, has made us forget that nature in general encompasses human nature. We also belong to that part of nature that is non-human, the human phenomenon having both a terrestrial and extra-terrestrial dimension. We take part in an essential way in the life which animates our entire planet, and we are an integral part of its planetary existence. By the very fact that life is a chemical reaction, our cells are susceptible to all the influences emanating from the Sun (magnetism, electricity and various kinds of radiation), the human being having been originally a drop of organic matter immersed in the grand network of cosmic emissions and in profound resonance with it.

If the idea of an interstellar void has fallen completely out of fashion, so has the idea of biological isolation. The human organism is no more dissociated from its constituents than it is from the systems of a higher order in which it belongs. Living beings are now considered to be elements in a vast system which covers the Earth.[31] Everything now appears continuous in nature and the living world forms an uninterrupted interwoven framework; all beings are derived one from another, and are bound together by the same movement across time. There is no difference in kind between the living and the inanimate, but only in complexity; the more refined the chemical analysis the more its governing laws are demonstrated. Moreover, the variety of the living world can be reduced to identical physicochemical processes at the molecular level. The evolution of this system, taking place at many levels in the structure, a hierarchy of integrons, goes through the major property of the organisation, 'the emergence unit: always capable of uniting with its kind in order to integrate into the system which controls it [...]. The cell is to the molecule what the molecule is to the atom: a higher level of integration [...]. From particles to human beings, a whole series of integrations, separations and levels happens, but no ruptures ever, neither regarding the composition of the subject nor regarding the reactions taking place there. Its 'essence' stays the same. From now on the analysis of molecules and cellular organelles becomes the business of physicists with the minutia of structures being revealed using crystallography, ultracentrifugation, nuclear magnetic resonance, fluorescence, etc.' [32]

These methods led to the discovery of the biological clock, the internal regulatory system that is in tune with celestial rhythms; from this sprang two new disciplines that are very close to astrology, chronobiology and chronogenetics. The first studies our biological rhythms which are in tune with cosmic time and are comparable to the influence of an exogenous temporality on an endogenous temporality. The 'temporal phenotype' is the variations in light, temperature, barometric pressure, gravitation and electromagnetic field which accord with circadian, monthly or annual rhythms.[33] The second came to be established by Professor Luigi Gedda, who directed the Gregor Mendel Institute at the University of Rome, and it showed the existence of a temporal genotype of a hereditary nature, this synchronisation 'operated by the presence in living beings of mechanisms that receive and, reproduce cosmic temporality that has been developed by life itself [...] by means of prolonged environmental selection,'[34] transmitted according to Mendel's laws of heredity and so therefore of a genetic order. It is apparent that, over the past fifty years, the various horizons of science have moved considerably closer to what constitutes astrology's way of thinking and have now reached a point where this could become a new field of objective study. All we need to know now is how physics, on which all the knowledge of the cosmos and of mankind depends, will respond when faced with the hypothesis of the art of Urania. The theory of astrological knowledge must conform to the basic laws of physics, which is now a universal science with its theories constituting the basis of our understanding of natural phenomena which we identify as real.

In the 1960s, we have to face a negative assessment: all claims by astrologers that they should receive physical status were categorically rebuffed, and this will remain the case while modern physics is what it is: it has established that the only conceivable physical actions are at short distance and have a finite speed of transmission which cannot exceed that of light whatever its mode, wave or particulates. That was the received opinion, but not anymore.

For the physicist, what constitutes the ultimate reality of the world is the watch-like arrangement of a group of small particles, fields and forces as described by quantum physics. In the microscopic world, as well as in that of the infinitely large, all objects are very far away, in huge numbers, separated from each other by comparatively large distances, isolated in space, while being in constant motion at high speed. This picture of the structural unity of the universe is one of great numbers, great distances, at great removal, enormous spaces and ultrafast movements, in which the only 'substance' is composed of space-time.

To explain this 'primary matter' they came up with a convenient theory: the principle of separability, that which is observed in the world when it is described by means of a model that is based on the notion of separate macroscopic objects. It was an analytical vision of a world compartmentalised by the fragmentary nature of its objects, whereby one can only imagine the influence of something close. The universe was broken down to its elements, each occupying one small region of space at any given time and only exerting a limited influence on the behaviour of elements distant from it.

However, this position was not universally accepted. Some physicists shared Albert Einstein's theory that a particle is only a 'denser' region of the field which encompasses the entire universe. In 1963 Jean Charon said:

> The elementary particles which constitute all matter should not be considered as separate from the rest of the cosmos, but as objects which, by what is known as their 'field' [gravitational, electromagnetic or nuclear], are coextensive with the whole universe. Naturally man, like all matter, is also 'made' from these particles which are coextensive with the whole universe: and so, in a way, man is united with the whole of the surrounding cosmos. He is in constant liaison with what one can call the cosmic environment. This cosmic environment, which at the end of the day represents the crux of all that exists, must also modify and act in some way on the personal consciousness of the individual. The influence of this environment is less

apparent because it is found in man's more or less
unconscious thoughts.[35]

Later, atomic and particle physics validated this idea of the
indivisibility of a whole by demonstrating—now not a
theory but a scientific fact—the principle of non-separability.
Bernard d'Espagnat, then director of the laboratory of
theoretical physics and elementary particles at the
University of Paris XI, provided the following definition:

> If the notion of a reality independent of man but
> accessible to his knowledge is considered meaningful,
> then such a reality is necessarily non-separable. By
> 'non-separable', we have to understand that if you
> want to consider the reality of parties that are locatable
> in space, then if such parties interact in a particular
> way at a time when they are close together, they
> continue to interact however remote they become from
> each other, this by the means of instantaneous
> influences.[36]

It goes without saying that astrology is particularly
concerned with the establishment of this fundamental
indivisibility. In principle, this sanctions astrology's
traditional philosophical intuition of a world of unity and
interdependence where existence is essentially linked to the
interaction of the one with the whole, each individual
belonging in the world. In place of things being fragmented
and of an effect that relies on proximity we now have the
concept of total synthesis and an effect that is total and
simultaneous. In its operational field where its system brings
the star and mankind together in space time, the problem of
the distance between these two objects is eliminated.

Thus, step by step, scientific knowledge advances
towards the recognition of human beings in their celestial
condition, well known by the poet and the sage.

We are citizens of the sky. Whether we know it or not,

in reality we live in the stars.

Camille Flammarion, *Urania*

We feel our deep kinship with everything that exists in the universe. Man 'descended' from primates, primates 'descended' from cells, the cell 'descended' from the molecule, the molecule from the atom, the atom from the quark. We were engendered in the initial explosion, in the heart of the stars and in the immensity of interstellar space.

Hubert Reeves, *Patience dans l'azur.*

Chapter 6 - The Statistical Assessment

It is important, first of all, not to hold on to appearances as with the type of astrological expression which leads to matters of faith, supposition, illusion and prejudice. To start with, we have to look under the surface to search for the facts, whether positive or negative, because only real evidence can give us the hypotheses, explanations and approaches needed to understand, if not reveal more about, astrology. Choisnard, at the beginning of the last century, said:

> The stars are related in a positive and demonstrable way with our innate abilities and as a possible way of knowing what these abilities are they allow a certain amount of study of the innate differences between men. This is a justification for the principle of judicial astrology among the ancients.

When it comes to certainty, it is possible that science has nothing better to offer than establishing the relationship between cause and effect; and yet there is no proof as yet of this causal relationship between human beings and the stars. To the despair of one of astrology's most fanatical opponents, the astronomer Paul Couderc, there is no proof to the contrary that any such relationship is not possible: 'It is a fact that there is no direct, undisputed proof that shows astrology to be wrong.'[37] That is not to say that you cannot hope for the discovery of the missing proof ... In 1971, Lucien Malavard, who was professor of science at the Sorbonne and a member of the L'Institut, declared:

> I, personally, have no problem with the idea of there being influences that we don't know about. One can well imagine that, in the centuries to come, many other material discoveries will be made, since, in the last thirty years, more discoveries have been made in physics and chemistry than have been made since the

beginning of the world! Perhaps evidence will be found and such influences demonstrated but for now we have no explanation. So my attitude towards astrological interpretation remains one of interest and curiosity.[38]

In the absence of anything concrete, we have to resort to the correlational evidence which is incomplete. In an exercise of this sort there has to be an anticipated outcome. We test a given configuration, for which past experience has already established the type of correlation expected, and the proof is in being able to repeat the provisional successful result, in a continuous series, with the given phenomenon being reproduced in a uniform way: for example, every thirteen months, at each Sun-Jupiter conjunction, we return to a climate of peace, détente and accord in the diplomatic process. This is a subject that we will tackle in the next chapter. Besides this type of experiment, the principal way to test the practical effectiveness of astrology is through statistics, proof being provided by the calculation of probability.

Having refused to get bogged down in a morass of hypotheses, Choisnard, a graduate from the prestigious Ecole Polytechnique (French Polytechnic School), was the first astrologer who could see the absolute necessity of using statistics as a way of proving astrological hypotheses. In order to establish some 'astrological facts' he used the law of correspondences which is defined as follows: 'In the birth chart a planetary aspect is said to correspond to a certain human attribute (their character or destiny) when this aspect is found more often with men gifted with this attribute than with other individuals.' Using this approach he began doing different surveys, and other researchers followed. Little remains of these small-scale investigations which were insufficiently focused and too scattered.

However it is worth mentioning two surveys that dealt with topocentric positions. Traditionally, having Jupiter at culmination (conjunct the MC) is a factor of success or social recognition. Choisnard collected the charts for two thousand people who were not known and those of one thousand five hundred people who had achieved success and become famous. For the first group, he obtained an overall frequency of 5.5% (corresponding to the theoretical frequency) and in the second an unusual frequency of 12%; he concluded that Jupiter culminating is a 'factor for celebrity'. In 1946, the astrologer Leon Lasson wrote a book called *Ceux qui nous guident* (Those That Guide Us) (Debresse, Paris) in which he presented a series of statistics which, although too small, were suggestive: these showed markedly that Mars was rising or culminating for 158 military leaders, the Moon was rising or culminating for 134 politicians 'elected by the people', the same with Venus for 190, Mercury for 209 orators and writers and Saturn for a small group of scholars....For each outcome Lasson came to the same conclusion as he had for Mars.

> For astrologers in every age, a planet which rises or culminates in the sky has a particular importance, and now our military show a preference for being born just when Mars has risen or has culminated [...]. Those, who through heredity or other causes, are predisposed to become soldiers are usually born when Mars has just risen or culminated in the sky [...]. There is a clear relationship between the sky at birth and the chosen profession, and for the military this relationship is expressed by the rising or culmination of Mars, this is in keeping with the teaching of astrological tradition.

This was the beginning of a highly unusual statistical experiment: it would be a huge investigation because, at bottom, there is nothing that suggests that human beings have any connection with the stars. While the obvious nature of some disciplines (such as graphology where one can see a direct relationship between the writer's character and its expression in their writing) makes verification unnecessary though they have established no substantial evidence, the paradox for astrology is that its characteristic of being highly unlikely gives it the status of irreversible probability!

Strangely, it is a declared opponent of astrology who we must credit with employing every means to obtain a statistical evaluation and, to his dismay, the results were unquestionably positive. Michel Gauquelin tested an initial batch of twenty-five thousand dates of birth taken from the civil records. He made a systematic inventory of whole groups of people featuring in biographical dictionaries and applied his audit to the same types of astronomical phenomena to obtain a set of results. His methods were double checked at various stages by leading experts in statistics. No technical errors were found and the counter-tests they proposed only highlighted the deviations obtained. Also his numerical results were looked at separately by various observers who produced their own statistics.

Michel Gauquelin was forced to agree that the 3,142 European military leaders, whose dates of birth were in the civil register, were born when Mars was rising or culminating (a probability of one in a million), that the 3,305 scholars from the Académies des sciences et de médecine (Academy of Science and Medicine) were born when Saturn was rising or culminating (a probability of 1 in 100,000), that the 993 statesmen and political leaders were born when Jupiter was rising or culminating a probability of 1 in 115,000), that the 1,485 sporting champions were born when Mars was rising or culminating (a probability of 1 in 5 million), and so on; the overall result for the 25,000 births exceeding five times the probable deviation![39]

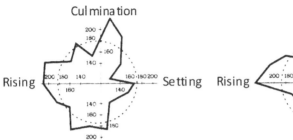

a) Position of Mars for 3,142 military personnel (marshals, generals, admirals, officers).

b) Position of Saturn for 3,305 scientists (academicians of science and medicine).

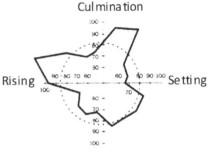

c) Position of Jupiter for 993 politicians (Heads of State, ministers, deputies).

d) Position of Mars for 1,485 sporting champions.

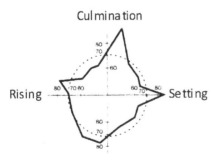

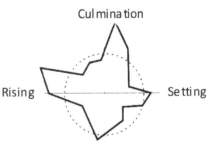

e) Position of Jupiter for 1,270 actors (stars).

Overall result for 25,000 cases five times more than the probable deviation!

An extract from *Man and the Stars*

These results mean that, even though his enemies were counting on it, the probabilistic field cannot be used as a means of rejecting astrology. A group of about thirty members of the Belgian Committee for the Scientific Investigation of Phenomena reputed to be Paranormal, known as the Para Committee, made up of rationalist scholars ever-vigilant in the fight against 'occultism', initiated statistical tests on a group of 535 sporting champions. Their dates of birth were collected and computerised by their specialists. This distinguished body that was blatantly anti astrology –Professor L Koenigsfeld of Liege, its president, expressed as much when asked – found the same conclusive results relating to the rise and culmination of Mars. With eloquent reluctance the assessment was published ten years later, in 1976. (Belgian Committee, Nouvelles brèves, no. 43.)

Another enquiry into Mars and sporting champions was thoroughly undertaken in 1979 with American athletes by a body of the same mind as the Para committee, the CSICOP (Committee for the Scientific Investigation of Claims of the Paranormal). Its publication, *The Sceptical Inquirer*, confirmed the result the same year. Previously, the rationalist revue, *The Humanist*, had the same experience and, in number XI-XII in 1977, attempted to get away with this very interesting evasion:

> If you are predisposed to believe in a Mars 'effect', Gauquelin's data will help to bolster your belief; but if you don't have this strong predisposition, the data might just support it pending further results, but not as far as admitting that there definitely is a Mars 'effect'.

So that was the position of our declared adversaries, at least, of those who had risked dealing with the question.[40]

It is not always possible to overcome our shame and fear when faced with astrology. When the results of testing astrology are negative statisticians know what to say; but if there is a positive result, then it is no longer astrology. When Gauquelin first ran his tests he flatly declared that these 'strange results' were just chance..., an 'accidental discovery'. The results were too 'new', 'unexpected' ...nothing to do with the doctrine of astrology [and did not have] any resemblance to the traditional laws of astrology'; better still, 'they even demolished all its theories ..., it was a new and powerful critique of this superstition'

In the luxury of this denial, he completely forgets the importance attached to the rise and culmination of planets by Chaldean and Ptolemaic tradition. It is worth rereading the *Tetrabiblos* apropos *the* profession and its achievements:

> The ruler of a profession is taken from the Sun and from the sign on the Midheaven. We have to consider the planet which, closest to the Sun, rises before it in the morning, and that which is at the Midheaven.[41]

> Also when the planets [...] are at the angles, they give to him who is born thus marvellous power and a worldwide empire [...]. If they are not at the angles, he [the subject] will live a lacklustre life and won't be paid well for what he does.[42]

Remember that Ptolemy had already associated Mars with success 'in the conduct of arms', Saturn with deep thought and Jupiter with statecraft. The 'discovery' that our statistician has made is more than two thousand years old: the predicted planet appears in the expected group (for example Mars for the military, athletes and physicians, Jupiter for politicians and entertainers, Saturn for scholars, the Moon for popular people, poets and writers), and they appear at expected points in the sky, on the celestial axes that Manilius calls the 'linchpins', the Ascendant and the Mid-heaven. These are two places of maximum concentration which are approximately equal (recognising the question of disagreement on this subject between various authorities on the tradition), and then we have the

Descendant and the IC, which are zones of concentration of secondary importance.

By reasoning like Lasson and many astrologers, at least our statistician had, involuntarily, done some astrological work: if individuals, who have Mars in a prime position, either rising or culminating, are markedly likely to be military leaders, wouldn't the roots of their professional vocation be found in their hereditary make-up?

Michel Gauquelin then undertook a second statistical exercise based on 32,074 births from the civil records. This study compared the birth charts of 16,037 parents with those of their children. This new survey confirmed the results of the first one: if the father or mother was born when a given planet was rising or culminating, the child usually comes into the world with the same planet rising or culminating. This phenomenon of transmission is observed equally for each child, male or female, older or younger, and doubles in intensity when the two progenitors have the same planet rising or culminating! The statistician concluded that there is a definite hereditary tendency to be born at one moment rather than another, following a parental precedent, and that this hereditary baggage implies that we are predisposed to choose a particular career path. Ten years later a second similar set of statistics was produced based on 37,112 births, which provided 18,556 comparisons: it produced the same results. 'If one considers the experiments 1966 + 1976 into planetary effects – 171,695 cases – the Chi-Square reaches a value that has little or almost no possibility of happening by chance: a probability of 1 in 10 million.'[43]

These results are not a revelation either. In his *Astronomia Nova*, Kepler stated, 'Similarities between the stars of close relatives are seen more frequently than between people who are unrelated.' What we have here is what we call 'astral heredity'. Choisnard, who studied it at great length at the beginning of the last century, defined it as follows: 'Human beings don't come into the world at random moments; nature tends to make births happen under a sky which conforms with heredity, the natal chart of the child having similarities with the charts of his progenitors.'[44] Certainly, Choisnard believed that he had established the existence of astral heredity shown by the zodiacal positions, the aspects and the topocentric positions of the planets. Only this last correlation had been demonstrated then but it is still worth mentioning.

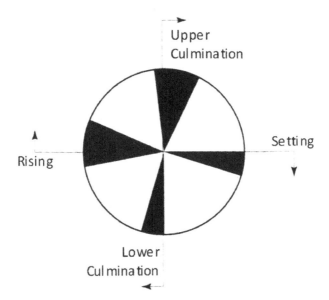

Planet at the birth of the parent

Michel Gauquelin carried out a third statistical survey as a result of the second one. He classified the 16,000 births that he had gathered previously for his investigation into heredity in order to compare them with the Earth's magnetic disturbance. As we know, magnetic disturbance, the international magnetic character (Ci), is given a value of 0 (calm day) up to 2 (magnetic storm). Gauquelin compared the 16,000 dates of birth with the 16,000 values corresponding to magnetic activity and he soon observed a connection between terrestrial magnetic disturbance and the planetary effect in heredity. He divided the material into two groups: those children born on a day of disturbance (a Ci of 1 to 2) and those children born on a calm day (a Ci of 0 to 0.9).

The number of hereditary similarities between children and parents is two and a half times greater when children are born on days with magnetic disturbance than when they are born on a calm day. Numerical precision makes the importance of this phenomenon more apparent when applied to planetary observations in the sectors where they rise and culminate. If an index of 100 indicates the absence of planetary effect in heredity (people who are not related to their parents) we find that the planetary effect exceeds an index of 105 for children born on calm days and an index of 113 for children born on days when there is disturbance. The difference is so considerable that, given the large number of observations, its chance of occurring is one in a million. This connection between planets and magnetism has been observed for Mars, Jupiter, Saturn and above all Venus.[45]

Michel Gauquelin, with this third investigation, has to be given credit for being the first to finally carry out this research into correlation but it has to be pointed out that the connection between astral determinism and geomagnetism was already in the minds of the reformers at the beginning of the last century when they were looking for a physical basis for astrological phenomena. In 1922, under the pseudonym of Flambard, Choisnard wrote:

As I indicated when I first wrote [1898 onwards], among the explanatory hypotheses for astrology, those that are in line with the dynamic theories of waves and vibrations have the advantage of bringing in all kinds of cosmic influences involving radiation, the influence and vibratory phenomena of sound, heat, light, electricity, magnetism, etc. If the Earth's magnetism, as is generally recognised today, undergoes variations that are dependent on the stars, it is hardly surprising that our vital organism which is immersed in it, feels the after effects; and it is not surprising if, as a consequence, man's individual magnetism is subject to the same laws. In short, this is an explanation, already proposed elsewhere, which has always seemed acceptable to me, at least provisionally, in the face of the experienced, observable and coordinated facts that have been established. The sexual rapport that brings men and women together has its laws of harmony. The connection between the astral influence at conception and that at birth were discussed long ago by Ptolemy and many other astrologers, without proof perhaps, but not without likelihood. 'Magnetic gestation' probably operates in concert with physical gestation; and nature tends to give birth to the newborn, if one can say that, in an environment of cosmic magnetic vibrations that conforms most to the hereditary magnetism which comes directly from the mother and indirectly from the father: From this we get the laws of astral heredity which are expressed in the frequent analogies between the birth charts of people who are closely related.[46]

This is the hypothesis which has been validated here, even if it is still full of mystery. So we come back to the data in the preceding chapter which founded astrological phenomena on the uranography of our planet, the instrument in an orchestra conducted by the Sun, which brings us nearer to having a theory explaining an influence of the cosmos on mankind.

Up to now we have been doing some necessary preliminary tests to see if our results would conform to traditional teaching. Having obtained these results, we can use the statistical information to look more closely at the subject being explored, dividing the mass of material into subgroups in order to find the differences or special features behind the invariance.

Thus, in his study of astral heredity, Michel Gauquelin compared the results obtained from a group of natural births with those of a group of induced births that had taken place in clinics where deliveries were by appointment and during working hours. The result was edifying: the astral correlations between parents and their children that were striking in the first group, fell in the second! The induced births, brought on artificially, happened at random and most of them no longer showed the correlation of having the same planet rising or culminating; the results showed an absolute fall in a survey comparing 1,440 births by Caesarean or forceps.

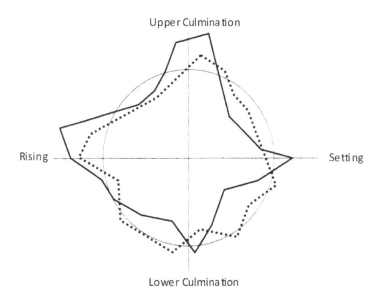

The intensity of the planetary effect on heredity depends on the magnetic activity.

This differentiation in the results again raises the question of the naïve idea that the stars might have an influence on individuals. Our statistician came to the same conclusion:

Does a planet influence a child at birth and leave the stamp of character? No, the effect of the planets is simply to trigger the birth at a given moment, because of a genetic sensitivity that the child inherits from the parents. The astral influence which is shown during the birth process is only evidence of the temperament that the child has […]. Yes, these latest discoveries distance us from the possibility of an astrological universe.[47]

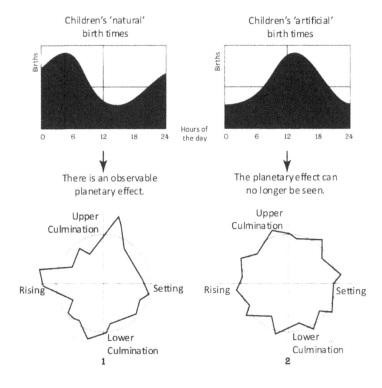

The planetary clock is no longer hereditary if the birth of the child is not natural.

Once again, Michel Gauquelin has forgotten two thousand years of history. In fact, although there is a historical tide of physicists in the line of Ptolemy and Morin, who feel that the stars really do have a tangible effect and that they are a sort of coercive force weighing on mankind, at the same time there is a whole symbolist tradition dating back to the Stoics and Plotinus who have never ceased proclaiming that the planets are more a sign than a cause.

According to hermetic thought, as I keep saying, the

map of the sky at birth is not some kind of show of celestial power come to influence us from on high but only a reflection of the tendencies that come from our interior disposition. Thus it is not the fact of being born at a certain time which determines how we are structured (in such a case one could bring forward or delay a birth to have a child 'to order' astrologically: a quarter of an hour earlier, the makings of a sporting champion, half an hour later, a big name in science). We have to reverse the proposition: it is the original human make-up which 'calls' and requires a celestial state made to reflect it. In short, one can say that one isn't as one is born but that one is born as one is; at least if you leave it to nature.

According to this hermetic tradition, if Venus, for example, influences our love life, it is not that a celestial body is exercising a transitive action which starts from a celestial point and arrives at a human point, it is that this planet is a symbol of the aspirations of the human heart, by virtue of a 'sympathy' between the astral Venusian element and the verb 'to love', since we are made of the same material as the universe.

The directive may well seem to come from the sky; if it is written there, above all it manifests inside the human being. Destiny does not take place outside the person. Humans are not dependent on an outside entity, in this instance a celestial body: they are only slaves or free people in themselves. In the universe where the one is coextensive with the whole and the whole converges in the one, there is no succession of cause and effect between a planet and a human being; on the contrary, the one and the other are held in an absolute simultaneity, the relationship between the astronomical external and of the human internal being one.

This traditional thought is expressed in the vitalist cosmology of the *Timaeus* and Plotinus was the main interpreter of its fourth *Ennead*. There we see the emergence of the notion of a sympathetic action.

Things that are similar, which are not touching, but

are separated by an interval, are in sympathy by virtue of their being alike. Without being in contact the things act and their action is necessarily at a distance. As the universe is a creature which has attained unity, none of its parts is in such a distant place that it is not still close, because of the tendency to sympathy which exists between all the parts of a single animal. When the patient is similar to the agent he is subjected to an influence which is not foreign to his nature.

This sympathy exerts itself via a channel of harmonic correspondence:

> [...] a correspondence similar to the way that, at each moment in a dance, the movements of the dancers both match and direct those of the others; there is no action of the parties on each other, nothing to connect them other than the intention of the dancer who performs as part of the whole without his having to will each of his gestures separately. In seeing the individuals of this group correspond to each other, we can take the existence of the one as a sign of the existence of the other and what's more without there being the slightest mechanical or physical influence between them. So the positions of the stars are only the arrangements of certain parts of the animal universe, and these positions correspond to those of the other parts according to a necessary rule. [Because] each being cannot live as if he was alone, since he is a part [of the universe], he is not an end in himself, but in the whole of which he is a part.[48]

Paracelsus expanded on this hermetic idea in his *Theory of Similarities*:

> Understand that the upper star [in the sky] and the lower star [in oneself] are one and the same thing and are not separated in any way. It is the exterior sky

which throws light on the interior sky. Man possesses a sky that is particular to him, which is like the one outside and has the same constellations. This is why man is subject to time: not by the sky outside but by the one that is inside. The planet in the firmament reigns over neither you nor me, but over that which is inside us. The astronomer who judges a birth according to the planets outside is mistaken, they don't affect man, it is the interior sky with its planets that acts; the exterior sky only serves to demonstrate and indicate the internal sky [...]. In the sky there is a semblance which possesses its likeness on Earth, and on Earth there exists a semblance which possesses its likeness in the sky. Saturn could not reign on Earth if there wasn't a terrestrial Saturn, and where it exists, it is active; however there is only one Saturn, not two. That of the Earth is the nourishment of the celestial Saturn, and this last gives nourishment to the terrestrial Saturn.[49]

Of course these philosophical theories will not exempt us from searching for a proof based on science for which they are no substitute, but at least they have the merit of granting us the biological reality by sweeping away the silliness of an astral impulse which, at the spontaneous moment of birth, would make the newborn strong or weak, lively or slow, cheerful or sad, happy or unhappy... their individual constitution, already formed from the time of conception, not depending on the moment of coming into the world. We have to look further than the idea of something mechanical, a physical action or a causal relationship, at least one that is direct. Nor is it a matter of adding a specific astral determinism to the determinism already known to genetics, biology, physiology, psychology, sociology... This astral determinism is only superimposed on these; it is expressed through them. In the words of Schiller: 'The stars of your destiny are in your heart.' A real knowledge of universal correspondences, astrology becomes a language with the sky as the signifier and the individual the signified. It deals, in a symbolic way, with the union of the signifier and the signified. The first does not determine the second, but expresses it; rather than being an agent, it is a witness. If the map of the sky is a picture of the individual on the same scale as the universe, the chart is not the creator, but it only reveals the being. Choisnard was thinking along these lines when he came to the following conclusion about astral heredity: 'the child does not have such a character, because he is born at a certain moment; but he is born at a certain moment because he has or will have such a character through heredity [...] Above all one is born under a certain sky because one already has such a hereditary character.

Michel Gauquelin made an equally important investigative breakthrough when he compared the results obtained for a group of notable professionals, those 'at the top', with those of a control group made up of individuals trained in the same profession but who were not outstanding: 717 sporting professionals who were not champions, 1,458 ordinary scientists, 2,123 politicians who'd never held office, and 2,840 soldiers taken from the rank and file. It is a general finding that in all the groups tested the correlations found are much more significant when the people concerned are representative of their group. Thus, the Jupiter which rises majestically at the angles in the skies of 604 film stars almost completely disappears from the horizon and the meridian at the births of 666 actors who are relatively unknown. Saturn did not appear for obscure scientists and neither did Jupiter for our simple politicians. As for Mars, it becomes more and more apparent the more one rises through the ranks of the army: while the soldiers with the most stripes have this planet prominently placed, it is less dominant among the lower ranks, and it never appears with the ordinary troops.

> So it is essential to have attained a certain degree of success, to have become famous, in order to observe some positive results. To put it another way, the more

an individual reaches the heights of his chosen profession the more he is likely to have come to the world in 'astral conformity' with his reference group. This tendency towards over-representation was observed for great heads of state, sporting super champions, Great War heroes, the sacred cows of theatre and cinema and the heads of painting schools.[50]

This author's interpretation, the same as that previously expressed by Lasson, was that having, for example, Mars as an indicator, corresponds to the option of an army career. Martian being the subject of heredity, Martian by the same token becomes the choice of career. This is an erroneous conclusion. Rather, as I have already stated, it is that this Martian indicator is more about having a disposition to succeed in the army, in the same way that having Jupiter at the angles is a sign of success for a career in acting. Because, 'it is not the fact of going into the army as a Martian that counts here; it is that, being Martian, one will be successful there.' Further on we will look at all the conclusions that must be drawn from these observations, conclusions also drawn by Michel Gauquelin who now talks about planets which favour success.

In his latest work he says, 'Is it really possible that the planets determine the choice of career? We don't believe so. It is not opportunity that is written in the stars, it is temperament.' Temperament... Brilliantly, once again, Michel Gauquelin takes us back two thousand years to where Ptolemy married the 'mathematical cause' and 'that which comes from temperament'.

From this came a new differentiating investigation which engaged the researcher and his team in some important work. Innumerable test results were pared down so that an average profile could be established for each professional category, and they looked at countless biographical studies so as to obtain thousands of files listing hundreds of character traits that were specific to each of the individuals who previously had been treated as a whole by the statistics. This was the result:

> Invincible champions, those whose names will be recorded in the pantheon for their courage and willpower, are twice as likely as other champions to be born when Mars is rising over the horizon or is at the meridian. These champions 'with their iron will', who have the character traits in the preceding list are more 'Martian than the others'. This is what we had to demonstrate. The percentage of these super champions who were born with Mars on the horizon or the meridian is twice that for the birth of Mr Everybody [61% instead of 33%]. On the other hand this same percentage for the less dedicated champions is lower than that of Mr Everybody [29% instead of 33%] [...]. The natal position of Mars is definitely an expression of temperament; it has little to do with one's profesional destiny.[51]

The same results were found for a whole list of other professional categories: the actor type has a Jupiterian temperament, in the way that the scientist type has a Saturnian temperament; Jupiter is found twice as often at the angles for extraverted actors than for actors who are more 'modest'; it is the same for Saturn for scientists who are more introverted.

The logical conclusion drawn from this series of investigations is that M. Gauquelin, changing from the choice of career to being successful in that career, and from this to his psychological determination or temperament, has, in a striking fashion, gradually recreated, as by extraction, the traditional planetary typology, associated with four planets: Moon, Mars, Jupiter and Saturn (and later, Venus).

The left clock shows Mars at the hour of birth of known champions. The diagram on the right shows Saturn for introverted and extraverted scientists.

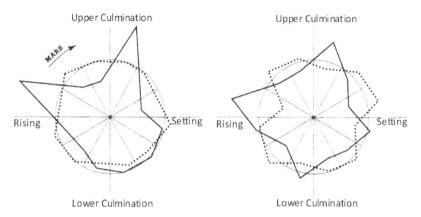

In the rest of his tests of astrology Michel Gauquelin did not find anything for the zodiac, the aspects or the other planets, so what is the value of his investigations? Is the method he used to investigate the zodiac satisfactory? He merely grouped together all the military, all the painters, all the musicians in his collection, and so on, and then counts the astral positions in all the signs of the zodiac for each category; nowhere did he find a particular concentration that put the accent on a given sign. If he had gathered all the angular planetary positions for the same professional groups, he wouldn't have done any better since, for a given professional category, while there is a planet that 'seeks' the angles, there is also another which 'stays away' from them (like the Moon, which is under-represented at the rise and culmination of the military and sportspeople, while Mars is under-represented in the same positions, for writers and musicians…) over-representation and under-representation tending to cancel each other out. In any case, in dealing with the angularity of a star, one is talking about a quantitative factor, as clearly understood by the tradition, while the planetary position in a sign is specifically qualitative. There is no special military, musical or pictorial sign; that is the lesson we have to draw from these undifferentiated statistics (There was no need to do it in order to know it). On the other hand there are, for example, musical or pictorial temperaments for each sign,[52] and while we are not really looking for them and are instead blindly fishing in the raw statistics, we are only wasting time with empty talk.

In 1985 Michel Gauquelin had to redo a third investigation into astral heredity, based on the birth data for 50,942 people, which had had a disappointing result. It minimised, while not altogether doing away with, what had been learnt before. The final outcome of his work that amalgamated his three categories (professional groups, key words and heredity) was the creation of a huge representative sample.

Again he was called before the *Comité français pour l'étude des phénomènes paranormaux* (CFEPP) (French Committee for the Study of Paranormal Phenomenon (FCSPP) in an nth repeat of the Mars and sportspeople scenario (*Science et Vie* [Science and Life], October 1982). Once again the proceedings ended in disagreement among members of the Committee; who argued about the choice of the selected champions. They had to be—according to the accepted protocol—'highly reputed'.

As a result one of them, Professor Suitbert Ertel (from the Institute of Psychology, University of Göttingen) protested in an article published in "*Correlation* Volume 17 Issue 2 in 1998 : 'Is there no Mars Effect?"

The Professor highlighted an obvious flaw.

> But when I looked at the standing of the champions chosen by the FCSPP by counting the number of times each was mentioned in eighteen reference books [a method he had introduced himself in 1988], I found that the FCSPP champions only had a relatively low number of mentions compared to those of Gauquelin in his first samples. Moreover the champions of the FCSPP who had a greater number of mentions showed a significant Mars effect which was not the case for the champions with a lower number of mentions.

This protest about the committee's imposition of these unrepresentative cases was in vain so Suitbert Ertel took over the investigation and independently approached nine of the FCSPP's competent researchers. Six responded to his call. The conclusion: 'The disproportionate number of births with Mars in the key sector that I found among the FCSPP's most eminent champions was independently confirmed by six researchers.'

One had the impression of seeing one's enemies blind, isolated and desperately clinging to one another while refusing to take the jump. The inquiry into Mars and the sporting champions certainly gave the best results astrologically but we need to hold it at this level and take it no further, because there are other results pressing which, though less important, cannot be dismissed. The tree of Martian statistics cannot hide a forest of similar outcomes which stand out because of their specific homogeneity: the rising and culmination of stars by professional group, character traits and heredity all in keeping with the astrological programme.

Now, with the start of the 21st century, we are going to lift ourselves out of the mire of the previous debates: more scheming and suspicion is possible because we are entering the smooth terrain of marriage and heredity, union and parental filiation which has authority and is unambiguous. An investigation into astral heredity which dealt with 75,572 subjects (1983-1994) had already been completed by Ciro Discepolo and his team. It was carried out under the guidance and control of the statistical authorities of the University of Naples and was reported in the *Ricerca 90* review. A significant frequency emerged from a range of cases: the tendency for the sign on the child's Ascendant to be the sign occupied by the Sun at the birth of the father or mother. This peculiarity indirectly reintroduces the debate about the zodiac; this common sign must have the value of being an intermediary charged with a characteristic that is transmitted from the parent to the child.

We have reached the milestone of the year 2000, which may well be viewed later as a decisive historical turning point in the unveiling of astrology thanks to the arrival of a new contributor. Armed with the resources of Insee, (the French National Institute of Statistics and Economic Studies) he was finally able to carry out the ultimate investigation, his material being the demographic data from the population census of 1990, an inventory of 56 million French people!

After all, until the arrival of Didier Castille the testing had only been of rudimentary samples, even if, in total, they extended to hundreds of thousands of people. Now we have complete access to the documentation and it touches the entire national population. Indeed it is the demographic in its entirety which is being surveyed collectively. In other words this will be the hub for the fate of astrology, the point where there has to be a clear yes or no. And we have to get to that point.

This turning point is important because of an unexpected astral intervention. This event was, in fact, the arrival of a new factor which was of huge importance. Until now an essential element had been missing from the case for rehabilitation. How was it that the Sun itself was absent in all the statistical records? A central vacuum which was disconcerting!

Astrology presents the solar system in an angular state. For too long the short-sighted talk about the poor planets that are much too small and much too far away, has hidden the fundamental reality of the unity of a living system where everything depends on everything else. The whole planetary configuration goes past the Sun, and such has been traditional thought. In Phoenician astrology, the planets were in submission to the Sun and were its assistants receiving their own power from this central, all-powerful star and transmitting it by acting in their turn. Censorinus claimed to be conveying the 'methods used by the Chaldeans' in saying that, if we are dependent on the planets they themselves are governed by the Sun. The Sun is the heart of the organism that is our cosmos, and it is from this that the modulating influence of the planets is conceived. How, then, have we come to abandon the sign of solar life? This enormous omission has now been remedied. Suddenly

Her Majesty the Sun has appeared on the horizon and for once she demonstrates the value of her involvement in the fundamentals of the human condition: both in mating and in procreation.

Marriage and the Sun

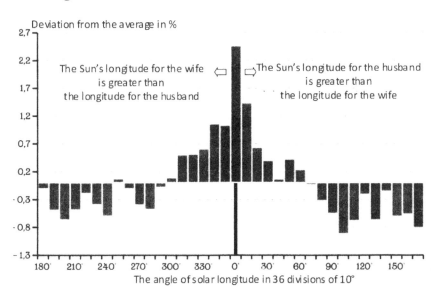

This diagram shows the distribution of the marriages according to the angle formed by the solar positions of the marriage partners. The vertical line in the middle (0°) shows the alignment of couples having the same birthday (but not necessarily the same year). Each degree of separation corresponds to the difference of a day between birthdays, a distance that spreads out to 180° on each side, the two extreme edges having birthdays that are poles apart from each other in the year.

Didier Castille had already contributed to a statistical exploration in the form of a comprehensive survey that Gunter Sachs presented in the French version of *Die Akte Astrologie*.[53]   Originally, Sachs' sample covered 358,763 marriages that had taken place in Switzerland between 1987 and 1994. The study compared the dates of birth of the husbands with those of the wives: it showed that the unions became more and more numerous the closer the birthdays were to each other.

There was even greater confirmation with the study of 6,498,320 unions which took place in France in the 21 years between 1976 and 1996. The results of the investigation are presented in *'Mariages au Soleil'*, (Sunny Day for a Wedding)[54].

These results for matrimony establish the value of the conjunction, the factor that tends to bring closeness and union: there are many more couples where the Sun of the man is close to the Sun of the woman, the maximum number of unions being made between people with neighbouring birthdays and even more with the same birthday. The psychological interpretation of this phenomenon would be that of a narcissistic effect or the attraction of like for like: birds of a feather flocking together.

In the investigation into Swiss marriages, the conclusion made by Gunter Sachs about the proximity of the birthdays was that the decision to marry is not unconnected to the sign of the zodiac that the partners have in common.

The grey squares correspond to the sign combinations for which the actual number of marriages is greater than the theoretical number. The indicator of the importance of each deviation (contribution to the Chi-Square) which is indicated under the value is interpreted according to the table opposite.

The diagram, with Didier Castille's explanatory comments, clearly shows a diagonal of over-representation for the partnerships of people having the same Sun sign, which is similarly found in a balanced population of 6.5 million French marriages. But the phenomenon extends beyond the sign It shows that really 'it is the angular difference between the solar longitude of the husband and the solar longitude of the wife which is special', their relationship owing 'more to the proximity of the solar longitudes than to that of the sign'. For the rest there is a regular progression of the matrimonial effect spread across the year: the more apart the birthdays, the less there are unions, and, inversely, the closer they are the more couplings take place.

	♈	♉	♊	♋	♌	♍	♎	♏	♐	♑	♒	♓	Total
Aries	934 ***	175	-72	-213	-31	-117	-173	-237	-105	-147	-59	46	564 684
Taurus	-196	992 ***	64	570 *	-643 ***	114	-179	-280	-517 *	163	-259	171	582 442
Gemini	288	166	1 029 ***	-159	-137	-111	-86	168	-271	-132	-119	-635 ***	565 465
Cancer	-235	-291	287	964 ***	92	8	-465	123 *	-164	-164	-23	-132	565 352
Leo	-141	-265	-30	-87	949 ***	146	278	-446 *	-194	-147	-45	-18	547 524
Virgo	-633 ***	-80	-160	14	321	972 ***	96	66	71	-125	-325	-217	538 762
Libra	-55	-85	-330	-405	201	247	922 ***	-2	57	-192	-280	-77	524 980
Scorpio	-344	-316	-105	-243	-305	31	249	1 281 ***	106	-46	-335	27	494 748
Sagittarius	-36	-361	91	-127	216	-374	333	-265	1 003 ***	-130	96	-448 *	497 582
Capricorn	164	-182	-346	32	-179	-346	-333	-236	83	1 068 ***	387	-113	522 877
Aquarius	-80	343 *	-58	127 *	-429 *	-529 *	-209	-241	-10	-46	1 059 ***	72	538 868
Pisces	334	-95	-369	-474 *	-54	-41	-435	68	-58	-103	-97	1 323 ***	555 036
Totals	561 791	581 311	571 256	565 511	548 505	540 358	526 700	496 698	498 076	517 497	537 788	552 829	6 498 320

The value of the contribution is:	The indicator is:	Difference significant to:
Greater than 7.88	***	at least 99.5%
Between 6.63 & 7.88	**	at least 99%
Between 3.84 & 6.63	*	at least95%
Less than 3.84		not significant

The distribution of marriages, according to the Sun sign of the husband and the Sun sign of the wife.

> One marriage in a thousand [6,417 for the group of
> 6,498,320 couples] shows a strange peculiarity: the
> spouses are born on the same day exactly. [...] In 1976,
> for example, there were 291 marriages between people
> born on the same day.

Of course there could have been a transcription error when
the birth was registered, but these marriages are nearly three
times more numerous than in theory, without the fact that a
great number of them were between people celebrating their
birthdays less than forty days apart.

Furthermore, this conjugal solar phenomenon is
accompanied – if not followed, due to the proximity of their
orbits to the central star – under those of Mercury-Mercury
and Venus-Venus, with the diagonals showing an over-
representation that is no less typical.

However, there is a star that has been shown to have
no particular role, the Moon, both in the Moon-Moon
connection between spouses and that of the luminaries in
their double relationship: Sun-masculine/Moon-feminine,
Sun-feminine/Moon-masculine. Yet we have to admit that, if
the results for the Sun, Mercury and Venus are in the
astrological sphere, equally the Sun-Moon relationship of the
couples should also figure there and it is difficult to let go of
that idea. Of course, it is not really good to take the easy way
out by calling on a possible qualitative value for the
correlation that is supposed to escape the quantitative
survey. Everybody will make their own judgement. In any
case it is important to recognise that the meeting of
complementary luminaries between spouses – we now know
– does not increase the overall number of marriages.

The solar crown of childbirth

We now move on to the children who are the fruits of
marriage. Didier Castille did just that and he gave his
assessment when he spoke at the second congress of the
Astrology Federation of Southern Europe in Montpellier on July

7th 2002. The conference was dedicated to 'The Relationship with the Other and its Many Expressions in Astrology'.

> These results hinted at some form of astrological heredity which encouraged me to carry on the experiment and in particular to look at the children of these couples. I continued the research using a different set of files, those of registered births which are computerised in the same way by Insee for the purposes of demographic analysis. There were fifteen million births in France between 1977 and 1997. The files gave the dates of birth, the date of birth of the parents, the sex of the child and sibling position for each child. They did not give the hour of birth, but they were adequate to look at the births according to the longitudes of the planets, only the position of the Moon being viewed with caution because of its speed.

The results of this second investigation replicated the matrimonial phenomenon: the birthday of the child tended to be close to the birthday of one of the parents; the child's Sun is more often nearer to that of the father rather than that of the mother, and most births happen around a common birthday.

**Distribution of births according to
the aspect that the father's Sun makes to that of the infant**

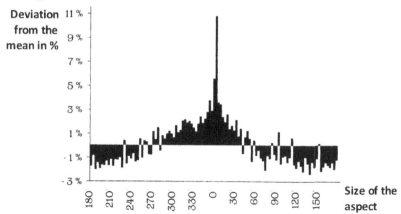

As is the case for marriages where most often couples have the same sign, the parent-child relationship follows the same pattern. For example, for this generation, in France, the family trio that came top in this investigation was one with a Taurus father, a Taurus mother and a Taurus child, 50% more numerous than the less frequent associations.

So, the Sun has now appeared in what used to be just a black hole and, under the pressure of the entire French population, has been shown to be at the centre of human life with its vital dual role: coupling and engendering, marriage and children. See how in each case the solar conjunctions form a narrow peak, the central summit of a circumflex accent with the two graduated downward slopes, along which stretch more and more conjugal unions and the offspring of these couples with the same birthdays. Matrimony and generation, similarly union and engendering: with this dual solar result of the same type, this has to be a decisive turning point in the fate of astrology.

From now on, with results like these, the best efforts of the anti-astrology lobby will be in vain and they will either have to be silent or engage in dishonesty. Certainly the fluctuations in the marriages – which oscillate between -0.9 and +2.4 – is small (even if it is stronger, if not downright obvious, for the births, since their spread is between -2 and +11%), but, it is more than enough to persuade them to take a risk and stop being stubborn,[55] because any self-respecting scientist presented with such a result knows where to stand on the question even if he or she is not yet in a position to understand the reasoning behind it. In any case people on the ground are already convinced by this argument because they simply have to compare their own dates of birth with those of their wider families. It is hard not to be influenced by these results, to ultimately let go of the preconceptions and prejudices, and science repudiates itself when it shrugs off this enormous problem without trying to throw light on it. There is nothing glorious about suppressing what should be brought to light.

In addition, the result was not unexpected: it was

received as being the stuff of astrological tradition as far as astral heredity is concerned. 'The inheritance' of the date of birth is the subject of the introduction to *Astrobiology* by Karl Ernst Krafft, published in 1939. It gave examples and began like this:

> The first problem that we had to tackle was that of the coincidence of the dates of birth so often found for members of the same family. These coincidence which relate to the month as well as the day, are found far too frequently to be attributed to chance.

In his early work at the beginning of the 20th century, Paul Choisnard had already mentioned 'the similarities between the zodiacal positions of the Sun' in parents and children. It is true that he advanced the same correlation for the Moon but is there such a thing as a researcher who never makes mistakes? In any case we should render unto Caesar that which belongs to him, and this is a great treasure.

Of course, this solar phenomenon can be applied to more than couples and their families. This is best illustrated by comparing the numerous points of similarity in the planetary patterns of those involved in the discovery of the heliocentric system, the founders of modern astronomy. Essentially they spent their lives making the case for the Sun being at the centre of the circling planet, and the Sun was their entire focus. In these circumstances the solar star in their charts is the signifier and the signified at the same time, the object is also the subject, microcosm and macrocosm coming face to face. Could there be a purer equation? So, what is being rolled out here is very important and the stakes are very high.

So, one could say that— in the same way that Napoleon had to have an exceptional configuration, his unique Mars[56]—the fate of astrology is being played out here: either their Suns are dispersed round the circle of the zodiac, scattered elements which are completely unrelated, the field free of any illusions (what would become of astrology then?) or we have the opposite and it is as if they are meeting up in a microcosm of common links that brings these notable people together across two centuries, the basis of a temple in which unity is the principle essence of the phenomenon.

Their six positions, in a double solar alignment, are grouped round two conjunctions separated by a sextile in a zodiacal diptych whose shutters fold back on one another. On one side the Piscean world of immensity, open to the infinite, the cosmic ocean that suits them best, and on the other the Capricornian seat, the basis of things at their most concrete, which in this case is mathematical order. Kepler and Newton, the two giants who discovered the laws of the solar system are links in a chain that goes back to Tycho Brahe; nothing could have been discovered by them without the rigorous enumeration of numerous planetary positions by the latter; similarly the third goes on to complete the work of the second. On the Piscean side the lineage follows the same pattern: Rheticus took over from Copernicus, who was captive to his work, and launched himself with the publication of a volume of the canon, the heliocentric revolution, as a result of which Galileo bursts upon the scene, his telescope pointed at the stars, to reveal a new astronomical world. And, in addition, more sovereign planetary figures make their entrance on stage, who are in convergence with these two solar nuclei (notably the Jupiters of Kepler and Newton which are both placed on the Sun of Copernicus). Now this grand poem made in space and time looks like an astral pantheon!

Copernicus	**10° Pisces**
Rheticus	**06° Pisces**
Tycho Brahe	**02° Capricorn**
Kepler	**15° Capricorn**
Galileo	**06° Pisces**
Newton	**13° Capricorn**

Here is a kind of crowning of the art of Urania. This is such a neat way of demonstrating the rules by which it is ordered. We cannot deny its existence just because we don't understand the cause. The rigour of mind required and the quality of this observation alone would be enough for an opponent with any self-respect to see a case for astrology.

It is significant that Pierre Thuillier, an impartial historian of science, finishes by wondering:

> [...] first of all let's concede that we still have a basic problem. What is the value of astrology compared to the actual sciences? It is an important and legitimate question.[57]

If only the rationalists who have become strangely medieval in their behaviour would stop gagging astrology and let it speak at long last.

We really are coming to the end of a time when we had to have real courage to defend astrology: its rejection is now becoming more and more ridiculous, it being seen less and less as an offence against reason, and more as a way of revealing the cosmic dimension of human beings, with an objective look at what the future holds for this knowledge.

Chapter 7 - Astrological Forecasting; the Facts

In *Le Retour des astrologues*[58] (The Return of the Astrologers), Edgar Morin puts his finger on the essential weakness of astrology when he criticises 'its lack of objectivity' and its 'empirical weaknesses'. One has to agree. Leafing through the specialised prose, we sense that there is not much by way of observation, or much that rubs up against reality. It would be nice to have more substance and less froth, padding and artistic vagueness; to have fewer great flights of fancy full of hollow phrases and to have the simple truth told in a straightforward way; we need to avoid the temptation of compensating for a lack of reality by indulging in suspect spiritualization. The authors of this specialised prose seem to want to have wings before they've tried to walk. However, it is not the affectation of the literary style which matters, but the astrological facts, and there are better things to do than dream astrology. If the astral signifier has any real foundation it is not dependant on the illusion of personal prediction.

Faced with these shortcomings, as well as the pointless speeches, based on a priori judgements, made by opponents, we have to return to the criteria that scholars have established for testing prediction. A proper demystification of astrology should be based on its strict application with the final word on whether it has any truth in it being 'what is left' after this reductive test of the evidence. Furthermore: why not judge it using the same speculative specificity that astrologers use? With the path of the planets being known in advance, isn't the aim of astrology to make forecasts?

It is easy to agree on how such a venture should be judged. Naturally, it is hard to establish the criteria for a forecast, especially an isolated one, so it is better to leave individual cases aside, because of the complexity involved, and go straight to mundane astrology with its wider scope. The public nature of historical events makes the judgements so much easier and the blueprint of the exercise can be simplified.

Before we begin, we need to have agreement on how the forecasts are to be evaluated. The same method of forecasting must be used every time to formulate the same type of forecasts. The forecasts must be in a continuous series with a similar prognosis being expected to result from the same configuration. Naturally, having several goes at getting the forecast right does not have the same value as getting it right the first time. Similarly, if a forecast and the indicated event are separated by a long distance in time its value is different to that of a short-term forecast. How we forecast also plays a role: obscure sibylline forecasts are all too familiar. They are often shrouded in mystery or cleverly written using evasive jargon with many meanings so that whatever the result the forecaster can save face. So the forecast must not have several meanings and must be stated in clear and precise terms. This should go without saying.

We now come to the practical material of mundane astrology, which uses the synodic nature of planetary cycles. A familiar example of these cycles is that of the luminaries. Each month, the Moon and the Sun meet at the same degree of their circular path round the zodiac. This meeting, as seen from the Earth, is known as their conjunction (0 degrees), which inaugurates the lunar cycle. The Moon gradually moves away from the Sun in a growing crescent. A week later they are a quarter of a circle (90 degrees) apart: that is the first quarter. One week later, at their opposition (180 degrees), the Moon is now face to face with the Sun, and ready to begin its waning phase. Next we have the last quarter and, now in the next sign of the zodiac, it returns to the conjunction or end of the cycle and the beginning of the next one.

The forty-five interrelated cycles of the ten celestial bodies (luminaries and planets) in the solar system give us our cosmological material, the temporal weave of its fabric graduating from the smallest monthly cycle to the largest of five hundred years.

From the beginning to the end of its recurring movement, the cycle is like a line in the universe, a thread that we can follow over time. Its course is punctuated by a series of successive phases that follow on from one another and, at the same time, it is a bipolar movement, of flux and reflux, of waxing and waning. In addition there is also a triple dialectical process going on with the initial conjunction being the thesis, the opposition being the antithesis and the terminal conjunction being the synthesis. The thesis is then renewed in the following cycle. It is a syntactic construction of rich ordinance, which enables us to perceive, in essence, the evolution of historic cycles. Because the information reflects only one level of reality its meaning is given using the language of analogy.

This cycle 'of becoming' is in fact structured like a helix: the circular movement returns to the same point (A to A) but, at the same time, advances perpendicularly (from A to I). What happens is not the result of a pure recurrence: the similarity created by the repetition is married to the diversity created by the unique leading to something completely new that opens up new landscapes worldwide. Naturally, we can only follow the closed circle, the sequence of the repetitive structure of history, and its unique quality escapes us. Such is the fertile terrain in the hands of the perfect practitioner who restricts his or her work to the relationship of such and such a configuration with such a current trend or corresponding historic climate.

If we are to believe Jean-Paul Sartre, the existential philosopher, on this matter, this approach is illusory: 'Neither is an existentialist going to think that man can find comfort in being guided by a given sign, on Earth; because he will think that man is going to interpret the sign as he pleases.'[59] Oddly, it is been forgotten that knowledge is something we can verify, the sign being read like a code. This is the basic orthodoxy for any scientist: we recognise something to be a fact because it is possible to reproduce it, that is to say that when repeating the same operation in the same conditions we obtain the same result. Here, the astrologer is perfectly placed to answer the demands of verification, with unlimited serial investigations.

THE PLANETARY CYCLE

<u>Conjunction 0°</u> - A: birth, engendering; the emergence of a historical movement; the seed germinates.

<u>Sextile 60°</u> - B: the plant grows; the movement materialises in tangible events; building.

<u>Square 90°</u> - C: crisis in growth; interior conflict causing a diversion or a rupture.

<u>Trine 120°</u> - D: very positive constructive phase, achievement, development; associative expansionist phase.

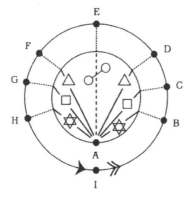

<u>Opposition 180°</u> - E: internal or external conflict breaks out; division leading to a testing time or a decline.

<u>Trine 120°</u> - F: after the crisis, recovery, getting back to normal; associative phase; defensive measures.

<u>Square 90°</u> – G: the equilibrium of the trine is thrown into question; defection, letting go, deterioration; crisis.

<u>Sextile 60°</u> – H: recovery, mending; revitalisation in a new set of circumstances.

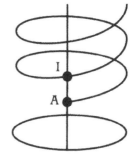

<u>Conjunction 0°</u> - I: end of the experience, metamorphosis or a re-launch to a new level.

Having established the operational setting, let's move on to the experimental forecasts themselves. It does not really matter that I am the author of the research because what matters is the procedure. I have chosen my work rather than someone else's because of the very high standards I have set myself. I came to astrology at a very young age and I suffered a major setback which profoundly shook my initial faith; my disillusionment made me more critical, and since then when undertaking experimental forecasts I never do things the easy way. When undertaking an experiment the moment of truth is when a particular type of result occurs at the completion date of the configuration being tested, and likewise all the way along the same continuous series. I had to rid myself of any illusions. My method was, if possible, to shut myself away in a remote faraway place where I couldn't guess at what was going on in the world, and depending only on the astronomical ephemerides, assign dates to history sometimes years and even decades in advance, the forecast thus becoming a gigantic leap in anticipating the future. It was the ultimate high-risk strategy!

From the possible experiments I propose two: one dealing with a fast-moving cycle, which has the advantage of repeating on an annual basis, and whose stamp can be seen across most of the last century, and the other regarding a very large cycle which relates to the long term and is applied to looking at history on a much greater scale.

The Sun-Jupiter conjunction

From among the 45 planetary cycles the astronomical phenomenon of choice seems to be the Sun-Jupiter conjunction.

The Sun-Jupiter conjunction is a longitudinal alignment of the Earth, Sun and Jupiter, reuniting the two celestial bodies. This celestial event happens at regular intervals and returns every thirteen months: while the Sun is making its annual tour of the zodiac, Jupiter moves forward one sign, the new meeting thus takes place in the following sign. I have chosen this phenomenon because its frequency means that the time lapse is relatively short (like the game with the greatest number of chips).

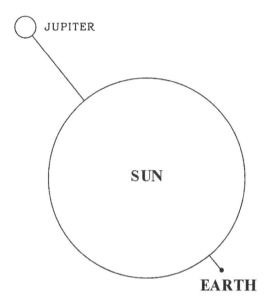

Astrophysicists have raised the issue of the geophysical impact of such an alignment, both at the conjunction and the opposition, because the geomagnetic conditions of such an alignment cause natural disturbances especially when another giant planet is involved. This does not mean that this configuration cannot keep its traditional reputation for being beneficial. The Jupiterian process with its humanitarian style is here valorised by the Sun, and tends to be translated into beneficial effects for society (détente, harmony, agreement, progress, civilising work…), the focus of its impact depending on the global situation at the time.

This configuration is thus ideal for demonstrating experimental forecasting which consists of systematically 'playing' the same piece, repeatedly throwing the same card, to test the expectation that same type of global climate will recur. In this instance, then, we can say that at the time of the aspect return there will be a return to happy circumstances with one completion date following another in a continuous series. This is how the phenomenon would manifest itself in theory; in practice, however, we have to take account of the fact that our configuration is not an isolated factor, but part of a group which will affect the manifestation in different ways.

First of all, our Sun-Jupiter conjunction will be configured differently according to its angular distance from other planets. Its positivity will express itself in a neutral environment and will even be enhanced, if it aspects other planets in a harmonious way: trine (120 degrees) sextile (60 degrees), semi-sextile (30 degrees) and also quincunx (150 degrees). On the other hand, the beneficial effect of its influence gives way to disruption in the case of a dissonant aspect: opposition (180 degrees), square (90 degrees), semi-square (45 degrees), and sesqui-quadrate (135 degrees). These limitations do not usually cause problems, because their counter effects can be predicted and so can be taken into account.

However, this configuration is not the only one to express itself in a beneficial way. Its companion is the Sun-Venus conjunction with its synodic revolution that returns alternately as an inferior conjunction with the alignment Earth-Venus-Sun or as a superior conjunction with the alignment Earth-Sun-Venus every 584 days. This conjunction has the attributes of a pacifying benefactress. More broadly still these two cycles can come together, either in conjunction or by their aspects, as if to lend each other a hand. Thus on 11 November 1918 there was a Sun-Jupiter trine just as on 8 May 1945; in the first case Venus was conjunct the Sun and trine to Jupiter and in the second was coming away from a recent conjunction with the Sun (as if assisting at the event) and is semi-sextile to the Sun and quincunx to Jupiter, with the implication of a harmonic triangle. This is a triangular configuration that we will meet often.

A timetable for the armistices

To go back to the beginning, it all started when my curiosity was aroused by seeing, in the ephemeris, a triple encounter of the Sun, Venus and Jupiter at around 10 degrees of Aquarius on 31 January 1938. I was not very knowledgeable at that time but the traditional attribution led me to expect something positive for the days around that date. At that time the Spanish Civil War was raging so there was every reason to believe it might end. That did not happen but on 4 February an Anglo-Franco-Italian 'gentleman's agreement' was signed on the Mediterranean, the only diplomatic détente that year. And it was at the Sun-Jupiter conjunction, which followed that combat ceased in Spain with the taking of Madrid by Franco in March 1939.

That is how I first became interested in this astronomical phenomenon. The conjunction of 11 April 1940 was to follow and was expected to be critical.[60] The German attack on Denmark and Norway had taken place on the 9th. The following conjunction, 19 May 1941, was equally critical; diplomacy having brought about a Franco-Thai peace treaty, and a meeting between Hitler and Darlan,[61] resulting in Franco-German collaboration. Nothing happened at the conjunction of 25 June 1942. The following conjunction (30 July 1943) marked the fall of Mussolini on July 25, followed by the start of negotiations prior to the Italian armistice of 6 August. With the Rumanian and Bulgarian armistices of 12 September as well as that of Finland on the following 19th, the conjunction of 31 August 1944 lived up to my expectations. The Second-World War was to finish on 2 September 1945,[62] as the planets came into the orb of the following conjunction at the end of the month.

Following these Sun-Jupiter conjunctions I continued with my study. After the war the tendency was expressed in a more diverse way. Under the conjunction of 31 October 1946, Dutch–Indonesian negotiations came to fruition (the Cheridon Pacific Accord 15 November); under that of 1 December 1947, the United Nations adopted a plan for the division of Palestine into a Jewish state and an Arab state (29 November), while a last chance India-Hyderabad accord came to a conclusion. The following conjunction, 1 January 1949, produced a 'clutch' of détentes: that day India and Pakistan ceased hostilities; 22 January saw the end of the war in China with the entry of Mao into Peking (after negotiations which began at the beginning of the month) ; equally there was détente in Israel ; on 10 January Indonesia became a sovereign state. After this, with the conjunction of 3 February 1950 there was the proclamation of the Indian Republic (26 January) and the conclusion of the Sino-Soviet pact (treaty of friendship, alliance and mutual assistance, 14 February).

At the beginning of the second half of the century, what is signified by our unique astral signifier becomes more disseminated but when a climate of war returns the Jupiterian tendency is again centred on its pacifying power, and is associated at first with moves that were defensive in nature. Thus, the American initiative led to the creation of a Pacific Pact under the conjunction of 11 March 1951, and following that of 17 April 1952, the successful negotiations ended on 27th May (under the Sun-Venus conjunction) with the Treaty of the European Defence Community (EDC). The pacifying note is seen at the conjunction of 25 May 1953, which accompanied the signing of guarantees between the Americans and the North Koreans and on 8 June, when there is a convention on the repatriation of prisoners; this unblocked the negotiations which led to the Panmunjom Armistice of 27 July, which in turn put an end to the war in Korea (under a Venus-Jupiter conjunction). Under the conjunction of 30 June 1954, negotiations which began with the coming of Mendes France to power, ended on 21 July with the Franco-Indochina armistice.

This series of observations led me to look at the question in more depth: I decided to introduce a control. I took the dates for declarations of war or the beginnings of hostilities and, at the same time, those of the armistices or the cessation of hostilities; I went back to the era of

Napoleon for which there were sixty well known events which fell into one or the other of these categories. In 1967, I presented this material in my book *Les Astres et l'Histoire.*[63]

Jupiter continues to move forward as the Sun approaches and then passes on. By adopting an orb of 12 degrees for the conjunction, the configuration is estimated to be 'operational' over a spread of 30 degrees, which is a margin equivalent to a month. This means that, in relation to the cyclic path of 390 degrees between each conjunction, we had one chance in thirteen of finding this phenomenon. For the sixty cases tested, we estimated that there should have been four or five of these conjunctions in one or other of the groups, yet I only found one conjunction among the military engagements, while there were nineteen among the cease-fires.--`

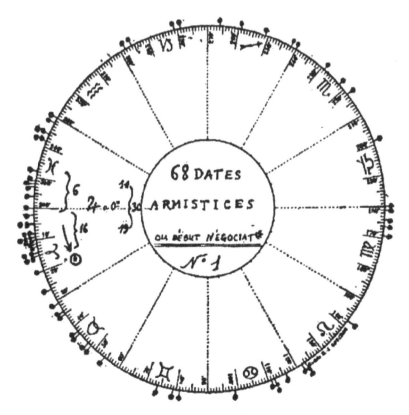

At Negotiation Beginnings

In the course of my investigation and well before its publication, a colleague, Henri Gouchon, redid his part of the operation which was based on 68 armistices, and his research resulted in the diagram above, published in *Les Cahiers astrologiques* (Astrological Notebooks) Number 110 (May/June 1964), which shows the distribution of Jupiter's positions in relation to the Sun fixed at 0 degrees. His conclusion was:

> Given that the signing of an armistice is always preceded by negotiations that are either short or long, we accept as being quite normal that at the moment of signing the Sun has often overtaken Jupiter by a certain number of degrees […], an armistice being the consequence of a state of mind which can last for a certain time. What it is important to state here is that in a run of armistices a good number are grouped around the Sun-Jupiter conjunction.

Gouchon's observation makes sense. The configuration is supposed to mark the time that the détente is operational, but the results differ. This is how it went for the Korean armistice on 27 July 1953: things were set in motion at the previous accord on 8 June. There were the beginnings of détente on 30 May when the Soviets relinquished their claims on Turkish Armenia. In the tense climate of the times, this move was followed, on 6 June, by the Soviet and Yugoslav diplomatic missions becoming embassies. Likewise, for the Algerian war, it was the preliminary accord between France and the FLN[64] in Les Rousses on 18 February 1962, under a triple conjunction Sun-Venus-Jupiter, which was the act of détente; the long drawn out formalisation of the armistice up to 18 March was only the confirmation of what had already been achieved. In the same way, if the fall of Saigon on 30 April 1975 (with the conjunction of 22 March) established the end of the Vietnam War, it was brought about by the Communist offensive. This began in the first fortnight of March and, in the second half of the month, the collapse of the fronts in Cambodia and Vietnam signalled the end of the war (we have also to take account of the management of a period of calm to allow the American soldiers to leave). This makes us aware of the care we must take in testing this matter, the researcher has to do more than just look at the labels.

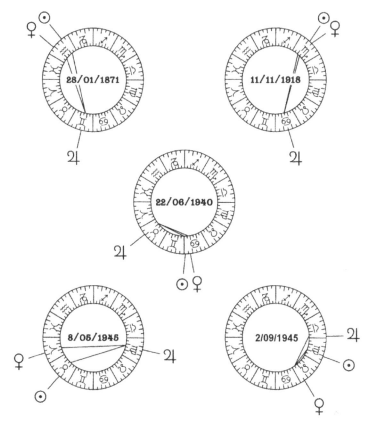

Five Armistices - A family resemblance: also, the Sun-Jupiter trine accompanied the defusing of the Cuban missile crisis of 28 October 1962, the nuclear test ban treaty signed in Moscow on 5 August 1963, and also the fall of the Berlin Wall on 9 November 1989 which put an end to the east-west divide.

Meanwhile, it is good to remember that the Sun-Jupiter cycle is only a cog that turns annually inside a vast mechanism which encompasses decades of general world affairs. It is no wonder that its timeline jumps from one section of history to another in a completely unrelated way, while keeping to the same positive course. When the conference of the four great Allies in the Second World War ended in Geneva on 21 July 1955, fourteen days from the conjunction of 4 August 1955, the world felt the new 'spirit of Geneva'. The Republic of Togo saw the light of day on 1 September 1956, three days before the conjunction of 4 September 1956. The scenario changed when the conjunction of 5 October 1957, was joined by Mars, giving it a certain sportive air: on 4 October we had the inauguration of space flight with the launching of the first artificial satellite, *Sputnik 1*. It is understandable that the point of impact of our conjunction was unpredictable.

Testing the forecast

I then set myself the task of testing what appeared to be known correlations, only this time I did not just look at the passive known events of the past that could be somewhat manipulated, nor did I simply try to anticipate something that was already on record. I had to project into the unknown so to be able to anticipate what was going to happen. When faced with a silent configuration which has obscure implications, and having no actual facts, the interpreter, more than anyone, is acutely aware of the rewards of success and of the bitter disappointment that comes with failure. For the astrologer, having only an ephemeris for support, finding historical events that will match the fixed astral timetable is like shooting blindly at an encrypted message, and what's more the relationship with the temporal has to be repeatable.

I started this work at the time of the Algerian war and this became my first test bed. I wrote about it in six short articles printed in the specialised revue called *Les Cahiers astrologiques*; the first three articles dealt with one date alone.

- The first (which appeared in number 72, January-February 1958) was given the title 'Will the Algerian War finish at All Saints ?' because of the Sun-Jupiter conjunction of 5 November 1958, which was also the subject of my talk, 'The best period for world politics in 1958'. In fact a conference on disarmament began on 31 October in Geneva and was a leading diplomatic initiative.

- The second (printed in number 76, July-August) recalled my original forecast which was more plausible now that General de Gaulle had come to power.

- The third (printed in number 77, November-December) picked up this theme with the hope that, 'under the favourable configurations of November, a compromise is on the horizon between the French government and the FLN'. And so something did happen which became the first step on the long road to peace: to everyone's surprise on 23 October 1958 President Charles de Gaulle invited the Algerian leader, Ferhat Abbas, to a meeting in Paris to discuss the future of Algeria. It was the famous call for the 'peace of the brave' that, following deliberations, the FLN on 29 October was to reject, but this first gesture went on to inspire others.

- The fourth text was a note (printed in number 83, November-December 1959) about the new conjunction of 5 December 1959: 'Therefore, is there a chance of peace around 18 November, and then on 5 December next? The coming weeks will reveal if [...] Jupiter deigns to direct its beneficial gaze on poor Algeria.' Something fresh happened that became the second step towards peace. Following his famous speech about self-determination on 16 September 1959 (Sun sextile Jupiter), General de Gaulle restarted the negotiations on 18 November (Venus sextile Jupiter). This time, the FLN accepted the invitation and charged its leaders, who had been arrested and interned on the island of Aix (Ben Bella among others) to initiate talks but now it was Paris which would break off negotiations at the end of the month.

- Given that there were no Sun-Jupiter conjunctions in 1960, the fifth text (number 86, May-June 1960) just noted the possibility of the negotiations restarting without great hope of a solution and three dates were given : around 15 February 1960 (Sun-Jupiter sextile), towards 20 June   (Sun-Venus conjunction opposite Jupiter) and towards 16 July (this trio once again). Two of these three corresponded to two known attempts at détente in 1960: one was on 17 February, when Ferhat Abbas made a public declaration, followed on the 29th by the sending of a note from the FLN to Paris by means of the French Embassy in Rabat; the other one was on 20 June when contact was made at last and two envoys of the FLN arrived in Paris for the start of the Melun talks which did not come to anything.

- Finally the sixth text, entitled 'When will the Algerian War end?' was from a conference organised by the Centre international d'astrologie (International Centre for Astrology) in Paris on 25 October 1960 (later published in number 91, March-April 1961). In it, knowing that the affair was a long way from being settled, I mentioned the possibility of negotiations being restarted at the new conjunction of 5 January 1961, with the chance of them evolving at the harmonic phases of the cycle (the trine on 28 May).

And so there were great strides towards peace under this conjunction: on 8 January1961 there was a referendum in France which resulted in an overwhelming yes for 'an end'. The FLN and the provisional government of Algerian republic (GPRA) replied on January 16 that they were ready for talks. This time the two parties were in agreement and negotiations followed the phases of the cycle: the first conference at Evian started at the trine of 20 May and the Lugrin conference at the end of July, under the opposition. The text ended by announcing the decisive fortnight of the Algerian peace sixteen months in advance:

> As we see, there is no trace of a really good pacifying configuration in 1961. The nearest thing to a peaceful tendency came at the beginning of 1962 with a Sun-Venus conjunction that lasted from the beginning of January to mid-February, its period of most influence being in the first ten days of February, where we find a triple conjunction Sun-Venus-Jupiter, as at All Saints in 1958. [...] A cycle was thus started and it seemed logical to suppose that it would lead to the peace at the end of its course, at the Sun-Jupiter conjunction of 8 February 1962. [...] only this concentration at the beginning of February 1962 is worth looking at.

Remember the facts. There was a new conference at Evian in December 1961 which dragged on for several weeks. The discussions started to be more productive towards New Year 1962. At the end of January and during the first two weeks of February the conference was in full swing and it ended with the Evian accords which put an end to the war. These accords were signed by the negotiators in Les Rousses on February 18 and were ratified by the French government on the 20th and by the CNRA[65] assembly, which met in Tripoli, on the 22nd. The hostilities ceased but there was more violence initiated by the OAS.[66] The two parties confirmed the accord at a second meeting at Evian and while everything was in place by 18 February, the official end of the war was set for 18 March.

The four successive Sun-Jupiter conjunctions of 1958 and 1962 showed the times of greatest intensity in these long negotiations.

Following this first endeavour, and having no war to

get my teeth into, I made do by pointing out the trends that were positive and peaceful in number 99 the May 1962 review. There I gave the salient dates for the near future. I only mentioned two forecasts that concerned our cycle:

> First of all, in the years to come, the largest 'pacifying impulse' will occur in mid-August 1963 when a Sun-Venus conjunction will be at trine to Jupiter. It would be very surprising if an episode of diplomatic activity leading to détente did not take place then.

So fifteen months in advance, we were able to forecast the warmer climes of the historic event regarded as the armistice of the Cold War: the atomic accord in Moscow on 5 August 1963, first signed by the Americans and the Soviets and then over the months by seventy-two countries. In the end more than a hundred signed up. It was nine years since Nehru and Mendès France had initiated the idea but had come up against the problems of verification. Immediately after that, in the same text, was the second forecast:

> In the last ten days of April and at the beginning of May 1964 there is going to be a triple conjunction of the Sun, Mercury and Jupiter [...]. There, as well as in mid-August 1963, we will see a huge push towards reconciliation, understanding, détente, and world health.

This nailed the dates for the most diplomatically charged two weeks of 1964 two years in advance : on 20 April there was a second atomic accord between the USSR and the United States (the reduction in production of uranium and plutonium) which restarted negotiations between the two great powers ; on 29 April, thanks to an American initiative, West Germany and the USSR forged relations which led to a visit to Bonn by Khrushchev in mid-September (Sun-Jupiter trine); on 4 May the Kennedy Round started; the most important commercial negotiations on world trade and enterprise up to that point.

On 8 September 1965, motivated by the war which started that year, I mounted a new 'predictive offensive' which was printed in number 119 (November-December) of the *Cahiers astrologiques* under the foolhardy title, 'When will the Vietnam War end?' Recognising that this war could last a long time, judging by the impact of two big cycles, I extended the investigation up to the end of 1970, scrolling through the dates of the Sun-Venus and Sun-Jupiter conjunctions and, as previously indicated, the steps towards détente, even though I had no idea of their peaceful impact. The simplest thing here would be to go over what happened in regard to each Sun-Jupiter conjunction since that of February 1962 when the Algerian War ended.

- **The conjunction of 16 March 1963: new** American-Soviet accord at the beginning of April 1963, resulting in the birth of the 'red phone'; Moscow and Washington are now connected by telephone.

- **The conjunction of 22 April 1964:** second 'atomic' accord between the two great powers; relaunch of European diplomacy and the Kennedy Round.

- **The conjunction of 30 May 1965:** a dissonant configuration accompanying a cease-fire in Saint-Domingo on May 21 1965 and increased American military involvement in Vietnam.

- **The conjunction of 5 July 1966:** during the last ten days of June, General de Gaulle journeys to the USSR under the banner 'from détente to understanding'; a European diplomatic movement begins with the Franco-Soviet accord of June 30. Moreover, after five years of negotiations, a green Europe became a reality on 24 July 1966.

- **The conjunction of 8 August 1967:** on 24 August 1967 at the disarmament conference in Geneva the

Americans and Soviets simultaneously presented two identical texts destined to serve as a basis of the treaty for the non-proliferation of nuclear arms. The same day saw the Nasser-Faisal agreement, signed on the 30th, which put an end to the war in Yemen. On the 26 the ten members of the IMF made considerable improvements to international credit.

- **The conjunction of 9 September 1968:** while negotiations on Vietnam in Paris had been stalling since May, in September, secret meetings between the Americans and the North-Vietnamese unblocked the situation and the American bombardments in the demilitarised zone of North Vietnam stopped on 1 November.

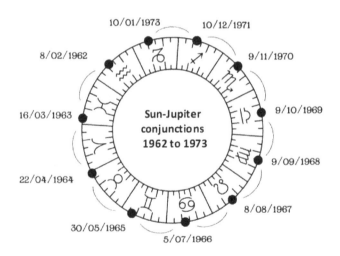

- **The conjunction of 9 October 1969:** a disarmament conference. Seven months of important negotiations between the two super powers on nuclear disarmament resulted in an agreement being signed on the denuclearisation of the ocean depths on October 8 1969. The evening before, on 20 October, at talks on the border issue, the USSR and the People's Republic of China, who had been clashing on the Ussuri River since

March, signed an agreement for a cessation of hostilities. Following the elections of 27 September Willy Brandt came to power in West Germany on a programme of reconciliation with Eastern Europe.

- **The conjunction of 9 November 1970:** five years earlier I had promised that this would be an important date in the peace process because it coincided with a Sun-Venus conjunction and I had hoped that it would concern Vietnam. The record: 2 November 1970, the Russians and the Americans meet at Helsinki for 'the big dialogue', a first agreement being signed on the 29th. On 18 November a German-Polish treaty was concluded and turned the page on twenty-five years of post-war history, re-launching negotiations on Berlin at the same time as the draft European conference on security. The same day the Sino-Soviet negotiations were restarted and ended on the 23rd with a commercial agreement. In the Middle East, after a provisional fragile ceasefire which lasted for three months, a new ceasefire was instituted on 5 November which would be effective for two years.

- **The conjunction of 10 December 1971:** after ten months of negotiations and twenty-one meetings the Berlin accord between the two Germanys, endorsing détente in Europe, was concluded on 11 December 1971. The 16 and 17 of December saw the end of the war between India and Pakistan. On the 18 and 19 of the same month a meeting of the Ten in Washington put an end to the monetary crisis set off the preceding 15 August : the so called 'financial armistice'.

- **The conjunction of 10 January 1973:** an American-Vietnamese ceasefire on 23 January 1973 puts an end to the military intervention of the United States.

Having exhausted the series of solar conjunctions taken from the article of 8 September 1965, I prepared some new forecasts for the continuing Vietnam War in an article written on 29 April 1972 which appeared in number 18 (second quarter 1972) of the review *L'Astrologue* (The Astrologer).[67] The article mentioned the extreme complexity of the situation: 'The end is approaching but it isn't easy to determine when the last piece of the jigsaw will be put into place because the settlement can be broken down into so many phases that ultimately the ceasefire might only be accompanied by a secondary aspect which would have been largely developed during an earlier phase.' Then I listed the phases of the Sun-Jupiter cycle in progress, the article finished thus: 'If not at the Sun-Jupiter sextile of 27 October 1972 then at the Sun-Jupiter conjunction of 10 January 1973?'

This is a mediocre result for the person making the forecast, but their disappointment is not as important as the astronomical timing, because this mild anticipation falls no less than eight months before a double event. Remember that an accord was finally concluded between the delegates, Kissinger and Le Duc Tho, on 20 October 1972, the same accord that President Nixon confirmed with the President of North Vietnam on the 22nd and that he proposed to sign on 31 October; on 26 October we learned of the existence of this accord, which was rejected at the last minute by South Vietnam. Yet it will be this same ceasefire accord, lightly revised, which will be accepted by all the parties on 13 January 1973; it is followed by a reduction in the fighting from the 15, and signed 23 January. The 'hot spot' of the final piece being put in place was to be found in the thirty-five hours of the Kissinger-Le Duc negotiations from the 8 to the 15 of January, that is to say, around the conjunction.

This experiment in forecasting continued with the writing of a 'timetable for peace that went up to 1980 and which appeared in *Le Pronostic expérimental en astrologie*.[68] In the absence of a significant state of war it only consisted of a list of dates for peace. Remember what is mentioned here regarding the conjunctions.

- **Conjunction of 13 February 1974:** the signing, at the oil conference in Washington, of an Atlantic document between the United States, Europe (except France),

Canada and Japan to deal with the oil crisis which had arisen the previous October. After the kilometre 101 talks between Israel and Egypt on January 18 there was a withdrawal of military forces (still on the battlefield of the Yom Kippur War) which began on January 25 in a climate of détente which lasted all February: the Suez Canal was cleared, there were Israeli-Syrian negotiations with the handing over of prisoners of war, and a resumption of relations between Cairo and Washington and between Tel-Aviv and Moscow.

- **Conjunction of 22 March 1975:** on 17 March 1975 an Iran-Iraq accord put an end to 46 years conflict over the frontier: this accord occasioned, with the cessation of aid to the Kurdish rebellion in Iran and the closing of the frontier by Iraq, a ceasefire in Kurdistan. On 18 March Prime Minister Wilson recommended the Commons to vote 'yes' in the referendum on Europe in order to keep Britain in the European Community. It was also the start of the death throes of the Vietnam War: The Communist offensive, which began in the first two weeks of March, led to the collapse of the fronts in Cambodia and South Vietnam in the second two weeks, with the laying down of arms; however Saigon did not fall until April 30.

- **Conjunction of 27 April 1976:** The United Nations conference on commerce and development opened in Nairobi on 5 May 1976, attended by the ministers for foreign affairs of 150 countries (previous reunions having been held in Delhi in 1968 and in Santiago in 1972). This meeting raised awareness about the beginnings of a confrontation between rich and poor countries.

- **Conjunction of 4 June 1977:** a new conference on international economic cooperation which was held in Paris from 30 May to 4 June 1977. The conference between the foreign ministers of nineteen Third World Countries and eight industrial countries was poor on results but kickstarted the North-South dialogue. The visit of Brezhnev to Paris on 20 June restarted Franco-Soviet relations.

- **Conjunction of 10 July 1978:** Israeli-Egyptian talks in London on 18 and 19 July 1978. The re-establishment of the interrupted negotiations engendered important events in the course of the cycle; the Camp David accords, at the trine of 1 December 1978 which led at the following trine (20 March 1979), to the Israeli–Egyptian peace treaty signed on 26 March 1979.

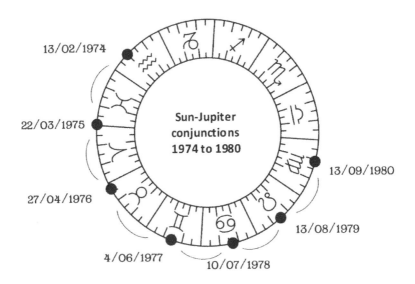

- **Conjunction of 13 August 1979:** the intense negotiations that took place during this August led to a new Begin-Sadat accord on 4 September 1979, accompanied by a first meeting between the Israeli authorities and Palestinian key figures. Also the peaceaccord of 5 August signed in Algiers which put an end to the war between Mauritania and the Polisario Front.

- **Conjunction of 13 September 1980:** an exception caused by a dissonant conjunction, similar to that of 1940. On 21 September a full-scale war broke out between Iran and Iraq. Nevertheless there was an accord signed on 31 August in Gdansk when the Polish authorities recognised the free trade union Solidarity.

A tree is judged by its fruit. With the exception of the above, that each of these conjunctions, taking place in an unknown future, was a strong indication of a happy outcome is difficult to refute. But the exact form and what will happen at each stage is unknown. In this regard our indicator is very short on information: we know it is good and that is all. The forecast only gives us a date that is qualified by the realising of a tendency, which is like having a verb without a determining object because this annual factor can be applied in so many different ways according to what is happening in the world at that time. Its own destination is generally beyond us, so it is as if this fragment of the configuration submits to whatever is happening in the news, Jupiter being a link in a chain of configurations that is difficult to decipher.

Even so we cannot just shrug our shoulders! It has 'something' that makes it a useful and informative little gem: you can see it in practice and it is a true indicator, the best we have in our possession. It is an unforeseen situation such as an outbreak of war that provides the interrogator with real knowledge because although future configurations are as plain as day in our ephemerides they are still incomprehensible. Yet it is in circumstances such as these that the art of Urania is most authentic. The experimenter feels obliged to research the issue and with very little knowledge looks at the blank screen of the future with its hitherto unseen configurations. After Algeria and Vietnam I looked at the latest wars of our time.

The Gulf War, which began on 17 January 1991, was the subject of an article called 'The Tempest in the Desert' written on 4 February 1991 and printed in number 93 (first quarter of 1991) of *L'Astrologue*. I had to submit four dates for a possible cessation of hostilities. For the first one I wrote, 'The Venus-Jupiter trine of 26 February is aspected by the Sun which is semi-sextile to Venus and quincunx to Jupiter.' Exactly on this same 26 February Saddam Hussein accepted the resolutions of the United Nations and there was an armistice on the night of the 27 and 28. The three other dates matched the post-war reconstruction.

The war in Kosovo in March 1999 was considered in an article entitled, 'The Balkan War', printed in number 126 (second quarter of 1999) of *L'Astrologue*. After flagging 'the 18 to the 20 of June [...] with the Sun being in sextile and trine (to a Mars-Jupiter opposition), things are likely to move forward'. The article ended with an interpretation of a Venus-Jupiter trine which was square to the Sun on 27 and 28 July: 'This allows me to formulate the chance of a ceasefire in the last days of July; in any case, the long awaited détente must take place then, if a conclusion is not reached sooner.' Certainly, the leader in Belgrade, Milosevic, had already ceded to the United Nations on 3 June and signed an armistice on 9 May, but on the ground the situation was tenser than ever in a contentious conflict and accentuated by the intervention of a Russian battalion at Pristina on the Serbian side. Finally on 18 June a détente was initiated between Americans and Russians and the 20 marked the end of a campaign of strikes (79 days), which delayed the implementation of the armistice while the Serbian forces withdrew completely from Kosovo. To finish, an unexpected summit of fifty or so heads of state was to meet in Sarajevo on 28 and 29 July, sanctioning a 'Marshall plan for the Balkans' which aimed at establishing peace with prosperity and democracy in this troubled place in Europe, the passage of time showing this to be the case.

The date of the American intervention in Afghanistan was 7 October 2001. This time the pronouncement was made in *La Lettre des astrologues* (The newsletter of the Federation of French speaking astrologers) number 24, December 2001 – it spoke simply 'of a détente in Afghanistan from 8 to 20 of November 2001', due to the Sun-Jupiter trine on 8 November. Taking international opinion by surprise, Kabul fell peacefully on 13 November and a few days later the Northern Alliance seized the whole country.

Finally, with the last Anglo-American war in Iraq in

2003 I was only able to tell my close relations of a likely rapid outcome with a Sun-Jupiter trine occurring on 29 March. Having started badly the military situation changed between the 4 and 8 of April, the day that Baghdad was taken and the Iraqi resistance unexpectedly collapsed.

It seemed to me that it was essential to extend my study of these Sun-Jupiter conjunctions as far as the end of the century in order to have a run of sixty and to give the sceptics something to think about.

- **Conjunction of 14 October 1981:** on 10 October 1981, there were huge pacifist demonstrations with millions of people marching against Euro missiles in Bonn, Rome, Brussels, London, Madrid and in Paris.

- **Conjunction of 13 November 1982:** this was the very November that President Reagan lifted the American embargo on oil and gas equipment from the USSR. This thaw happened on the eve of the release of Lech Walesa due to the demise of Brezhnev on 11 November; followed immediately by a resumption of disarmament negotiations at Geneva under Andropov and also a détente between Moscow and Peking.

- **Conjunction of 14 December 1983:** a new thaw throughout this month which led to a conference of the big powers in Stockholm on 17 January.

- **Conjunction of 14 January 1985:** a decisive turning point in détente (the arrival of Gorbachev) with the Schultz-Gromyko meetings on the control of armaments on 7 and 8 January in Geneva.

- **Conjunction of 18 February 1986**: the signing of the final act of the European Union on 17 February in Luxemburg. This month Gorbachev launched *perestroika* and *glasnost* at the 27th party congress, while on the 13th flights resumed between the United States and the USSR, and the dissident Anatoly Sharansky was freed and exchanged for western spies in Berlin.

- **Conjunction of 27 March 1987:** the situation was

neutralised, no tangible manifestations.

- **Conjunction of 2 May 1988:** from 14 April to 15 May the Geneva accord was accompanied by the withdrawal of Soviet troops from Afghanistan (considered to be the end of the war), followed by the American-Soviet summit of 29 May in Moscow when a treaty was ratified to eliminate some missiles.

- **Conjunction of 9 June 1989:** the libertarian uprising of Chinese students in May, which resulted in the Tiananmen Square massacre on the 3 and 4 June, triggered huge demonstrations of support in Canton, Shanghai, Hong Kong, Moscow and various European capitals.

- **Conjunction of 15 July 1990:** German unification took place in the middle of the month, with the green light from Gorbachev who accepted the inclusion of the former GDR into NATO.

- **Conjunction of 17 August 1991:** coup against Gorbachev who turned against its authors the failed putsch precipitated the breakdown of the regime.

- **Conjunction of 17 September 1992:** the popular ratification in France of the Maastricht treaty on 20 September.

- **Conjunction of 18 October 1995:** after a similar ratification in Germany on 12 October, Maastricht was put into effect on 1 November. European-Chinese relations, which had been frozen, since the 'Peking Spring' resumed on 2 November.

- **Conjunction of 17 November 1994:** on 26 October a peace treaty was signed between Israel and Jordan (with the Venus-Jupiter conjunction). On 8 October, a UN international tribunal was created in reaction to the genocide in Ruanda.

- **Conjunction of December 18 1995:** on 21 November the Dayton accords were signed; they dealt with the peace process in Bosnia-Herzegovina which was put in place in December.

- **Conjunction of 19 January 1997:** there were general political upheavals in Eastern Europe. Daily pro-democracy demonstrations on the streets of Belgrade in Serbia in January led to an electoral victory on 4 February which destabilised Milosevic. In Bulgaria in January street demonstrations in Sofia led to a new government on 12 February in Romania the December elections gave the presidency to a Christian Democrat. Boiling point was reached in Albania where the state started to totter.

- **Conjunction of 23 February 1998:** under the mantle of the UN an accord, which narrowly averted a new war against Saddam Hussein's Iraq, was signed in Baghdad.

- **Conjunction of 1 April 1999**: a critical conjunction. NATO's bombardment of Serbia started on 24 March; the doctrine of humanitarian intervention, a legal initiative, allowed a programme of negotiations to be imposed on Belgrade.

So there is strong evidence that the Sun-Jupiter conjunction has a positive effect. There is no doubt that its progress covers a great number of the most representative episodes of détente in the history of the second half of the 20th century. Admittedly, most of the time, the circumstances do jump about randomly from one historic event to another. Nevertheless, in its series of cycles, its sequential unity gives the impression of a chronological thread running through history with the many event points placed on the same line in the universe. The course of the long negotiations before the end of the Algerian War is a good example. Remember, also, the trio of conjunctions in 1969, 1970, and 1971 with détente in Berlin and the duo of 1992 and 1993 with Maastricht. The four successive conjunctions of 1969 to 1973, which were in tune with the conquest of space, are another example.

Naturally, the Sun-Jupiter conjunction does not cover the totality of peaceful events. The forecasts made for the latest wars remind us of the contribution of Venus as well as the particular frequency of harmonic triangles formed by this trio.

Actually, the Sun-Jupiter trine is frequently found on its own: around 11 November 1918 and 8 May 1945, at the armistice of Hungary on 20 January 1945; at the referendum sanctioning the independence of Algeria on 1 July 1962; at the détente of the missile crisis in Cuba on 28 October1962 ; at the signing of the Israeli-Egyptian peace treaty on 26 March 1979; at the supreme American-Soviet agreement on disarmament on 7 December 1987...

Harmonic triangles turn up constantly : the peace treaty with Japan on 13 August 1951, American invitation to Khrushchev to go to the United States on 13 July 1959, the Oslo accord at the White House between the Israelis and the Palestinians on 13 September 1993 and the confirmation at Cairo 4 (Oslo 1) on 4 May 1994. Let us not forget that the Munich Pact on September 30 1938, had dissonant aspects with the Sun semi-square to Venus which is square to Jupiter which is sesqui-quadrate the Sun, and this illustration of corrupt fruit reminds us that though we are conducting a purely quantitative survey we must not forget that each configuration has a qualitative value.

At the end of this voyage into the unknown, critical or sceptical readers must carry on with their own investigation to see if the astral blueprints of times to come can help them to follow Ariadne's thread of history. This would be the best way to make an honest judgement about the validity and worth of this cosmo-sociological work. Here are the dates for future Sun-Jupiter conjunctions:

- 21 November 2006
- 23 December 2007
- 24 January 2009
- 28 February 2010

Give me a Sun-Jupiter conjunction and I'll have you talking about astrology!

A historic forecast

Having now tested this indicator, chosen purely for its annual renewal, we move on to a tour de force which covers history on a much larger scale. We were only able to study one cycle but, as it unfolded, we were more than compensated by the size of its impact on the world scene. As well as having recourse to previous conjunctions which were used as a control we now applied the same method of testing to the whole cycle through each of its successive phases. So, I made the following proviso and forecast:

> For example, the Saturn-Neptune conjunction of 1917 and the Russian Revolution of the same year could be a mere coincidence. One can only talk of correlation when one finds out that the revolutionary movement in Russia started under the preceding conjunction of the same two planets of 1882 and that the history of the Soviet regime has really followed the different phases of the cycle 1917-1953, and also that it is continuing with the new current cycle. So that, having observed a large number of successive correlations, we will feel justified in predicting a milestone for Communism and the Soviet Union at the new Saturn-Neptune conjunction of 1989.[69]

It is this Saturn-Neptune cycle that we will be discussing here, and about which I made two official forecasts for the conjunctions of 1953 and 1989, the duration of the cycle being 36 years. Prior to the presentation of this forecast I need to explain how the operation was conducted and how I arrived at the results.

A cycle is a line in the universe: of time, space, movement and substance. It is the nature of the two planets involved which determines the substance of the manifestation. In the planetary concert Neptune resonates with the public mood, the popular beliefs, with the collective faith of a people. Saturn places this last at the lower level of a disadvantaged world; the planet has its roots in human misery, with beings who are frustrated, suffering privation and want. So the Saturn-Neptune undercurrent may take on the character of revolt and its conjunctions can accompany collective revolutionary movements; moreover its tendency is to harden (Saturn contracts), to concentrate, to radicalise in the style of the extreme left. So, looking at the five preceding conjunctions this is what was found.

- **Conjunction of 1773:** the Boston Tea Party of 16 and 17 December was the start of the revolt of thirteen English North American colonies which led to the independence of the United States in 1776.

- **Conjunction of 1809:** what started in North America spread to South America. In 1810, in the Spanish colonies of Latin America, there was an uprising, which led to the continent becoming independent in 1811. In addition, in Europe, the upheaval caused by the Napoleonic campaigns shook people out of their torpor; European nationalism arose from these national struggles and is more active than ever with the following conjunction.

- **Conjunction of December 1846:** in 1847 the Communist League was founded. It had its first congress and Marx and Engels launched the Communist Party manifesto. Also, in February 1848 there was an explosion of patriotic, liberal and proletarian ideas and a revolutionary movement spread across the European continent.

- **Conjunction of 1882:** between 1879 and 1883, in the space of a few years, in ten European countries, socialist parties sprang up which claimed filiation with Marxism. Their electoral successes meant that this was the first time that these diverse organisations made an appearance in the national political life of European countries.

- **Conjunction of 1917:** Russian revolution; on 7 November 1917 the Bolsheviks took power and instated the Soviet regime. A year of mutinies in the armies deployed in the field and of revolutionary awakenings in Latin America.

This series is suggestive... Moreover, the comparable path in the cyclical process, complete with secondary aspects (semi-square and sesqui-quadrate) as well as Soviet history is just as persuasive.

- **Conjunction (August 1917):** the October Revolution, the Soviets seized power and established the 'dictatorship of the proletariat ' under the direction of the Bolshevik Party with Lenin and Trotsky. The country, isolated from the world, was in the throes of a civil war and had also to cope with the intervention of various foreign armies.

- **Semi-square (October 1921):** chaos and the New Economic Policy, NEP. A critical year with typhus, famine, and industrial and agricultural collapse. In March the Kronstadt rebellion shook a power reduced to going back to liberal capitalism (NEP).

- **Sextile (December 1922 to September 1923):** coming out of war and chaos. A new regime was established which became stable and the country's frontiers were secured. On 30 December 1922 the treaty of the United Soviet Socialist Republics (USSR) was signed creating a federal state which, by July 1923, had its own constitution. In the same time period the regime was recognised by several states and the conferences that took place in Genoa and The Hague (1922) marked the entry of the Soviets into international life.

- **Square (January to November 1926):** Stalinist dictatorship. The death of Lenin, in 1924, gave rise to power struggles, in particular the clash between Trotsky and Stalin. The years from 1925 to 1927 saw the exclusion and then the exile of Trotsky and the rise of Stalin's dictatorship, which forced the submission of the high-ups in the regime.

- **Trine (March to December 1929):** the Five-Year Plan. In 1928 Russia was very backward economically. A first Five-Year Plan to construct grandiose industrial buildings went into operation in October 1928. A gigantic surge in the means of production allowed them to catch up after centuries of being behind; the USSR became a new force in global markets while an economic crisis hit the capitalist countries.

- **Semi-square (February to December 1931):** problems with the farmers. With the bad harvests of 1931, the collectivisation of the countryside provoked a peasant revolt which caused a reversal in agrarian reform.

- **Opposition (March 1936 to January 1937):** Moscow trials, Anti-Comintern Pact, Spanish Civil War. Even though the second Five-Year Plan allowed the USSR to become third or fourth among the industrial powers, the regime was in crisis. Stalin eliminated the old Communist and Bolshevik guard of the October Revolution in the course of two trials (19 August 1936 and 23 January 1937). The second liquidated the military high command (Tukhachevsky and seven marshals and generals). While the working class agitated in the United States and France (The Popular Front of May 1936), Franco's coup d'état in Spain in July 1936 erected a barrier against Communism as did the Anti-Comintern Pact (Germany-Japan-Italy) which was signed on 25 November 1936.

- **Semi-square (May 1940 to March 1941):** war. Despite efforts to avoid the menace of the Anti-Comintern Pact, the USSR was attacked on 22 June 1941 by Nazi Germany and members of the European coalition.

- **Trine (July 1941 to April 1942):** military resistance and the Anglo-American-Soviet alliance. Some gains. The failure of the Reich's blitzkrieg against the USSR. The reorganisation of Soviet Power, assisted by Anglo-American aid. Resistance swiftly followed by victory over the Wehrmacht for the Red Army. The USSR gained prestige and was stronger for the ordeal.

- **Square (July 1944 to April 4 1945):** end of solidarity with the Allies and a climate of revolutionary crisis. The war over, solidarity with the Allies broke down with the advance of the Red Army into Eastern Europe, where they installed pro-Communist authorities (tension with Poland and Turkey). There were various revolutionary movements (Greece, Belgium, Yugoslavia, Italy) which all failed except in Yugoslavia.

- **Sextile (July 1947):** economic recovery and the creation of Cominform (organisation of Communist parties). The fourth Five-Year Plan (1946-1949) erased the devastation of a ruthless war, and between autumn 1947 and spring 1948 countries in the Soviet zone became part of the Cominform (22 September1947). In the climate created by the communist victory of Mao Tse Tung in China the soviets dominated central and eastern Europe.

- **Semi-square (August 1948):** Yugoslavian crisis and the Berlin blockade. On 29 June 1948, the Communist world split because of divisions between Moscow and Belgrade. August 1948 was the month that the Berlin blockade began and lasted for over a year. In addition there was the Lysenko affair and the death of Zhdanov.

- **Semi-sextile (14 February 1950):** coming out of a Sun-Venus-Jupiter conjunction, the USSR and the new China signed a treaty linking the two great Communist homelands; Saturn was at 17degrees Virgo, between Pluto at 16 degrees Leo and Neptune at 17 degrees Libra, so that they were united with a semi-sextile separating Saturn and Neptune and another semi-sextile separating Saturn and Pluto (the cycle of Communist China).

So I doubled my bet that the continuous cyclical series of conjunctions showed a correlation between the Saturn-Neptune cycle and the destiny of Communism along with that of the Soviet Union. Given such a historic analogy, I took the risk of making a completely original forecast (there being no precedent in this genre: it was therefore a first) which appeared in the newspaper *L'Yonne républicaine* on 1 January 1953:

> Given that the Russian Communist Party was born under the conjunction of 1882 and that it took power at the one of 1917, one has to think that the year 1955 will be an important one for the USSR. In fact, the Communist regime will be at the end of a cycle at the same time as it is renewed, and at the end of a cycle we can expect an internal reorganisation, perhaps a new generation of statesmen in the Kremlin.

To everyone's surprise (no one knew he was ill), Stalin died on 5 March 1953; this marked the end of the cycle with the new conjunction (November 1952-July 1953). To the text of my forecast I added this:

> As this is the renewal of a cycle, there should be a bounce in the Communist cause in the world, or at least in the revolutionary cause. Soviet politics will find echoes in nations which until then had been hostile or indifferent to it.

In fact, Moscow went on to find a new revolutionary vocation supporting the cause of decolonisation and Afro-Asiatic nationalisms (the Bandung Conference took place in April 1955): it ended its isolation by politically supporting the 'third world' which then became a neutral front.

Encouraged by this success, I immediately embarked on my biggest predictive exercise yet. I began with this succinct statement: 'At the conjunction of 1952-1953, Stalin dies and the USSR undergoes a complete metamorphosis; it starts a new cycle for which the completion date is 1989.' This text is from one of my articles printed in *Défense et illustration de l'astrologie* (Defending and Illustrating astrology) in 1955.[70] It was as if I was making an assignation with history thirty four years ahead of time and it was to become the leitmotiv for a whole series of forecasts centred on the same theme and related to this same far off due date.

I confirmed this undertaking for a second time in my book, *Le Pronostic expérimental en astrologie* [The Experimental Forecast in Astrology].[71] After repeating the forecast I had made for the conjunction of 1953, I added:

> Encouraged by this success, would I be given more credit if I took the next Saturn-Neptune conjunction of 1989 seriously as the herald of a new 'grand premier' for the fate of the Soviet Union or world Communism?

I intended to perform a double act, which was to carry out in quick succession, albeit at long distance, two similar exercises in forecasting using the recurrence of the same phenomenon. I had to fix the date which would mark a crucial turning point for the future of Communism without having any details about the content of the timetable.

I had done something similar, more than twenty years previously, in my work *Les Astres et l'Histoire* (The Stars and History) which came out in 1967. For 1989, there was a mention of a 'triple planetary meeting, the most important astral reunion in the whole of the 20th century', Saturn leaves an encounter with Uranus to join with Neptune and these last two planets go on to form their own conjunction in 1993. Each cycle having its own range of assignments, the two Saturnian encounters allowed me to look at the relationship between two historic giants.

> [...] the Americans and the Russians representing the capitalist principle and the Communist principle [...] both these two runners are at the end of a race, with its final destination in 1988-1989, at the end of which

the world will start to renew itself and give birth to a new society. There is no doubt that a great crossroad in our history will be reached when the three lines cross between 1988 and 1992.

I provided a graphic illustration of the three cycles meeting, Uranus-Neptune, Saturn-Uranus and Saturn-Neptune, in my book *Astrologie mondiale*[72] (Mundane Astrology).

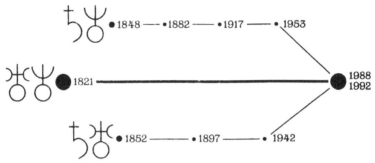

When one knows that the Uranus-Neptune cycle evolves in parallel with the fortunes and misfortunes of our so-called capitalist society, in the same way that Saturn-Uranus marks the salient times for its right wing (imperialist, totalitarian, fascist), while the Saturn-Neptune cycle times the distinctive phases of the left wing (syndicalist, Socialist, Communist), it is conceivable that the fusion of these three cycles at the same place at the same time could signify a crucial time of renewal for the world.

I had already given my interpretation of this great configuration in *Le Pronostic expérimental astrologie*, (The Experimental Forecast in Astrology).

[...] the most significant year being 1989 with the triple opposition of Jupiter to this conjunction. The fate of humanity for the 21st century could be pinned to this. We have seen our modern capitalist society evolve throughout the great Uranus-Neptune cycle since it began last time. Starting with the last Saturn-Uranus conjunction in 1942 and the last Saturn-Neptune conjunction in 1953, we saw the United States on one side and the USSR on the other being catapulted into a competition for world supremacy or for being the worldwide formula for society. Now these two runners have come to the end of the race at the same point in time as if they are merging into a single stream. This common unique destination of 1989 is the historic date when the world will be ready to renew itself in order to give birth to a new society and it will happen at the time that the three planets cross.

Below is the map of the sky that accompanied this text.

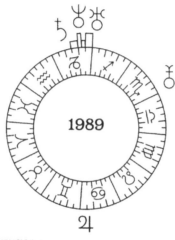

In 1980 I reformulated my forecast for an article called 'Nostradamus' in the *Club du livre* [The Book Club]. Telling the reader about an exegesis of Vlaicu Ionescu, according to whom the Soviet regime would last 'seventy-three years and seven months' and disappear in June 1991, I gave an account of my own experience of working with cycles, logging aspect after aspect and eventually concluding:

> Anyone who undertakes such work eventually acquires peace of mind. One can believe it or not believe it, it does not change anything. There is absolutely no doubt that the USSR is expected to go through a crucial and decisive turning point in its history when the Saturn-Neptune cycle renews itself

with the conjunction of 1989. What is more, circumstances demand that this large conjunction will form at the same time and in the same place as the two others, preceded in 1988 by a Saturn-Uranus conjunction (with a 45-year cycle) and followed in 1992 by a Uranus-Neptune conjunction (with a 171-year cycle). For the years 1988-1992, suffice it to say that this triple astral reunion, with its major planetary upheaval, heralds changes in society throughout the world and notably in Russia. The astronomical phenomenon relative to this country falls between December 1989 and March 1990, but it is likely that there will be a shift of a year to a year and a half for the consequences to manifest. That is why ultimately the Nostradamic end date perceived by his exegete Ionescu may be recorded by history.

From Paris to Vienna, along with Stuttgart, Capri, Madrid, Rio de Janeiro and Zurich, I was faced with the same issue as the one I had had to confront between 1983 and 1987, that of trying to formulate, in different ways, what it was that the great actors on the world scene had in common that would bring them together at this great planetary crossroads.

As the key date approached I recalled the climate of revolutionary fervour at the time of the great conjunction (*L'Astrologue*, number 80, fourth quarter 1987). Finally I got to the nub of the matter in the 'gale warning' I gave in my article, 'Orages sur 1989-1990' [The storms of 1989-1990] (number 85, first quarter 1989):

> So the Jupiter-Saturn opposition alone (from September 1989 to July 1990) indicates a critical turning point for the European Community, which will be involved in a new crisis and will have to go through a very testing time before reaching its historic maturity in 1992.
>
> But above all, we must not forget that Jupiter then moves on to form an opposition to the Saturn-

Neptune conjunction during this same period of September 1989 to July 1990. [...] This could be the time that revolutionary movements come to a head, with popular uprisings, huge street protests and the risk of powers being toppled. One cannot help thinking of the glorious feats in countries that have been oppressed such as Romania and Eastern European countries that have been kept under the yoke like Czechoslovakia.

Let's summarize here what did happen in this historic year 1989. It all started with the Peking Spring's explosion. On 17 April a student demonstration started in Peking. It continued, and when it was prohibited on the 25th and 26th one million young people marched in growing numbers to Tian'anmen Square. Gorbachev's visit on 15 May re-launched the movement which was joined by the entire population; every day, until the massacre of 3 and 4 June, a million Peking residents demonstrated against the imposition of martial law. Also millions marched, in solidarity with the students, in Canton, Shanghai and Hong Kong and huge demonstrations of support were organised in Moscow and various European capitals. It was the first popular shake-up of the regime since its foundation.

The same spring there were signs of nationalist unrest in Georgia, Lithuania and Moldavia as well as the Balkans, while the Soviets bowed to reform and had elected deputies in congress for the first time. In April a breach opened in Poland where, thanks to agreements being torn up by Solidarity, the country adopted a non-Communist government on 12 September. Hungary followed suit with a similar result on 13 June and it took down the iron curtain which separated it from Austria. This triggered a massive exodus of East-Germans over the summer, with those who stayed organising impressive street demonstrations. Gorbachev's visit on 7 October, precipitated the fall of the German Democratic Republic. Abandoned by the Soviets, Erich Honecker resigned on the 18th. Next, on 9 November, the Berlin Wall fell; this was a point of no return. Bulgaria, Czechoslovakia, Yugoslavia, and finally even Romania (25 December) followed. With the exception of Albania the whole East European Communist bloc disappeared!

At the end of the same year, with the secession of the Lithuanian Communist Party, demonstrations and secession in Mongolia and civil war in Azerbaijan, the USSR was already just a shadow of its former empire. The final blow came with the failed putsch in Moscow on 19 August 1991, which caused the downfall of the KGB and the Soviet Communist Party. It was accompanied by the dynamiting and toppling of statues and the race to independence of the provinces of the USSR. In December 1991 these were finally replaced by the Community of Slav States. It was the end of the vast Soviet empire that had dominated the 20th century.

This account of a major turning point in the 20th century with all its historical fireworks gives complete validity to the forecasted date which was fixed more than thirty years previously and constantly restated (remember that this political earthquake surprised the entire world). And this is without counting - the planetary crossroads also heralded the re-founding of society - the arrival of the Internet (1990-1991) that, with the spread of personal computers across the world, utterly transformed globalisation. We have the impression of a finger pointing to the truth of mundane astrology which is that it is in close contact with history.

Thus, at different levels, the mundane path of the Sun-Jupiter conjunction and the horseback ride of the Saturn-Neptune cycle show the extent of astrological forecasting. Those who want to learn more can look at some new explorations of history in 'Le destin de l'Europe' [The destiny of Europe] on my site, www.andrébarbault.com. Also 'Bilan des cycles planétaires' [An Assessment of Planetary Cycles] covers more than two centuries of the Jupiter-Saturn cycle. Finally, I have set out an enlightening 'Un bilan prévisionnel' [A Forecast Assessment].

While it is a fact that astrological forecasting works and

that it can be a useful means of persuasion, it is also the case that, in its present state, the information it provides is very scanty. Our knowledge is still very rudimentary. When searching for reliable precise reference points, our initial results only give a basic outline of the forecast which leaves the option of several outcomes (as in the research on the end of the war...). These results shouldn't lead us to believe that we can forecast everything going and stick our noses into everything like some columnists. I have to mention the exaggerated claims that are made in the game of divinatory one-upmanship. We have only got to examine the rash of predictions for whatever presidential election to see their absurdity. The fact that they repeatedly get it wrong does not seem to put an end to such tittle-tattle. We are far from being able to afford the luxury of this kind of forecasting.

Throughout my life I have tried to wrest the secrets from the configurations in attempting to anticipate the future and I'm always at risk of being dreadfully wounded by a forecasting disaster. But that is not surprising and it is also not surprising that I, more than anybody, have had to submit to the wonders of such charitable co-workers who are so good at protecting themselves from the exposure of prediction. Besides, I claim absolutely the right to make mistakes because they are formative. Had I had even more setbacks, my work would not be any less valuable. Seeing how forecasts work out are steps toward the better tracking of planetary cycles. In short, who thinks that they are clever enough to wear the crown in Urania's palace? [73]

We are still only at the laboratory stage when it comes to forecasting. Treating forecasts in this way is new territory. We are at the very beginning. The qualified researcher still has a lot to learn but it is rewarding work. Even if it has a long way to go before it is fully developed, astral - forecasting has a real future and the good practitioner will definitely find some real gems.

As a start, let us end the prejudices of detractors, and write large the predictive power of the astral signature to signal historical events and forecast what is to come.

Chapter 8 - The Psychoanalytical Key

When new students begin to study astrology, they immediately fall sway to the hidden power, invisible, silent and anonymous, of tradition. However capable they feel of mastering the subject, it will take them over.

Hardly have they leant over their first chart before their sense of self, their sense of being 'me, here and now', is obliterated by the immense shadow of this enduring and universal tradition. It is as if their actions become lost in the never ending repetition of the same actions, by which millions of others just like them have rooted themselves in the past with their heavy dependency on traditional methods. In any case, there is a vague feeling that they are discovering the secrets of this 'traditional science' as if the truth will be revealed once they are admitted to the sanctuary.

As a result of this feeling of initiation, without being conscious of it, they are taken over by a magical mentality super ego: even if they don't want to, they start wearing the mythical pointed hat; they become trapped in the 'paradigms' of another age, and they assume the prejudices and received ideas belonging to the furthest reaches of the mind where the sorcerer wearing his starry robe is able to fascinate the part of the unconscious that engages in magical thinking. It is not easy to let this go...

Just because there is truth in astrology it does not mean that the whole astrological tradition must be received as truth. Pascal said, 'What makes one believe so strongly in the effects of the Moon is that some of them, like the movement of the sea, show it to be true.' And yet when first introduced to this truth we are encouraged to answer to the demands of the absolute, the tyrannical influence of this super ego which accepts everything: false aphorisms, doubtful correlations, absurd methods of interpretation, the senseless search for divinatory objectives which is always unsuccessful.

By the beginning of the last century, the French Choisnard School had started to create some order by looking at problems in a scientific way and introducing a number of rationales into astrological practice. They banned the old ways of teaching astrology which involved the teacher who, elevated by the prestige of the tradition, blindly communicated knowledge that was unregulated and sometimes erroneous or doubtful but which was received by the pupils as if it was founded on faith.

In the middle of the 20th century, astrologers concentrated on putting the correspondences between the sky and mankind on a solid footing and also, more importantly, giving the practice of astrology a psychological basis. With a group of friends at the Centre international d'astrologie (International Centre for Astrology), in Paris, I did some important work in this field which led to several books being published. Basically the research aimed to build a basic symbolism for different celestial bodies (Sun and Moon, Jupiter and Saturn, Uranus and Neptune), then on establishing the correlation between the astrological factors and various existing typologies.

This is how I described the situation in a statement I made at the time: 'The contemporary astrologer is playing an instrument (in this case, the planets) but he only knows a few isolated notes in an unknown key', therefore we need to 'go back to basics', to 'rewrite the concepts', with a view to 'fully getting hold of these symbols [...] lifting astrological knowledge to the same level of understanding as modern knowledge.'[74] The result was the following programme.

Astrology is to knowledge of life what mathematics is to the physical sciences. Its abstract symbols are too removed from the empirical data of real life for it to be able to assimilate them directly without the help of science. The correspondence between celestial indices and human phenomena can only be put on a solid footing using well-founded techniques. Only the well-founded techniques of science have the necessary qualities to establish the rules of correspondence. That is why our research had to make use of a number of disciplines, as points of reference, and to which we have to incorporate astrology and its original values. We must structure our knowledge in the same way as the different sciences. We won't be able to use the astrology of tomorrow as a tool for the mind to just throw itself into things without exercising proper judgement. On the contrary it will be an instrument that makes use of well based knowledge and which puts the researcher directly in touch with the make-up of actual phenomena, the only valid reference. [75]

By using this approach, we were not afraid of being accused (as we had been before by the purists) of debasing astrology. Far from it! Astrology has the prestige of having given the homo-analogic laws to the other sciences because it has, more than any other natural phenomenon, the most stable and rigorous system of numerical, spatial and temporal relationships. Alchemy, medicine and psychology were all originally modelled on astrology, just as many of today's sciences come from mathematics. Now, on the contrary, when we look for a model among the human sciences for the simple reason that these are better structured, astrology, as a self-sufficient autonomous practice, disappears, is integrated into the body of other disciplines, becoming just one of their branches: cosmo-biology, cosmo-sociology.

This was the way we set about our work and we made the decision that however gifted we were in the psychological sense we would not just improvise in our own way; we had to take the new thinking that was enriching modern psychology and structure our knowledge in the same way as an established discipline. So, when Michel Gauquelin rebuilt the planetary types using some particular typologies, he only underlined what we had already achieved: we did not have to wait for him to establish the correlation between Jupiter and extroversion and Saturn and introversion...

Besides, the end point for him was only the beginning of an avenue that we had already largely explored. Indeed, precious as his contribution is, his results are only valuable as a first approach and they only scratch the surface of psychological reality. A type embodies an array of character traits, but what is underneath the character trait? It is a 'predisposition'.

François Jacob declared, 'The cell is to the molecule what the molecule is to the atom [...]. With the cell, biology discovered its atom'. And so predisposition is to psychology what the atom is to physics and the cell to biology. To understand the importance of researching into predisposition, you have to give it analogically the same level of value that the biologist gives to the cell: 'the basic unit of all living things, [it] ensuring that life continues, [...] it is the necessary origin of all organised bodies, [...] possessing all the attributes of life'[76] (the properties of what is living must be attributed to it)... In other words it is important that predisposition becomes the focus of research, getting inside its world because it is only from the inside that we can begin to understand the story of humanity and to know more about the future of mankind.

Now this research has its foot in the very epistemology of astrology, which has to be taken primarily as a human creation. We had to go back to the origins of astrological thought, 'discovering' what life was like for the Ancients, grasping the way in which the phenomenon affected them, this point of origin being the best way of understanding how we arrived at our current astrological knowledge.

Indeed, mankind is at the basis of astrology, because the phenomenon of astrology is inside us: we discovered it because we live it. And, because it is born in us, so we contain the root or mother cell of the astrological universe. Here, the action and the thing acted on are linked, the one determined by the other, like the sign and the thing signified, also like the thing sought and the mind which discovers and interprets it. This one-way action reminds us that science establishes objective causal relationships between things, even though here, as in divination, there is only a being projecting the shadow of its own structure on to the screen of the world.

Even though the main anthropic cosmological thrust of astrology makes the people ramble, it nevertheless provides a tiny springboard of knowledge for astrologers and forms the basis of their astrological thinking which is guided by intuition. This type of happenstance can for example explain the declaration by Abbey Charles Nicoullaud, under the pseudonym of Fomalhaut, in his *Traité d'astrologie sphérique et judiciaire*:[77] 'Beyond the orbit of Neptune there is a planet with the name of Pluto.' This planet was discovered in 1930 by Clyde Tombaugh. He chose the name after it had been suggested by a little girl and the community of astronomers ratified his choice.

Far back in time, mankind made the gods and the sky in its own image and, with the power of collective worship by which human beings are uplifted when they encounter the world, the human being signified stands before the astral signifier to which they correspond through the projection of the collective unconscious. The psychic power expressed is, basically, the meeting of anthropomorphism and cosmo-morphism: mankind finds itself in the world and the world is assimilated into mankind, signified by means of a universal symbolism organized by analogical connections. That way, if there is a deep relationship between the stars and man, it is due to the stars being anthropomorphic and mankind being cosmomorphic centred in a living unity.[78]

Today, we cannot see any transitive phenomena coming to us from the stars that would give support to astrology but, on the other hand, we are familiar with the phenomenon of transference which operates the other way round, placing the human heart in a distant celestial body. Emerging from profound darkness, human beings began to define themselves by thinking of the psyche as a reflection of the natural order, even structuring it like a diagram of the universe.

Leading on from this, the only question was whether an actual homology could exist between the make-up of the interpretive code that we were studying and that of the real world, something not completely unthinkable: reality being taken as a continuous environment, the universe is not only outside us but also in us; human beings being inseparable from the continuous environment that bathes them and inseparable from mankind and the universe are our thoughts. This accords with the anthropic principle: given that there is an observer, the universe has the properties required to engender both itself and him, the one being ontologically linked to the other.

In other words, the human mind has the universe within it, and nature is composed from the same matter as that within us. So we could conceive that the laws of creation and of universal reality could be reflected in our psychic creativity and mentality, which does not stop us imagining a twin complementary process in which the universe becomes the thought and the interior representation becomes the layout of the world. We would have the kind of system in which the signifier is an analogue of the signified, the signification resting on a homology of their respective structures; so considerable properties can be transferred from the signifier to the signified. In any case, there is well-founded research of a system of signification in another system, which is exterior and concrete and which became the model for interpretation: the life of the human soul relative to nature and relative to the celestial configurations. The analogy between the two entities and the two systems allows the known to be assimilated into the unknown. This gives the unknown some structure, and therefore some sense. This is how the structuralist idea of a seminology of astrology came about in the universe of the word.

Astrology is encapsulated in these popular images: man, by introjection, astralises himself and assimilates himself into a celestial body and, by projection, humanises the celestial body by placing himself in the sky, this identification of the human soul with the universe being his psychic foundation.

In his book *Fondements et avenir de l'astrologie*[79] (Founding Principles for the Future of Astrology) Daniel Verney, a scholar graduated from Ecole Polytechnique, found a good way of expressing this unity by giving definition to a code which if it 'enables man to decipher reality, to read this writing that is the world, must be because the human brain is also an integral part of the world and that it is organised, or written, in the same way, which is in accordance with a specific universal structure'. And the place where this unity is most alive, where this inscription or writing is most expressed, is in the deepest part of human nature; in the continuity of man, nature and the cosmos.

Astrology then, with its internal source, came from the ancestral innermost depths of the collective soul with its anthropo-cosmological make-up. Jung gives a psychological rationale for this inherent source on which the coextensive universal nature of human beings is founded and in which macrocosm and microcosm unite, the first being to the second what the second is to the first:

> In as much as personality [...] is unconscious, it cannot be distinguished from what all its projections contain, which means that to a great extent it is identical to its surroundings, corresponding to a kind of mystical participation. This situation is of the greatest practical importance, given that it explains the particular symbols by which this state is translated in dreams. I want to talk about the symbols in the world around us and the symbols in the cosmos. These form the psychological basis for the representation of man as a microcosm, which, as we know, is connected to the macrocosm by the components of character formulated in astrological terms.[80]

In psychoanalytical terms, the links between the macrocosm and the microcosm are in the unconscious, making the human heart the cell of the astrological universe. The links between mankind and the sky use human emotions as a support and as a means of connecting identification according to two states: the projection which anthropomorphises the star and the introjection which cosmomorphises mankind.

Astrology's general condition as a knowledge comes from this psychic anthropo-cosmological origin. This is the keystone not only of ancient general astrological belief systems, but also is the root of the philosophical theory of macrocosm-microcosm on which this royal art was founded, as well as the material itself (the substance of human emotion) which is at the heart of astrological practice.

In regard to our epistemological exploration, astrology, from the time of its birth through to today, is a system created by the human soul for the human soul; with astrology we can search for and configure the psyche in regard to the universe, its mirror. From this we can define its phenomenology: the human soul is at the same time the subject and object, in and related to the universe. That is to say that the unconscious – where the tendency has its roots – is the realm of the astrological phenomenon: it is the 'place' where astrology originated, from where popular astrology derives its beliefs, from where scholarly astrology takes its philosophy of life, the place where the practising astrologer constantly operates... Not to mention the way astrological phenomena manifest intrinsically, operating by way of unconscious processes. It is therefore natural that, first and foremost, the system for decoding and interpreting astral language is psychoanalytical hermeneutics.[81]

It is natural that human beings were central to astrology's foundation since it is in human beings that it finds expression and manifests itself. We just have to let our feelings express themselves in order to reveal how connected we are to the world around us. We feel as if we live in others or that others live in us, as if we had no boundaries. Jung declared that 'the soul could be a mathematical point and, at the same time, be as immense as the planetary world'; in fact, at this unconscious level, mankind has expanded to the size of the cosmos, as equally the cosmos is condensed in us, and is living in a world of symbols with the world of symbols living in us. The poets sing abundantly about these states of participation in the cosmos: Verlaine was inhabited by an internal autumn and his violin soul was 'the same as a dead leaf'; Poe immersed himself in the world of the dead and drowned in his gloomy waters. Baudelaire wrote:

> Like lingering echoes, which afar confound
> Themselves in deep and sombre unity,
> As vast as Night, and transplendently,
> The scents and colours to each other respond.

So it is that in the temple of nature, across the long line of correspondences established by the range of our particular affinities, human beings are really united with the world and even feel at one with their own star. Here, finally, macrocosm and microcosm are one, united as they were initially at the creation, at the centre of all sensitive experiences involving our emotions: in dreams, in games, in love, in poetry, in faith… One can understand why its enemies have called astrology an ersatz religion, and why Bouché-Leclercq defined it as 'a faith that speaks the language of science, and a science that can only find justification for its principles in faith'. Faith certainly has a lot to do with feeling, but that does not make the beating of a heart a religious state. This is all very confusing.

However, the truth is clear: astrology is a knowledge of the soul (this word always to be taken in the psychological sense and not the theological one); its subject being the unconscious universe of the psyche, it establishes a bridge in the dialectic between the astronomical exterior and the human interior, and provides the algorithm for the symbolic union of the signifier and the signified.

Let's return to the original condition of astrology facts: the birth chart places the native at the centre of the world, surrounded by their celestial constellation. The configuration is anthropocentric and provides the very cosmic representation of the subject. Positioned in this way the astral diagram relates only to the person concerned, and to that person's view of themselves. It is egocentric (in the widest sense of the word) and completely subjective as beautifully illustrated by Anatole France when he said, 'My life amounted to very little but it was a life, that is to say at the centre of things, at the centre of the world.' More importantly, being placed at the centre of the cosmos adds to the worth of the native, making them the purpose of creation. The 'here and now' of the birth chart leads to the idea that the newborn infant is the humanisation of the universe at that time and place. Victor Hugo gives a sublime evocation of mankind being at home in the universe.

> My soul of a thousand voices
> That the God whom I adore established
> At the centre of all things, resounding echo!

Though the macrocosm acts as a mirror for the microcosm, the image it sends back can only be perceived in a psychological way, subliminally, in the inner depths of the mind, that we now call the unconscious. It is not surprising that the cosmos speaks to mankind in this symbolic way: the great book of nature is written in the mother tongue of the instincts, and the letters are moulded in the clay of animal life.

Before Freud, when astrological symbolism was not comprehensible, we would have had to accept this criticism from Paul Couderc: 'This symbolism is the sort of thing found on playing cards and has as much value: we print a heart on a bit of card and from then on this card is able to tell you about your love life.' This charming astronomer is actually a contemporary of the father of psychoanalysis but he seems completely unaware that, for example, in dreams, myths and cults, the image of the Sun generally symbolises the father, the eye or the phallus, and that the Moon has symbolised femininity since time immemorial, all over the world, in myths and legends, for poets and in the dreams of all men.

Nevertheless it does make us wonder why, before we had psychoanalysis, the astral symbols grouped together completely unconnected aspects of life in a seemingly illogical way. It is just about conceivable that Mars should relate to the military as well as to sportspeople, and it is not hard to see what these two occupational categories have in common. Many sports are only games that have come from combat: boxing, wrestling, fencing, javelin and a game of rugby that simulates war. If no force is used it becomes about speed or skill. In the more refined sports, like tennis, in tournaments the players dispute like knights of old with the racquet replacing the rapier and the foil; even chess pieces are armies and the players rival strategists.

In all games in sport there is a duel, an adversary to beat. But what is the link between a soldier, a sportsman or woman and a doctor who is also a fully-fledged member of the Martian family? Even considering the strength of character required to confront the hardships of life that are created by illness, blood, human suffering and the struggle against disease, this line of reasoning is not really convincing at a rational level. But perhaps illness is an attack on the body, a state of war for the individual concerned, and the doctor is the soldier responsible for combating it. This is where we have to use reasoning by analogy, and the symbolism we have been given to decipher is a language that expresses feeling, the verbs used by the individual's unconscious; today it is recognised as the fundamental process behind all the manifestations of the psyche.

Reasoning by analogy is a way of thinking used more by artists than by scientists because it passes through the feelings before joining the usual internal processes that use its thread to weave a destiny according to an analogical motif. This ability of the soul to weave is immensely powerful: in infancy we don't need the help of fairies to turn a pumpkin into a carriage or a clog into a glass slipper; since the dawn of time, every day, in every country, children are able to change a piece of wood into a horse, a rag into an adored doll or a lead soldier into a heroic figure, changing an insignificant object into the most important thing in the world. It takes some strength and the restrictions imposed by family and society to curb these wonderful flights of the creative imagination; without ridicule, scolding and other gibes there would be no limit to these marvels. Yet it is not true that they die with childhood: they are just transformed with age and other flowers start to grow in this private garden. The symbols always remain where we are most receptive and where the imagination is able to make myths come to life.

The diagram showing the planets in their configuration around the newborn infant represents a cosmos that is inseparable from the interior being. In relation to this interior being, that exercises so much power in infancy and which never entirely loses its influence, Schopenhauer said, 'the world is a representation of ourselves': it is not actual events that count, what it shows is our feeling response to what happens. Here the values held by our 'inner constellations', as understood by Paracelsus, mark us through the medium of our sensitivity which animates our life, constructs it and realises it in an analogical way, like a Chinese shadow projected on to the screen of the outside world. Valery said: 'Events are the foam of things. It is the sea that interests me.' It is this sea deep inside me, which my inner being. In many ways life is much more real there than in the sphere of the visible happenings of 'real' life which are more or less superficial.

The dynamics of this interior being are housed deep down at the source of the soul. The roots of sensitivity, from the cradle of humanity and bathed in the atavism of the most primitive human being, are in a lower level of the psyche, where the instincts are embedded; it is in this dark night of the being that 'astral determinism' lies. And the analogic leitmotif of astrology must be understood in the light of its own data. In order to establish the thread between the astral phenomenon and the human act, the most important rule of interpretation is always to see beyond the immediate effect, to look at it from the inside. Therefore, in emotional impulse we retain its primacy as much as its primitive nature, the unconscious beneath the conscious, the subjective value underneath the objective evidence, the dream underlying experience, the structure underlying what is presented; in a word, the inner life lived by the being.

In the way that symbols operate, where the mind in flashbacks reconstructs the processes of the inner life, the polymorphism of the actions and expressions of life is reduced to the concept of an original theme. Everything that happens in life, from illnesses to being in love, from material or social problems to moral concerns, whether consisting of actions, visualisations or feelings, goes back to a fundamental psychic root. Thus, each planet represents a power which carries life and from birth to death, unfolds a given script, expands on the given sketch and develops a story by confronting us with life's problems.

We have to follow – as in how a particular desire is expressed in different ways all through someone's life – the proceedings of the symbol itself, to track the successive guises through which, using different masks, the drive becomes associated with an outcome and, why not, to discover the eternal archetype that lies behind its multiple transitory expressions.

For example, it is important to understand how, at different ages, starting from childhood with its important first events (teething, crawling...) the symbolic range of the tendency symbolised by Mars (the oral-sadistic stage energy, according to the Freudians' vision) is lived. The particular position of this planet at birth (its position in the diurnal course in the zodiac and the aspects it makes to other planets) is the prior configuration into which the beginning of the Martian adventure tends to adjust. This is here the theme of the destiny of aggressiveness and the response to the world's aggressiveness, whether expressed in a positive way self-assertion, conquests and passions, or in a negative way with fights, threats and acts of aggression (road accidents, alcohol or tobacco abuse, debts, rowdiness) in our modern society.

Astrology has been judged as if it were a physical vision of the world, which it isn't, and not as a psychological view of life. The signs, then, are taken as being the 'dreams and charms of a knowledge that is pre-rational' (Michel Foucault). We know that until the 16th century it held an important place in the learning of western culture, the world of resemblance (sympathy, signature, analogy), the non-rational being its anthropomorphised generalisation to the outside world.

Now astrology rests totally on the epistemological configuration of the world of resemblance, which has been in retreat since then in scientific circles; except, however, with the exploration of the unconscious, which is not just chance. The justification for the use of this principle lies in the material being studied: we now know, thanks to psychoanalysis, that the world of resemblance plays an active role in psychological life, and even constitutes its inherent reality.

So therefore, the semiology of astral signatures is perfectly acceptable when strictly defined as a category in our knowledge of the psyche and therefore as a system of similitudes that touches on our interior universe in the same way that our unconscious structures itself symbolically and creates an analogical image of the world. The unconscious life of the psyche is thus: it justifies the thought which interprets and recreates the facts.

We now come to the main criticism of astrology, the argument that gives the best justification for rejecting it: having come from the far distant past it is the product of an animistic and magical vision of mankind, which is relevant only to a way of thinking that preceded logic and science. But is the modern world so proud as to believe that only rational, scientific thought is capable of anything! The example of astrology even proves that that primitive mind was efficient. Indeed, if this argument were true, the conclusions drawn, because of the prejudices of our own collective mentality, are no less false!

In fact, we have simply not been aware that astrology, having come from the psychological (which we have explored), makes this its object: the astral signifier has been totally confused with the human who is signified, the astrology-subject and the astrology-object, thus mixing up an obscurantist approach and what comes under an obscure world, our inner darkness. To understand and work with the irrational phenomena of the unconscious, the psychoanalyst has to follow the processes of the primary psyche; it does not mean the psychoanalyst thinks in a primitive way.

Astrologers also work in this area, and the 'semantics of astrological discourse' and the fundamental processes of the psyche are part of the same board game: symbolic language, symbolic categories and an identical analogical palette, repetition automatisms, transference, displacement, contraction, over-determination, substitution. Astrology deciphers and reads the chart like a psychoanalyst interpreting a dream.[82]

So we have judged astrology as if it was a kind of archaeology of the mind, without knowing that it relates so well to the real interior archaeology of mythical thinking and behaviour which we still have in us and which influences our faith, our reason, our desires, our objectives, to such an extent that the hurried assumption that it is a 'false primitive knowledge' has changed into 'the true knowledge of primitive human beings'.

Because, as I have stated before, the signs of the zodiac being the work of a primitive mentality, with chimeric creatures such as a goat combined with a dolphin in the case of Capricorn or a rider with a horse in the case of Sagittarius, it does not stop people, every night all over the world, fusing together elements of their souls to create original compositions. In their dreams they go on making centaurs and become centaurs, in a way that is very similar to some zodiac signs.

These silent powers which people their sleep, sometimes in the turbulence of a nightmare, an imaginative fantasy or the persistence of an obsession, which has a subtle but real effect on them and on their lives, are the same as those which animate the myths, the religions, legends, folklore, stories, the imaginings of people and which continue to inhabit the soul of humanity, like the pagan gods of Olympus in the depths of each soul. This reverberation of the deep psyche is astrology's truth zone because this is the umbilical cord that links human beings to the cosmos, their profound humanity being seated in the unconscious.

The human soul as subject and object... It is not surprising that applying the expertise of psychoanalysis to astrology has led to it becoming methodologically based; by psychoanalysing it, we find the psychoanalytical essence of astrology and we can structure it according to the psychoanalyst's code of interpretation, without having the constraints of belonging to any particular psychoanalytical school. It is by using this method of 'interpreting its interpretations' that it was possible at last to find its missing logic.

At the heart of this debate is what epistemologists call the 'episteme of analogy'. It is not that they have been unsuccessful in analysing the way this type of thinking works, but rather that their thinking stopped at the idea that the logic behind the signs, the old relationship of analogies and signatures, came from unsophisticated minds, and so was not compatible with our scientific way of thinking. Gaston Bachelard, for one, did not avoid this too narrow framework of interpretation into which contemporary epistemology is set, thanks to Michel Foucault in particular, and which only considers it as a bygone conception of the world where the mind couldn't tell the difference between the sign and the object, the sign and a name, the name and its meaning. In short, there would only have been a kind of infantile thinking which must have resulted in false reasoning.

It seems that the true nature of episteme has entirely escaped these epistemologists, who can only see the shell without seeing the fruit inside. Yet this is real fruit that has to be carefully gathered in order to preserve its essence. With the new idea in physics of the indivisible whole in a reality that is infinite in space-time, the theory of macrocosm-microcosm is represented in a completely different way that rests on the structure of mind and nature being homologous. Since mankind and the world are one, and consciousness and its object only exist because of each other, the principle of resemblance comes into its own and in nature is considered as a signifying activity, where the sign is a natural thing because it is an integral part of universal life. The physicist Bernard d'Espagnat, who dealt directly with the theory of microcosm, was right:

> According to this hypothesis, as we know, the brain and the human mind, one of the most complex combinations in the universe, still have some structures that quite clearly show their independent origins. The hypothesis cannot be proved. However it is plausible because it accounts, in a schematic but basic way, for so many things as for example in the way, as discussed already, that it is possible to apply mathematics to phenomena [...] If this is so, one can see that the idea of an independent and structured reality whose permanent structures would be, at least partially reflected in the human mind, explains the physical laws that we observe. I would say that such an idea, far from being worthless and superfluous as often claimed, is on the contrary quite reasonable [...] It becomes essential then, to start again to research the correspondences which may exist between an independent reality and the concepts of the mind, these correspondences being, at the moment, hypothetical.[83]

The field of astrology has a perfect array of these correspondences in which analogies are understood using the language of signs. Nature is in itself an active signifier which gives things semantic properties. So the signs provide a simple natural database intended to be perceived by man, a perception that gives the human soul an understanding of its own essence thanks to the connection between the identity and its double, between the symbol and the symbolised, the signifier and the signified.

This is an reflexive way of knowing things where the world infinitely mirrors itself. From time immemorial things that are alike have reflected each other in a mutual transfer of their images between the Creator, the creation and its creatures. In the same way human identification, dealing back-and-forth with the internal, is an introjection of the external, and the external is a projection of the internal, just as the sky reflects mankind, the creation reflects the Creator; reproducing a common model which is both human and cosmic. The unity of man-cosmos is like holograph where the part, the elementary particle, contains the whole: the whole of our genetic inheritance is in each of our cells, just as each human being carries within them the whole of the cosmos.

When astrophysicists finally say that 'the whole universe is mysteriously present in every place and time in the world'[84]; what for them is the outcome of scientific thought, has always been the stuff of everyday for astrologers, for whom the new born infant is like a condensed universe. For them the new born is a moment in time in a particular place in the universe that becomes a human being.

This brings to mind the traditional vision of an encoded sacred world language, used to write the great book of nature, where the celestial signs are able to deliver a divine message because they are the bearers of an initiatory discourse drawn from a treasured universal mother language which can penetrate hidden meaning and reveal life's mysteries.

For Leibniz, if there was a universal science it would be subdivided into three separate sciences which would correspond to three important areas: the god of theology, the soul of psychology and the world of cosmology.

'I wouldn't deny that astrology is the "golden language" of analogy, one which lends itself to the greatest exchange between man and nature by establishing a whole network of points that correspond with each other. Nothing shows a more ardent desire for harmony (in the sense that

Fourier understood the word)...' André Breton in an interview about astrology (*L'Astrologue,* number 4, 1968).

> Like long echoes which from a distance blend together
> In a mysterious and profound unity

What Baudelaire expresses so well is known to all poets because they live it. What is a poet if not a decipherer, he said, the artist becoming the servant of the gospel of correspondences. All the authors of the 19th century symbolist movement from Swedenborg to Baudelaire, as well as Nerval, declared the same thing. For them the poetic act comes from a unity of thought which re-establishes the unity of creation which is the source of the fundamental analogy between mankind and the universe. Not everything is expressed by scientific equations, but areas that are still forbidden to science are not forbidden to people inspired by what they know in their hearts, which is that the royal art of the stars could be the common ground where science, poetry and religion meet.

We can appreciate the richness of the content of this episteme of similarity, knowing that it is to be found at the centre of all human experience. Even though it cannot stand up to the test of physical cause, which the laws of physics demand, it is still the language of the perceptions. Astrology has rightly been said to defy reason because of the way it uses its logic. In short: if reason comes from our determination and has nothing to do with our stars, in reality it is from the irrational, the unreasonable and unintelligible, of which it gives an account through this episteme, if at least we understand by these terms the archetypal behaviour of the psyche with its mythology, the birthplace of the imagination and the 'faces' of the heartbeat, that is to say all that occurs in our unconscious.

That the episteme of analogy is not a good way of reasoning about the material world is so self-evident that we have to ask if this way of thinking would be more suited to another sphere altogether. Should we have faith in such an approach when it comes to the exploration of human beings? Shouldn't we just be satisfied with observing that the analogical thought of this episteme is a knowledge that goes back to the dawn of humanity and the dawn of knowledge, because, it is the nature of what we are investigating that determines how we investigate it; and here, we must go back to the root of things in the night of mankind.

Today's astrologers can be reassured: it is not they who create a horoscope by giving meaning to the pawns on the astral chessboard, to the celestial charts, and their analogical reasoning is not just a feeble way of thinking from the time of the dinosaurs. As soon as an astrologer is a good one, astrology makes him a human depth psychologist: its concern consists in him being at the top of his art. In any case, he must bear in mind that he will never be a happier and more qualified servant of his muse than when his own psychology is closed to the indivisible nature of human personality (individuum = indivisible), when he forms an intelligible and understandable whole with the world in its very entirety

Besides, the theory of similarity is not the only idea used by astrology that is outside the sphere of science. Going back to its origins in order to understand its basic principles, one can see that it is founded on a metaphysical rationale that is speculative and transcendental in style, and naturally completely closed to today's scientific mind.

From the Pythagoreans to the Neo-Platonist Christians and including the Orphics and the Platonists, i.e. the world of traditional hermeticism, the same thought of man as microcosm has perpetuated along with the most important idea in the Bible that God made man in his image. The astrological system comes from the very nature of things through the similarity of man as a copy of the world which is itself a copy of God. Thus we see the astrologer setting off on a discovery of the significant relationships by which the Creator signs his work, the transmission of the same image being the line of his thought.

The idea was established very early that the language

of the world, conceived as being the way that the divine archetype was realised in a spatial way, was mathematical in essence, the celestial writing providing its own plan of human creatures which have the same essence. It is mainly thanks to Kepler that we know about this great journey of the mind. He took this tradition from Plato, Proclus and Nicholas of Cusa, and developed it to the highest state.[85]

This is how he came to return to the Pythagorean sphere: the sphere and the polyhedrons, as well as the circle and the regular polygons, are the primary materials used by the Creator. We can see him at work on a conceptualised system proper to give an ontological dignity to different mathematical entities: point, radius, arc, angle, ratio, figure.

Applying Euclidean reasoning to the study of regular polygons (sides, angles, perimeter, surface), his speculations about the circle and its divisions furnishes mathematics with a symbolic language which, because of the primordial ontological value given to the sphere, has the function of being the ultimate connection with the essence of God, this sphere which is the symbol and the rationale of geometric beings. This is why, with its divine nature, the circle, the fundamental pattern of life, serves as the archetype for all things: 'Regular figures are studied for themselves as well as for being archetypes; they are perfect in themselves...' (*L'Harmonie du monde*).

The ontological value of being the origin of all understanding that he gave to the sphere from the circle, the matrix of mathematical relationships and a model representing nature and the human soul, allowed Kepler to believe that, in the relationship between the symbol and what is symbolised, this universal operator allowed him to go back to God, the absolute and final cause, the ultimate giver of meaning. It is the Creator's signature on his work which gives a symbolic quality to mathematical entities, mathematics becoming the common language between God and man, and consequently their mediator, the need for this language relating to the original value of the sphere which serves as the archetype of creation.

We see Kepler starting with the relationship between the curve and the straight line, expressing what it is that binds and separates the Creator and the creation, passing by the perfect curve (such as the surface of the sphere), and ending with the sacralisation of the geometric figure with the dogma of the trinity (the assimilation of the Father at the centre, of the Son on the surface and of the Holy Ghost in the equality of the relationship of the centre to the periphery). The relationship between the centre and the surface gets special treatment, the central point representing the origin of the sphere, and the surface, its extensiveness generated by an infinite emanation from the centre itself.

According to Kepler the radius, which is a straight line from the central point to a single point on the surface, is suggestive of the creative act, engendering and reproduction. Infinity emanates from this centre and radiates in all directions to cover the surface. Polyhedrons, derived from the sections of this archetypal sphere are the supporters of life. It is from the syntactic analysis of this monad and its offshoots (the dyad, triad, tetrad, pentad, hexad…) that we get the theory of astrological aspects which are regular polygons of the circle. This is how the diagram of the human soul placed in a perfect circle was arrived at; the innate perception of these fundamental mathematical relationships by the intuition of an instinct inhabited by archetypal harmony becomes the capture of its own essence by the soul.[86]

As generally understood, Pythagorism is about the cult of harmony, of proportion and of order in the universe, where all the parts are interdependent, where a number is an idea of a thing and where mathematics is a faithful reflection of what is. This allowed him to look for an ontological truth by creating the world using theorems in which the numbers and geometric figures are themselves invested with particular intrinsic properties.

Now, even though this way of seeing things is strange to us, we shouldn't just dismiss it in a century that has shown that mathematics primarily reflects the operational capacity of human beings. Materialism evolved around mathematics, Pythagoras coming before Democritus, finally the only thing left was number, the most stable entity. Returning to the Pythagorean notion numbers are the essence of things; numbers functions and mathematical symbols are seen as being fundamental.

'All is geometry' is often quoted by physicists specialising in the theory of general relativity. However, it is abundantly clear that modern physics expressly forbids the idea that the mathematic descriptions of the quantum theory could be ontological values. They only consider it as something that provides the rules which allow them to make predictions about their observations. The contemporary scientific mind is fixed on this matter; but should it be making judgements that are beyond its boundaries?

Moreover, assuming the human field should be wider than its actual sphere, we have to allow the use of astrological discourse that restores the noumenon and applies it to some key ideas (like the four elements which we will apply to the world of painting in a coming chapter). Remember that if the horoscope, a diagram of the human unconscious, casts human beings in the same mould as the celestial configuration at their birth, no other anthropocentric representation corresponds so well to the fundamental condition of the ego.

For while the search for the psyche has led to the human phenomenon being represented diagrammatically, its unique and essential existence comes from its egocentric foundation and its subjectivity: human beings now have an ideally and perhaps unavoidable concept of themselves as coming from an inner centre which has external forms of expression. This idea contributes to a consubstantiation of the human soul and the circular-spherical, to the geometry of the configurations of this space and the harmonious or dissonant relationships at the heart of the being. This is what astrology is founded upon and what gives it strength and grandeur.

At our current state of knowledge, we must guard

against narrow certitudes and be tolerant of personality clashes and opposing schools. For example, in one school, the stars cannot be actors in a play based on our interior world: they are types who have their own role in the outside world. The map of the sky is not merely a representation of the native; it is only an accurate diagram of their cosmic environment to which they respond as if by reflex. Here the project changes completely.

It will always be tempting, and even necessary, to look for ways of modernising astrology, but in allowing it to be exposed to the double danger of being precariously balanced between its ancient heritage with a tradition to which we owe everything and scientific determinism itself, there is a great risk of it being impoverished if not denatured. Also perhaps it is hard for astrologers to support and defend astrology.

Is it any wonder then that it is sulphurous, troublesome and dangerous for our current scholars? In 1975 the world press made a great deal of a petition in the American review *The Humanist* which condemned astrology; signed by 186 scientists, of whom 18 were Nobel Prize winners. They did not report, however, that 114 others, who also included Nobel Prize winners, did not respond when invited to sign.

How do we find the voices? And how do we compare deceived reasoning with intuition when it bears such a powerful idea? According to surveys more than half of the people in the West believe that astrology is well founded. So rather than playing around with their prejudices it would be better to get to the heart of the problem and, at last, discover the truth.

Chapter 9 - Determinism and Free Will

At the very source of the known tradition, Ptolemy tells us that the power of the celestial torches is limited, our will receiving no laws from their movements; there followed two clear maxims cited by Thomas Aquinas and repeated from author to author, *Astra inclinant, non necessitant*[87] and 'The wise man rules his stars, the fool obeys them', to which one could add this third: 'Heaven helps those who help themselves.'

It couldn't be called a fatalistic doctrine, and yet it is easy to be despondent. Here again is the astrophysicist Jean-Claude Pecker: 'Astrology in every age is absolutely deterministic, imperious, inevitable' (*La Recherche*, Number 140, January 1983). On the other hand, astrology has become 'fatalised' by the pressure of the superego with its magic mentality that belongs to popular tradition and astrologers have themselves given in to it.

In *Life is a Dream* by Calderón the lengths that the king goes to in order to avoid the misfortunes portended by the horoscope become, as in the story of Oedipus, the very means of its accomplishment.

La Fontaine said that we cannot escape our destiny, 'You meet your fate/Often by the way you try to avoid it.'

'Oh, my God, how useless it is to try and escape one's destiny!' Madame Roland exclaimed before the scaffold...

Stars, fortune, and destiny: it is all the more difficult to separate these terms when they are so rich in profound resonances. It is this trio, loaded with magical thinking, which have caused astrology to deteriorate from its initial psychological knowledge to a divinatory art whose unscrupulous claims are instinctively incorporated into the mysterious machinery of the marvellous. Akin to the pronouncements of the sibyls expressing their oracle, this vestige of a primitive mentality satisfies our thirst for the absolute which requires perfection and infallibility; it is as if Fortune, blindfolded but sure, automatically and punctually regulates everything and a high science, involving initiation, has descended from a fabulous past and must deliver the inevitable verdict. On the one hand there is nothing more ridiculous than a seer who makes a blunder; and on the other, a successful prediction has the power to fascinate. It is this core idea of the absolute that we have to crack to end this unhealthy growth in magical thinking.

There is no harm though in looking into the matter of whether, and by how much, we are determined. In analysing this problem we must start with an important exclusion. What we call astral determinism, which is supposedly shown in the birth chart, is entirely removed from the external conditions which must affect the native: their ethnicity, the geographic climate, the context of family, their education, their economic, social and cultural circumstances. Everything that these factors represent in the life of the subject, the chart gives no account of, because the celestial mechanism turns indifferently for all the individuals on the planet.

It is obvious that the chart has to be interpreted with this exterior world taken into account. When an opponent solemnly declares that it is false that the heir of the Nabob and the son of a pariah who are born under the same sky have the same chances and the same destiny, this ingenuous individual is trying to gather cherries in Alaska. Ptolemy specifically mentioned this case to show the importance of the exterior factors that he had to marry to the 'celestial causes'. Today in France, when it is well known that two thirds of the men who rule and direct all areas of society have come from a very narrow fringe composed of the upper or propertied class, while from among the workers and the cultivators, who recently still represented three quarters of the active population, less than one tenth manage to emerge from their ranks, it is well understood that, from the beginning, with two men born under the same sky, the son of a great CEO born in a beautiful part of the capital and the son of a labourer lost in a hole in the country, their chances of social elevation at their communal Jupiterian culmination are very unequal. When he was dealing with the same subject Thomas Aquinas found a good way of defining this relationship between the effects of the environment on destiny and the heavenly cause that rules the interior destiny: 'All that is received is received according to the nature of those who receive it.'

If we already know what is not in the chart, we will be surer about what can be found there: the internal universe of the being. Furthermore, only the part of this 'interior' is potentially included or prefigured at birth. 'At the beginning [at conception] the seed received a temperament imprinted by the surrounding sky', declared Ptolemy, for whom the 'diversity of the seed gives nature its principle power'.

Applied to the generic essence of terrestrial creatures it is like the ray of sunlight that causes a rose to blossom into a rose and a violet into a violet. But there is still a war going on between what is innate and what is acquired. There are still those who hang on to Locke and Condillac with their concept of the tabula rasa of the newborn, the untouched modelling clay on which the environment prints its indelible marks.

Yet the 'materialists' who hold to this idea (by which they rule out the notion that human beings are born unequal) should be aware of the fact that the roots of character are deep-seated in the body, which is received once and for all at birth.

The psychoanalysts who, for a long time, believed that personality came overridingly from an individual's personal history, have had to make adjustments; in his later work, Freud recognised that 'psychic reality has more meaning than historical reality', this psychic reality is no other than our interior being, which subjectively processes our experience and determines the way we react.

As a living organism, the being is also a living milieu which develops the individual in its own way, using the person's own inner resources together with the possibilities presented by the outside world. We have to remember that astral determinism deals strictly with what is innate, our constitution and tendencies, and that it is only concerned with our inner powers.

Yet if the world of the tendency was the expression of the rule of absolute law giving the impression that the individual was tied to it hand and foot, astrology could never have been contested! One can only truly discuss what is ready to be discussed. So it is not by accident that given the scale of humanity and at the singularity of each human being there is a diversity of points of view and alternatives.

Thus, all over the world, we first see astrology reigning unchallenged in antiquity with the universe clinging to mankind like Nessus' tunic. Greek theatre, the tragedies of Euripides, the *fatum* of the Latin people, destiny for the Ancients whether a blind or capricious force or a well regulated power on an irrevocable course, dominates the feeling of being alive; man's greatness will be to submit to his fate, accept it wisely and live with the consequences. Out of this milieu of collective psychology came the great mythologies of Euro-Asiatic polytheism with their content full of celestial values.

These myths are the public arena of human endeavour portrayed as an exemplary model. As the astronomy of our interior sky, astrology finds strength and vigour in these mythic creations; it is the life of the gods that is translated in us, the human being becoming the theatre where their stories, their struggles and their exploits are acted out; the planets embody the gods like the sidereal ballet that they create around us witnessing the dramatization of our interior mythology.

How outdated this must have seemed with the Cartesian revolution when mankind no longer believed in the gods. With the trunk no longer nourishing the branch, astrology starts to wither and it goes into decline in the same way as the myths which, having lost their evocative power become synonymous with error, illusion and falsehood. Mankind no longer feels crushed by the forces in the world; the mysteries of the heavens begin to be tamed by the telescope, with no awareness that the spiritual content has been lost.   While the self-willed cornelian[88] hero wants to be himself and be master of both himself and the universe in order to subjugate destiny, the cogito of Descartes, 'I think, therefore I am', led to the reign of reason and to everything that is most autonomous in man: finally tearing down the veil of cosmic destiny, like an animal breaking its shell to emerge into the light of the outside world, this man liberated from his interior night believes himself a free to think and act, the philosophers proclaiming his freedom in the world.

In such a world what was astrology to do when the rug had been pulled so radically from under its feet? It did at least gain something by being stripped of the popular old beliefs to which it had been enslaved: being able to go swimming with only the weather, and if you had the time, to care about; and trimming your beard without wondering if the Moon was waxing or waning...

Everything has now changed with the resurgence of astrology in the 20th century. With Freud's discovery of our inner darkness, we discovered that this liberty was an illusion, and this happened in a general outburst of rational frameworks and, above all, as life was being rationalised. Today, many psychologists dare to advance the idea that the gods of mythology are not dead: they continue to live in the hearts of mankind, since aspects of mythic behaviour survive in human beings and are inherent in the human condition.

Jung himself was the first person to maintain that the powers of these gods continue to live in us even if the ancient pagan gods have gone from Olympus and are no longer believed in: 'All the forces of nature act like the Olympians did, full of gods desirous of being favoured, of being served, feared and adored.'[89] When today's psychoanalysts plunge into the depths of the psyche, they discover a universe with everything in it where there is a close and extended commonality between the soul and the world. They even state that its backdrop is woven with the embroideries of these myths and their natural symbols.

These symbols seemed to him to be like nebulous forces inside himself, which under various guises go back to the source of a universal eternal power whose invisible action animates the stories of Zeus as well as the images in our dreams, the games of children, the passion in lovers, the inspiration of the poet, or even the 'isms' of our modern ideologies, the images used in branding in advertising and other tricks of the consumer society.

A product of civilisation, astrology is also a product of character; if the first has its highs and lows, the second has its beliefs and its rejections. On the human level we accept or reject according to our temperament. For example, we can see the difference between those who are predominantly Gemini in nature and those who are predominantly Scorpio when they are faced with their destiny.

Made with an internal bipolarity in which the thinking being often keeps an eye on the feeling being, the true Gemini type can live with a dualism which prevents them from taking themselves seriously and from taking things seriously. There is nothing more alien to them than the sense of destiny with its implication of a preoccupation with character, the figure they cut, their bent in life, the mark that they will leave behind.

While this sense of destiny goes very deep and weighs heavily, a passionate being (like a Scorpio), life's path for a Gemini is slight, light, wandering; it is not even a real path, it is a collection of stages on a route which remains barely sketched out. The life of a Gemini is full of surprises and changes. It is not established in advance at all but, on the contrary, can be adapted to all circumstances; all is provisional, transitory, with a feeling of availability, of disengagement and with a large range of possibilities that they are at liberty to explore, even to change their minds completely.

Having a dualist nature gives us the ability to make choices and to diversify, to be secretly associated with the opposing party, to hold to both sides at the same time, and to regard victory and defeat as separated only by the thickness of a sheet of paper. Marked by a triple conjunction in Gemini, Jean-Paul Sartre became the advocate for an interesting form of psychology; he naively believed that he was depicting the whole human race, but he was only positing a variant of the Gemini type to which he belonged.

He said that the essence of human nature was to not have a nature; man 'does not find either in himself or outside himself the capacity to attach (...); in other words, there is no determinism, man is free, man is liberty' (*Existentialism and Humanism* (Methuen, 1948). Being nothing first of all, since there is no human nature, man will only be what follows, and he will be what he goes on to do; he is not only what he thinks he is but what he wants to be, being nothing other than what he does.

In short, we are only what we choose to be, taking into account the society from which we evolve. But under the Plutonian 'accent' what we are is not far from what we are not, the authentic and the inauthentic, this existentialist 'you choose yourself' is bordering on self-negation, artificiality, an absence of meaning, emptiness.

Nothing like that with Scorpios who characteristically are in charge of themselves: they express themselves fully, have a great sense of ego, are strongly supported by their gut instincts and, more than any other type, have a sense of destiny. They are interested in their own character, in whether they are cutting a figure, are forced to take themselves seriously, live life to the full, and live according to what they intend to be their legacy.

They want to be defined by destiny, have a need to make themselves by inscribing their actions on this destiny which lifts them, alone, up to the 'divine game of heroes'. For this animal with its power over itself and others, it is about being the champion of a cause, and seeing it through to the end with all the consequences. It is about becoming ferocious or admirable, spitting fire if it has to, sulphur, bile and ointment, both ostracism and sympathy; it is straight from a tragedy of Sophocles. This is the world of André Malraux's heroes, of Malraux himself and of Charles de Gaulle, who lived out his affinity with Scorpio to the full.

It is easy to see that Sartre would reject astrology (he

takes as his basis the denial that human nature exists, even though this is only one of a given kind as represented by his type of person that he is putting into anthropology), as much as Malraux is respectful of its mystery as of the ancient gods.

In a general way, the a priori relationship of human beings with astrology is based on the supremacy or the damping down of the unconscious in the structure of the personality as well as the relationship of the self with the unconscious.

It is not hard to understand that if we feel ourselves moved, stirred or invaded by the groundswell that is held deep inside a dominant unconscious we will be inclined to believe this, just as someone whose self is structured and whose conscious self is dominant will be inclined towards scepticism; the master of interior forces, combined with the resources of vitality and the will, will feel perfectly autonomous and would find the language of determinism spoken by astrology very strange; this is what can also be experienced by someone who feels supported and protected by an ordered and powerful religious faith.

Equally, in the first category, there is a tendency towards scepticism when someone, fighting their subconscious, is cut off by fear or denial from their interior night. The exception to this is the people who are closed off in a neurotic way, who are more hostile than sceptical, and can only be thought of as 'prophylactic sceptics'. They always stick to their own version of the truth and are not interested in a knowledge which does nothing for them or has little to teach them. At least they should guard against generalising this negativity which is only found in people of their condition.

Indeed, people who are in the first category are right to give astrology credence because, having a nature that is sensitive to their psychological harmonies and dissonances, they find the language of their stars intensely evocative and a precious source of information.

In addition to the astrological relativity at the base of a particular case, each person has a general disposition to be in accord with at a certain level of soul. The psyche contributes to what we believe since it is through the psyche that astral determinism is expressed. In the same way, there is a general disposition, at a certain level, to not accept the reasons that we may be sceptical or even the fact that the world of thought, that of the diurnal life of the conscious, is what constitutes our interior zone of autonomy, independence and liberty (with the exception of insidious unconscious bias).

This is why when our psyche is dominant we lean more towards faith or have a real sensitivity to the astral tendency (more so in the case of children than with adults, with women more than men and with those who are in love or are poets and mystics), or, conversely, that we lean more towards scepticism, usually accompanied by an erasure of this astral determinism, when the powers of logos are strong, especially in the case of the rational man, whether Cartesian or classical, who gives priority to the structures developed in his mind, favouring impersonal order and objective values while erasing their subjective feeling of being alive.

It is equally the case that due to the compensatory processes of the unconscious, hyper rationality sometimes causes the enslavement of psychic monsters condemned to being repressed.

If then there have been such diverse opinions throughout history as with those living in the same era, the tendency is only an aspect of the larger reality that life presents to us. I wouldn't hesitate to go further by saying that the great paradox of astrology is that it needs free will for it to be saved and that its purpose is to give the lie! Free will, lack of determinism, or determinism having nothing to do with astrology, it does not matter.

The school of life teaches us this lesson. One day it was suggested that, as an experiment, I looked at the case of twin sisters, born only a few minutes apart, who were now around forty and who had totally different lives. Knowing nothing about them, I drew up the charts which were practically the same and which had, in common, Saturn in a dominant position on the IC at a dissonant angle to two planets, one in house VII and the other in V.

Immediately, I reasoned that in both cases there would be a feeling of having being 'orphaned' and that it would be a constant theme in their lives. This would have repercussions for their love lives and would affect their lives as women, wives and mothers, and a tendency to feel emotionally frustrated would be dominant in them both. The sisters soon recognised themselves in this description which applied to them both and which was lived out in two different ways.

One of the twins was not married and suffered both because of her involuntary single state and the fact that she had reached the age limit for having a child: these were the twin themes that preoccupied her in life. The other had married young and her marriage had completely failed; she found herself very alone within the marriage, living a celibate life with a husband who was practically non-existent; moreover she had several children, but she had also missed out on the experience of motherhood because the pregnancies were too close together; her children soon left her and she found herself alone again; that was the whole story. From the very beginning they had felt as if they were living in a psychological orphanage. The two women remembered spending their early childhood feeling that they had no mother and that they had grown up together and consoled each other like orphans. Having defined this common psychological situation, which they both immediately recognised, it was impossible for me to identify from their charts which was single and which married.

It is in these limitations of the practitioner that we find the very limits of astrology, the wise interpreter being satisfied with just revealing the forces that determine the future and, using this basic information to show the range of possible situations, with all the similarities, equivalences or substitutions that may result.[90]

Let us not forget that astrological language relies on

analogy, in interpreting a chart we have to find out how the association works (old age and 'the evening of life'…), and only retain what is held in common. The isomorphism of the 'like' establishes the logic of an echo with the comparative approach adhering to something similar which, however, is not the real thing. And then it is mixed with the complexity of human nature. It is good to remember the main thing is that we carry a purpose within ourselves that directs our lives.

Our ego – that which, with a feeling of belonging to ourselves, we take in hand with an autonomy which has its own laws – wants to be the master builder of our lives, and it is the driving force, the architect of a future, programmed in its image. But this centre of consciousness and core of the will is only one element in our pluralistic being, similar to the majority shareholder of our capital.

Apart from the influence of all the other elements that help to make up a person, it can be that it is not the ego which has the last word in the debate that goes on inside us: we don't always do what we want. It can even happen that, not understanding its emotional or instinctual potential, the ego turns its back on the deeper interests of its being, putting it in an awkward position regarding its true nature.

In such a case, having strayed from its vital energy, the planet no longer works with us or helps to bring its natural affinities to fruition; estranged from the goal to which it was assigned by a lesser ego, it only bears the fruits of the commitment undertaken. Here its configuration is no more than a factor guiding the decisions the ego makes, providing the tone for what we have decided to do and it is a fact that, when we create our own life story, very often we don't know what the story is, consciousness having planned the route while the guiding tendency directed the steps.

We can believe that we are free; that we are fully in charge of ourselves with our resources all entirely at our disposal, without realising that the pawn that we are moving forward on the chessboard of our destiny is trapped, manipulated by a power so hostile that we are driven to our downfall. The possibility that we have this inner sense of inevitability indicates the usefulness of revealing what lies deep within ourselves. If the influence of the configuration is like that of the soil in nourishing the plant, people make their configurations according to how they use them, having a choice of what they sow. We will see a little later on, in the case of marriage, what the consequences of this shift in the nature of the configuration are on the circumstances of the configured.

We also have to remember that people have to liberate themselves from their fundamental blindness when looking at themselves. In the beginning, because we don't know who we are, we don't know where our talents lie—and others don't know any more than we do—which is why there are so many adolescents who cannot decide on their vocation. Alfred de Vigny dreamt of military grandeur and Stendhal wondered if he could be a Turenne or a Molière. Pasteur had a talent for drawing and pastels, and would certainly have gone to the school of fine art if he'd had careers advice at that time. When Manet saw Renoir painting at age 33, he confided to his entourage: 'Ah! Poor man, what he's doing is appalling! Charity demands that we discourage him; he'll never come to anything.' And so Renoir would have been dismissed by his elder and turned into a notary or a bartender.

So here we have someone whose first condition is that of pure potential. This is the lot of our tendencies: they come from a latent unconscious state and finally manifest themselves consciously. To start with, they are nothing other than a potential in search of development and they wait to be revealed. The being is hardly outlined, just dotted in. Every step it takes is illuminating. On one hand the tendency is a natural aptitude, and on the other it is the route that must be taken to reveal it, something to be conquered. There is a great difference between a rough piece of wood and the wood that is in a bishop's cross or in a range of stringed instruments just as there is with plain copper and a lighted candlestick or the sound of a trumpet. This is how we are as much the creator of ourselves as the created.

This is the relationship between the native soil and the gardener as the physicist Robert Gouiran evokes with his 'man-ephemeris' (as an image of the structure of time and space), the astralised part of ourselves, and 'the reactive man', the source and cause of ourselves, free beings, autonomous. The quality of the linked relationship between the one and the other is of more consequence than the astral charge itself. The choices made depend on how effective the person's resources are, whether opportunities are exploited and perhaps even on discovering the pearl that is deep inside us, to the extent that the secret part of ourselves is working for us. The most important thing then is for our direction in life to be in harmony with our inner tendencies, in the way that a Martian is most successful when playing sport or fighting in the army. The worst thing we can do is swim against our own vital current, ignore it or discredit it.

We need to respect the old adage 'Help yourself and heaven will help you', which carefully puts heaven after yourself. It is naive to believe that a good supportive configuration will automatically bring success in a given operation if one is not in a state to cope with it. It would be like taking an exam without having knowledge of the subject matter; in a case like that the good configuration in question only offers a more modest result. The configuration only helps us to be victorious if the desired goal is already within reach and only a little bit extra is needed in addition to the necessary input. Naturally, the best way to make it effective is to fully engage with the project and put our all into it. These are the conditions in which the influence of the configuration is most effective. In this situation the diurnal self and the nocturnal being of the deep psyche are united.

Because we are practitioners tasked with obtaining the best results and making as few mistakes as possible, there are two chief observations to be made: firstly, we must give astral determinism less importance; secondly, we have to accept that the nature and expression of this determinism is complex and subtle and so can escape the inexperienced observer. There is some distance, like between the two ends of a chain, between the perceived basic tendency, which is buried in the night of the being, and the bare facts presented in the broad daylight of the life being lived.

Let's get beyond embroidered legends of astrological marvels: these inner powers to which our stars are witnesses only have a second hand influence on our bank account and don't impose career choices on us or assign the best date for a wedding. It sketches out our internal life more discretely, revealing more subtle analogies, seeking out the deeper truths that are hidden behind what our destiny appears to be at first glance. Besides, let us not forget that astral determinism only represents what is innate, our bare selves. We can only know what the internal constellation of an individual is like without knowing what the external environment has been. It is this external environment which forms the acquired character and neutralises or amplifies the innate character.

This original tendency is only fully deployed when in perfect juxtaposition to this milieu, the world outside becoming a sounding board for the interior cosmos. This generally only happens in the case of a destiny that is outside the norm: an exceptional phenomenon, something supreme, a huge success...We can see the amplifying effect of childhood accidents, the effects of family, educational, economic and social, when the basic tendency expands dramatically or shines through into an exemplary life.

Yet, when one looks at the role of the tendency that is given to all those born under the same sky, the feeling tone of what is experienced, and the role of the history of personal accidents brought about by the environment, which furnish the conditions of existence differently for each of them, one often has the impression that the astral determination of someone's constitutional type that we observe only has second place in the being like that occupied by a number that comes after the point. Without going that far, the unity of life we are looking at is a synchronisation of the genome, the environment and the astral signature.

These limitations are enough to write off divinatory astrology, whose job is to play dice with the unknown. But, besides that, there is an astrology that a psychologist would understand, conscious of the limits of both astral determinism and of interpretation itself, which is a way of approaching the mystery that Goethe defined as follows: 'Each being has the reason for their existence inside themselves.' These are Don Néroman's memorable words spoken in 1937 (*Que nous réserve 1938?* [What Does 1938 Have For Us?], Plon):

> As long as the public imagines that astrologers can see the future, that they can prophesy, that they can help them win the lottery, this unfortunate science is tossed between the jeers of the sceptics and the supplications of the naïve. The public must be told the truth: astrology adds another light, the light which illumines our route, the light which shows us a gaping hole for example right where we expected to find a bridge, but it is not a fairy wand which uses magic to make the bridge that has vanished reappear. For example, astrology can tell us what sort of career a child should be guided towards; but it does not tell us that using the magic in a horoscopic book of magic spells; you have to observe the child, in the usual way and then use the additional light provided by astrology (…). Likewise, if the astrological interpretation indicates natural gifts that direct observation does not recognise, you must blow the lamp out. But if we do find that the interpretation is in line with the facts, we would be better able to understand those facts, we would know for example if a taste formed at seven years old ('I want to be a general, or a sailor') is ephemeral and unimportant or indeed solidly founded and pressing.

So it is not about replacing the information provided by recognised disciplines, but about making it more complete. Choisnard's formulation comes from this: 'Astrology is a geometric means of seeing if a psychological judgement is right or wrong.' In short, as Don Néroman said:

Astrology does not claim that it can tell you from the outset that you will have a serious accident after you have walked for 37 miles, it just wants to warn you that at the 37th mile there will be danger. And, basically, it is not difficult to choose between prediction and advice. Between a gypsy who predicts my death at the Cross of Noailles and a local council which helps me to avoid it by putting up a warning signpost, I prefer the council.

Because we shouldn't underestimate the value of this approach to the information about future character that it can provide, even if the light that it throws on this subject is too often like that of a little candle in an enormous cathedral. We know that it isn't events that are written in the chart, it is the tendency on to which they are grafted which, keeping within the range of its own symbolism, is liable reinvent itself according to circumstances; for example when there is a date for something that is strongly Martian in nature it can correspond to accidental danger, a dangerous surgical operation, the risk of a law suit, a confrontation or a collision in some area of life.

The information given isn't concerned with the outer wrapping or, if you prefer, the type of event, but with its feeling content, its affective nature; thus when something Martian is indicated there will a problem to do with aggression or a climate of destructiveness. What is said to be the prediction of an event (having chosen well from those possible) is generally a grasp of one or many indicators that have effectively come in to the overall composition of the event that has happened, but what these factors can foresee is very limited. They are only a facet or a partial dimension of everything that this event represents in the human story.

Without going as far as finding out what the future holds, it nevertheless gives us a reasonable knowledge of life's rhythms, a way of determining the high times and low times in life's many currents and of forming a partial estimation of the future which enables us to plan ahead.

The chart acts like a celestial identity card, providing a symbolic representation of the universe that tells the story that each person carries within them. It represents the personality in a spatial way, laying it out geometrically and placing the force field, where the personal life is played out, at the centre. Through the play of the interactions and interferences, harmonic or conflicting, between the bodies, the psychological functions represented by the astral diagram encode a certain 'sense of destiny'.

If the tendency cannot help us to forecast in the short term, at least we can analyse the content and look at the meaning of the event that has taken place. Life often leaves us struggling with an embarrassing range of possible interpretations when something happens. The actual circumstances of the event remain an enigma, leaving us in limbo, suspended between hope and anxiety, between what could be trivial and what could be the very worst.

A reading of the chart can guide us to the right conclusion by allowing us to decide the 'value' of the event in relation to the person's system as a whole. This ongoing story, for example, refers to the manifestations of this inner fate (the aggression shown, the guilt, self-punishment, anxiety...), as it goes through each transformation, while we wait for what is possibly going to materialise.

It is by going to the interior source of our being that we can 'follow ourselves' and find the meaning of our destiny. In this way it is possible for it to help us get a clearer idea of ourselves and make sense of the experiences which have made us what we are. We discover what makes us unique by affirming or restoring our inner presence so that we fully accept ourselves and are open to the world.

Interpreting involves an intimate collaboration between the interpreter and the interpreted. This is the best basic way that we are able to compare the two pictures: that of the planets with their initial potential and that which is lived, an assessment of what the subject has become. It is thus possible to establish to what extent, how and in what form they allow the vital impulses to express themselves, whether they made good choices that were in accord with themselves or whether, on the contrary, they have turned their backs on some of their essential tendencies and are now awkwardly placed in regard to their deeper reality, perhaps having even lost their centre of gravity.

Finally, as we have seen, it is in this question of the accord or discord of the person with themselves – their relationship with the tendency more than the tendency itself – that interest in the limits of astral determinism rests! Here we return to Jung's useful way of looking at the question: 'Not adapting to our inner cosmos is a failing which is liable to produce consequences that are just as harmful as ignorance and incompetence in the outside world.' [91]

Ultimately, it is only at this second level that all becomes clear. Going back to the statistical assessment which showed that the tendency, by itself, is far from being tyrannical: we can see that a dominant Mars on an angle of the sky in no way compels people to join the army (if it is the army rather than another Martian route that the individual in question must follow)!

Besides, we know, when their tendencies are not yet clear, how uncertain the young are about their choice of career. They are often passively impressionable, dependant on parents, on friends, fashionable professions, the extraneous considerations of the job... It is not then because we are Martian that we will choose a military profession or another Martian career.

Statistical surveys give us much more information about what people do rather than what they are or, in other words, whether they have made good use of their tendencies. Hence my own conclusion which seems to be valid: 'It is not the fact that, as a Martian, you go into the army that counts here: it is the fact that you will be successful in the army by being Martian'. (Note that this angular Mars is really only observed at the highest levels of the military hierarchy.)

It works in this way because people with a Martian nature are going to be 'in their element' in the army; being aligned with the principal dynamic of their dominant tendency, they have a greater chance of flourishing there and of completely realising themselves and therefore of having more success than others.[92] Michel Gauquelin had come to a similar conclusion when he declared 'it is rare to be successful in an artistic or literary career if one is born with Saturn on the horizon or the meridian'.

In the beginning, the tendency is quite a small thing: an impetus that we have to become aware of, a discreet internal nudge easily neutralised by the influence of those around us, a state which is experienced only when it comes into contact with the world. This is the way most people learn. On the other hand its realisation becomes so much more, being the sum of its attainment, a feeling of plenty, of success, if the reverse is not the case. Here we can evaluate the accord or disaccord between the innate and the acquired, or, more precisely, whether the basic tendency extends along an adopted path which corresponds to it, or we find that the first and second phases are incompatible. This is where we discover that the world of selective affinity means something, because when a tendency resonates harmoniously with the environment it plays a crucial amplifying role!

'When we interpret, we have to search for what nature really intended', Choisnard said. That is a good introduction to questioning the enigma of the birth chart, but as soon as we resolve this problem the interpretation involves finding out in what way and how far the being has conformed to nature, because the key to his future success is in this key sentence: 'Become that for which you were born.'

After a long practice this is the conclusion I have come to about the weight that should be given to things: besides the actual astral phenomenon, there is as much, if not more, of an astral phenomenon for the person concerned; that means that, inside the being that has been astralised at birth, there is dialectic between a configuration and a configured. The value of the thing itself (the tendency) is passed on through the relationship between the thing in itself and the use that is made of it by the one who is configured (to the point where, according to this quip in the end there are no configurations, there's only the configured).

In this dialectic, the astrality itself is assimilated into the world of the tendency which represents what we are, and our own astrality is developed according to how we use it, what we do with it, with the future being the elaboration over time of the second state from the first. Thus we can talk about there being a dialectic between the nature of the terrain and what the gardener plans to plant there.

If, in extremis, we use astrology to give ourselves much more awareness of our deeper nature, we do this in order to match its essential truths as perfectly as possible with ourselves; just as the agronomist is advised to grow the type of vegetation that is most appropriate to the quality of their soil. 'Let's sing in tune with our family tree', Cocteau advised, which here becomes: 'Grow strong at the centre of your cosmic field.'

All that Edgar Morin could find to say about this quest to discover our deeper nature and our ability to conform to it was that it is 'bourgeois astrology'. He probably does not realise that the Essene astrologers were mainly concerned with determining the spiritual essence of each individual. Above all it is hard to understand the reasoning behind this criticism and for the latent distrust of modern man vis-à-vis his psyche.

It is curious that he treats his psychic life in this coy way, as if he is ashamed of it. It is true that he would be mostly aware of it when feeling unbalanced: in the way we feel our stomach when it is upset (considering that, at least, we see our stomach or we can see it). Yet, if the stomach can cause us problems, the psyche causes even more, more often and, more importantly, because these are the problems of existence!

So, it is not really appropriate then to invoke narcissistic complacency, female vapours or any other negative egocentric motivations when talking about astrological questioning. Let's calmly return to Jung: 'It is worth observing the silent workings of the soul (...), man is worth the trouble that he takes to look after himself (...)' No doubts, then, that it is best to conform in the most harmonious way possible with his deepest nature.

With this influence that works by ricochet, I've come to the conclusion that it is a mistake to decipher the chart according to what the subject is doing, when it would be better to understand it in terms of what they would rather be doing in order to achieve the harmony that brings success. This relationship between the configuration and the configured appeared in a critique by Molière who hoped to trap astrology with an insoluble contradiction. It happens in Act III, scene 1, of *The Magnificent Lovers*, in the scene where the author pits the astrologer Anaxarchus with himself about the indecision of Aristione's daughter, Eriphile, about her marriage.

ANAXARCHUS : Wouldn't it be better, Madame, to end things to everyone's satisfaction, by looking at the light that Heaven can throw on this marriage? As I told you, I have started to cast the mysterious symbols according to our art, and I hope to show you soon what the future has in store for this wished for union. After that, can you still be undecided? Won't the glory and prosperity that the sky promises to the one choice or the other be enough to determine it, and the one who is ruled out cannot be offended when it is the sky that has decided who is to be preferred.

ERIPHILE : But, Seigneur Anaxarque, are you able to see the future so clearly, that you never make a mistake, and this prosperity and this glory that you say the sky promises us, who will guarantee it, pray?

ARISTIONE : My daughter, you always have a little bit of doubt.

ANAXARCHUS : But when at last I have made you to see what the Heavens have marked out for you, you can settle the matter yourself, according to your own wishes, and it will be for you to take what fortune brings from either choice.

ERIPHILE : Anaxarchus, does Heaven mark out both fortunes that await me?

ANAXARCHUS : Yes, Madame, the happiness that will follow if you marry the one, and the disgrace you will have, if you marry the other.

ERIPHILE : But as it is impossible for me to marry them both, it must be written in Heaven, not only what must be, but also what must not happen.

CLITIDAS : There, my astrologer is embarrassed.

If only the satirist knew how right he is by embellishing an artificial scenario in order to entertain us with a good farce. The young Eriphile cannot find herself torn between a good or bad choice because the configuration that accompanies such a matrimonial project sets the seal on which party it will be.

Indeed, the same configuration may manifest in different ways but always keeping within a set of situations that are equivalent symbolically. We cannot not fix on a solution when the latent has not yet become manifest, in other words demand similarity between what must happen and what must not happen. People are free to express the tendency in the best possible way, except when something is out of their control, as, for example, when there is psychosomatic transference.

The best way to explain is by going back to what the astrologer observes, and, since we have been discussing this scene in *The Magnificent Lovers,* let's see what he discovers about the marriage. Half a century ago, practitioners were mainly preoccupied with forecasting the date, at least approximately, to within a few seasons, on which the subject was likely to marry. Observation had shown them that, in general, the event fell at a time of life that was rich in configurations indicating love; this would encourage them to believe that the date for the marriage was already established and that they were easily capable of making a forecast.

Now there is a new generation… and practitioners assess things differently. By leaning more towards the observation of cases, they can see how situations can differ: at the time when couples decide to legalise their future love life, some are in the wake of the most beautiful and highest love configuration of their lives, others fall under a passionate configuration, no less powerful but negative and critical, while there are still others for whom this historic get together takes place under a weak, even derisory, secondary configuration.

We then find that each of these three types of configuration corresponds to an equivalent situation: in the first case a happy and successful union (at least in the beginning), in the second, a bad matrimonial experience that is troubled and painful, and in the last, a weak uncertain emotional history.

Initially the search for the most representative love configuration for the date of a marriage relied purely on a conventional way of thinking that produced unreliable results. It is clear that marriages can take place under very different configurations; people don't always seal their unions at the peak of their romantic destiny when their tendencies would be magnified. Some marry in times of difficulty, make misjudgements about character, or overestimate their feelings when swept along by romantic love (the contrary can happen when a regrettable rebuff is based on a misunderstanding of character), or are just not aware of how pale and indifferent the climate is when they consent to marry.

With all this going on, astrologers have no hope of announcing the date of a wedding, but they have gained some insight. The marriage that is freely undertaken under a particular sky is the image of the astral note of the moment: with excellent astralities, delightful nuptial.

The configuration does not indicate what is categorically going to happen: it only expresses the psychological impact, the human content. The anecdote related by Aristotle about Thales wanting to predict the olive harvest and falling into a well while looking at the sky has become an illustration of the interpreter forgetting the essential. All the configurations that occur in a lifetime are deciphered not separately but by looking at the state of the person and the conditions of life at that time: it is generally what they are involved in at that time which decides what they will make of their configuration, so what happens can be surprising.

So astrology is no weaker for being in agreement with Alfred Adler when he says, 'What we bring into the world is not important; all depends on what we do there', since life - as Violette Leduc aptly said - is ' about using liberty to overcome destiny'. Without wanting to elevate our own destiny to the level of the Golden Legend by erecting our own pantheon, we can always hope to find the most advantageous way of living in accordance with our astral note, by using it to gain knowledge, our interior as well as our exterior milieu.

At least all this is helpful in facing our own responsibilities, when it comes to that gap between our possibilities and our limits where our rights and duties are found. Knowing that every lamentation in the genre of 'My Saturn is to blame,' can be answered straightaway by Kepler's maxim: 'I don't give the government of human affairs to the sky.'

Finally, at the end of our long journey to the heart of the astrological experience, we find that the concept of astral time first held by the Ancients was well founded. We have a lot of sayings that are reminiscent of it: 'Destiny is the power that brings order to the beings who have strayed' (Proclus); 'Bad things will only happen to he who does not know how to be in tune with the times' (Machiavelli); 'There is nothing in the world that does not have a defining moment, and the art of good conduct is in the taking of this moment' (Cardinal de Retz).

Again, we shouldn't have a narrow way of looking at things, like the people who think they are occasionally affected by perturbations in the cosmos (at times of sunspot activity, for example), and feel that it acts like a stranger who is hostile towards us. In reality, astral time is the bearer of fundamental information, because of the implication that its true role is that of a regulator and organiser giving structure to the cosmos.

Here, we come back to the specialists in the field of cosmic clocks, who say that 'wellbeing depends on the relationship of our biological rhythms with the rhythms of environmental factors', and that 'the biological and psychological harmony of our organism depends on our rhythms being in tune with those of the universe', proclaiming that harmony between man and nature is sovereign.

Finally, we do not break away from our configurations, and struggle against them to go contrary to things: our liberty should flourish in the areas expressed by our tendencies, and even magnify their essence in a sort of hymn to the microcosm ripened by the Sun of our spirituality.

Chapter 10 - The Astrologer's Art

An apprenticeship in astrological knowledge which is supposed to lead from an obscure faith to an informed understanding is a difficult affair.

Whatever the motivation, we begin not knowing what we are going to find, while bringing what we don't know about ourselves. And there is no guide. As there is no university teaching in the faculty of human sciences, that is the way it is. The usual way that we are tempted to start is by coming across a publication and we each have to train in our own way, more or less at random with no way of (at least in the beginning) judging the quality of what we are learning, it being chance whether or not we come across a good school.

Having found a suitable course of study, neophytes often find that they start binning the postcards from their mythological albums like old fashioned stereotypes, and gradually get rid of the vestiges of their own ignorance (senseless illusions, the vanity of misleading seductions), and the shelter of dead-end mumbo-jumbo, verbal juggling, shams and various hobbyhorses. Next, they find out that apart from what they gained from studying, they have a great deal to learn about themselves; they discover that real learning is to be found in what they bring to the exercise of interpretation, their own attempts at reading the maps of the sky. Having overcome the risk of coming a cropper by falling into the clutches of the nebulous imagination of a dreamt up utopian astrology, disconnected from reality, they naturally want to do their best to educate themselves.

Before they can become an expert on the subject – if it is possible to be one, and who can make such a claim with a knowledge that is still at the construction stage? – they must carefully gather their facts. The danger they run is in staying with the vague perception of a flickering light, of a chart that gives hardly more than a glimmer of understanding, communicable only in an evasive way, a languid impression with marked omissions… with nothing advanced by way of clarification. It is in trying to connect things that are not really connected that the mistake is made, taking a coincidence for a real link; remember that real connections do exist as well as those that it is futile to follow up.

We have to pass through this no man's land where the discrepancy between the words and the things produces a strange sense of unreality with truth not separated from falsehood and nothing is said that has any substance. As we increase our knowledge, a self-regulating phenomenon comes into play with intuition coming to the aid of the mind and the practitioner then feels whether or not they are on the right track. When we are right, the knowledge we are applying feels like the power behind a drive belt. If we wander off or get lost, the belt slips off and the engine is left idling. The sense of unease that we feel tells us when we are grinding straw and chaff instead of grain. When the interpretation is right, the truth that is conveyed resonates as much with the interpreter as with the interpreted, uniting them in a spiritual way that is very profound because they have the benefit of evidence. Not only is it impossible to not believe it but, more than that it provides a ray of light which has the advantage of being the truth, even if its content is bitter when it is revealed or confirmed.

This is how training works with astrology: it is a sign that we are gaining real knowledge when we cease to feel ill at ease in the skin of an astrologer. Becoming an astrologer who is healthy and happy with their astrology is something that takes a lot of time and effort.

It is not just a question of it being an intellectual exercise, a distillation of knowledge. Any communication of knowledge puts in play psychological problems because of the particular relationship that is formed between two people. There is almost a relationship between the content and the container. As you can imagine, an interpreter who is still young and inexperienced, even without the prejudices of their age and lifestyle, does not have the experience needed to address someone who is considerably more mature and whose cultural background is on a higher level than theirs, since it is inevitable that we can only understand someone's world within the context of our own. We cannot go beyond our own limits. In addition, a lack of psychological awareness can place a barrier between us and what we are looking at. The most common intervention is when we project, in the psychoanalytical sense of the word, our own potential complexes and unconscious fantasies on to the person whose chart is being interpreted, which then interferes with the interpretation. In such a case the interpreter is telling their own story and does not realise that they are not truly interpreting the chart in front of them. For example, a practitioner with marriage difficulties who does not have enough awareness of the problem to put it on one side is very much at risk of 'seeing' marital dramas when there is no justification for doing so. So it comes down to the fact that astrologers are much better when they remain impersonal, can efface themselves behind the astrology and let it speak through them as through someone who is transparent.

Equally, another way that an interpretation can be short-circuited is by the problem of mutual subjectivity. In *Nouvelles Conférences sur la psychanalyse* (Five Lectures on Psychoanalysis), Freud dedicates a chapter to dreams and the occult in which he tries to demonstrate that seers merely express the thoughts, and more especially the unconscious desires, of the clients. He cites the case of an intelligent and cultivated young man who is very attached to his sister and would willingly have married her if that were possible. Jealous of his brother-in-law, he consults a female astrologer who predicts that 'the person in question would die in July or August following food poisoning caused by crayfish or oysters' (!). 'What's strange', Freud's patient says, 'is that my brother-in-law adores crayfish and oysters, and last summer he was the victim of poisoning by oysters. He could even have died.' Freud's conclusion was: 'I rather think that the astrologer made the prediction to correspond with the desire of the client: "my brother-in-law won't give up his taste for oysters and one fine day he'll snuff it!" I confess that I have no other way of explaining this case…'

Nevertheless, over and above the relationship between the interpreter and the interpreted, there is the power of the astrological fact itself, which conveys information independently of them both as has been accepted by those around the fathers of psychoanalysis, Ferenczi and Jung. It goes without saying that the prediction in question, told in the vulgar, naive way of fortune telling travellers, is far from being an exemplary model. In the circumstances, though, the Viennese master was right to perceive what happens all too often in many consultation rooms where so many dissatisfied wives would be quite happy to become widows. This particular parasite appears to have confused things by exercising their gift for the paranormal, but then there are a lot of people who use the chart like a medium of clairvoyance… In short, the danger is that astrologers will put themselves in the forecast or let their clients put them there unconsciously, to such an extent that astrology does not really come into it, because it has been suppressed by either one of them. In any case, the more astrology is allowed to contribute to the forecast the less it is tainted by this psychic substitute which is the interference caused by the subjectivity of those involved.

I would also add that while the practitioner is free to try and prove themselves by providing information, there is a risk that they are taking on an inappropriate role, which the client tends to make them play (that of guide, mentor, confessor, spiritual adviser, therapist, even high priest…), while the role that is best suited to the exercise is that of a counselling psychologist.

The inverse of not wanting a consultation for fear of learning about oneself, something that is easily camouflaged by a mocking contempt, is the unhealthy need to believe everything the consultant says: it invites an inappropriate idealisation of the consultant, whose knowledge is overestimated and subject to one-upmanship. This calls for the corrective response of having a practice that is pared down, adopts the right tone, and has a modest approach. But there's worse.

In the consulting room, the client is too often governed by the unfortunate belief that everything is determined. No doubt this is justified when the critique draws the client's interest or curiosity into a childlike process which has the result of being disempowering. Believing that they are submitting to their fate and passively waiting for what is going to happen to be revealed, this type of client adopts an amazing inertia which de-motivates them from having control over their lives.

So astrology can serve as an alibi for a certain kind of cowardice in dealing with life, by putting themselves in the hands of strangers, depriving themselves of freedom of choice and justifying their resignation by saying 'It is Saturn's fault.'

The most incomprehensible clients are the ones that are not interested in knowing themselves because they believe they know their own character and consider that it is useless to talk about it. With no psychological knowledge they are reduced to hanging on the words of the forecaster while clinging to their skirts. They expect the astrologer to make their decisions for them and in helping them the astrologer becomes their guardian and astrology becomes a drug.

With this kind of clientele the traditional consultation, in which information is purely psychological, starts shifting towards a consultation that is more like psychotherapy. The client is often motivated by a kind of neurosis and, without knowing it, is looking to the consultation to offer some kind of help. If fear of living sometimes causes some people to beware astrologers, it leads others to have an unhealthy dependence on them, giving them the role of confessor, by confiding their secrets, the role of keeper of their conscience by their soul-searching and sometimes even the role of therapist by releasing their emotions. A nervous condition that hasn't responded to medical treatment can occasionally be resolved in the process of an interview because of the light it can throw on the conflict which is at the root of the paralysis. A normal consultation can certainly include encounters of this kind and this is also what, when successful, with a good rapport and quality communication, gives the consultant not only a feeling of having learned something valuable, but also the sort of satisfaction that comes from all deep encounters with themselves. In this way a consultation can have the benefit of self-therapy. The desire to know is the primary motivation that commonly drives a consultation, but underneath there can be a call for help, a need for assistance. It is this underlying demand which must be understood by the practitioner, so that the service they can offer or the help they can give does not get lost in the intellectual exercise of throwing light on the birth chart.

The previous case, where the person's neurosis demands something of the consultation that it cannot give, is quite different. Paradoxically they risk clinging on in vain and sometimes reach the point of not being able to do without. Astrologers of the sorcerer's apprentice type sometimes respond to this type of demand and take pleasure in the delicate exorcism of little bits of the neurosis and in being told that they are 'doing good'. However, they must realise that, being only astrologers, they are not prepared or made for this work; in any case they cannot take the place of a psychotherapist or a psychoanalyst. All they can do is help the person to do without their services by gradually making the session more like a lesson than a consultation, so that without realising what's happening they become able to read their own chart.

Now we come to a particular issue: the power that astrological knowledge confers on the astrologer. It is not surprising that in the middle of the 19th century Szondi, a specialist in psychological testing, considered that astrologers – like psychologists, psychiatrists and graphologists among others – had paranoid tendencies, a dominant compulsive need that is related to an inflation of the psyche, an exaggerated sense of self, a need to be important. The fact of taking an individual, being able to more or less read them, understand their processes and figure out something about their future can give the astrologer the obscure impression that they are somewhat in cahoots with destiny, have a small place at the table of the gods and are helping with the distribution of fortune and misfortune to humans. There's nothing really wrong with that up to a certain limit, but one step more and our astrologer starts putting on the starry robe and pointed hat and taking themselves for a wizard who thinks they can join the debate and interfere with the verdict. We can recognise this inflated individual by their confident manner that makes us feel that they are imposing their version of the future instead of deciphering ours.

This dangerous intrusion by the interpreter is met by the infantilism of the interpreted: considered as the author of destiny, the first is perhaps glorified and given a halo for being the giver of good news, but woe unto them if they become the bearer of bad news because, now, it is not Saturn who will be to blame but them... We can see that the subjective relationship between the interpreter and the interpreted is not neutral; it can be an obstacle to a clear reading of the birth chart, which is best approached as transparently as possible, without forgetting this essential fact: as well as their knowledge, which qualifies them to use psychology and even analysis, the cardinal virtue is to love their neighbour.

We also have to recognise that people come to a consultation blindfold, like Fortune, vulnerable to being told the worst as well as the best. Unfortunately there's no doubt that if some people could be told that they were heading towards a tragedy they would be horrified, and it seems that it is a good thing that nature has placed a veil of ignorance in front of our eyes allowing us to have our illusions and our hopes. It is understandable that people don't like to know the bad things that can happen to them in advance and don't want all the worry that would cause: what good does it do to add the unnecessary pain of apprehension to the ordinary troubles of life? Shielding yourself from anxiety is to behave like an ostrich which puts its head in the sand, but even so it is a legitimate reaction which must be respected: a forecast must never be imposed on someone who has not asked for it and does not want to know and the astrologer must stop themselves if someone's existence is going to be poisoned by a revelation. Those who take the risk of having a consultation generally do it because they prefer to know, even if the revelation is unpleasant, because the advantage of lifting a corner of the veil is that they can arm themselves against their fate as well as reassure themselves by cushioning the impact of the setback and by being ready to exploit its opportunities.

Another problem is 'the effect of the packaging' of the information being forecasted: the same situation or event can be carefully worded or thrown out in brutal language reminiscent of 'divinatory terrorism'. There are sadistic astrologers who take pleasure in frightening people to satisfy some feeling of power, just as there are stupid heavy-handed ones who are no better. Announcing a happy occasion that is really wished for is not innocent either: 'We count the minutes we have left to live and we shake the hour glass to hurry it up' (Alfred de Vigny). It would be better, sometimes, to have the surprise of a happiness which swoops down on us unexpectedly rather than be subjected to the power of the future which, apart from the pain of waiting, creates an obsession around a date on the calendar that alienates us from reality. Having something that is pending like that leads to a de-motivating passivity, as if destiny has promised something and we just have to hold out our hands to receive the precious goods falling from the sky. To build our lives we must permanently engage with it so the forecast must do the contrary by mobilising the person, guiding them wisely and making them want to contribute to the delivery of the event by helping them to take greater control of their lives.

In addition, it is often the case that forecasting a set-back, a run of bad luck or hard times is more successful than announcing happiness, because all dissonant configurations are manifested like a current going downhill, flowing under its own momentum, while harmonious configurations come from an upward movement: there is no effort involved when a tile falls on your head, but you have to be in the right state of mind and put in the work to achieve a result that is not a foregone conclusion. A propitious forecast that is a failure is like an iridescent soap bubble that bursts, and it is common to feel disillusioned when the reality of expected happiness is not as good as the dream. In the circumstances, the conscientious prognosticator stimulates some involvement of the person in the forecast and in their contribution towards its realisation.

Nor should we forget the part played by a misinterpretation of what is said. Speaking about the theatre, Tristan Bernard said: 'The author writes a play, the actors perform a second one and the public sees a third.' Substitute astrology for the author, the astrologer for the actor and the client for the public, and you can see why Kepler said: 'Forecasts should only be read by people who are learned, intelligent and calm.' The problem can be one of communication and the listening process itself sometimes malfunctions. Sometimes there is a refusal to hear: unconscious forgetting, a reinterpretation of what is heard, or even a speaking disability. Perhaps, then, we have to have achieved a particular level of self-knowledge in order to hear the message when we are given it. Generally we will hear the truth in our own time, when we are ready to receive it; otherwise, however well it is expressed, it won't be heard.

We also have to acknowledge that, between leaving the astral signifier and arriving at the signified human, it is possible for Ariadne's thread to elude the hands of the interpreter, either by a softening of the symbolism, where analogy leapfrogs from one thing to another and goes all over the place in an annoyingly inexact way, if not losing in a spiritual mist, formulated in such an abstract way so distant from real life that its terminology hovers in a vacuum and could apply to anything at all. An accomplished approach to interpretation involves using simple everyday language which is in touch with reality.

A time when you might decide to have a consultation is when there is an important decision to be made and either you are feeling uncertain about it or you would like what you have decided to be confirmed. So the consultation usually leads to a decision being confirmed or not validated.

Those using the consultation to confirm a decision are healthy people who use their intuition, their natural ability to come to their own decisions, to guide them when planning their projects. The person feels that they are conscious of having a programme or life plan which gives expression to their awakening tendencies as they seek satisfaction by aiming at a goal. This is exactly the kind of interior programme that can be seen by the interpreter as well as its alignment with the future project that they have fixed on. Thus there is an accord between the interpreted and the interpreter and it is rare that they can both be wrong.

Having a consultation that does not affirm their decisions can happen to anyone—who hasn't made a mistake? But usually, it concerns people who often make mistakes in their life choices, people who are complex, contradictory or immature and don't know themselves. The case of a young woman who wants to get married but who then becomes disillusioned comes to mind. Here the expectation of happiness and the marriage being declared a failure are clearly at odds. Before pronouncing on a negative finding the interpreter must naturally question whether it is not they who have made a mistake but, since light has been shed on what isn't working, they can present the future from a different perspective, with a happier outcome.

This ability to throw light on things is at odds with the dreadful prejudices of a contemporary evil which is ravaging our society. The problem of the big divide which makes us strangers on this Earth has never been so acute. 'This divorce between man and life, the actor and his setting, literally has a feeling of the absurd,' Albert Camus declared in *The Myth of Sisyphus*. The art of Urania removes this impasse by advocating the relatedness of human beings to the universe, by building—or rather re-building—an immense arch which connects them to all the conditions of their exterior milieu, because they are beings that are centred in the world and who participate in everything; first of all it specifies their unique nature and, just as importantly, makes them part of a universal whole. This is where we part company with an existentialism which de-individualises people, seeing them as being nothing in themselves and only able to be what they manage to be, without really knowing how or why.

They seem to think that everyone is arbitrarily suited to perform any action whatever and can produce the same results, that everything is equally available to everyone without bias, whereas what happens when we act is that the latent becomes manifest because we have operated a process of selection which leads the act along the path for which we were made, so a lunar type would cut a sorry sight in the boxing ring just as a Martian would be very ill at ease playing the lute. This connection to our specific affinities is well known and has always been an indication of talent, as the school of Boileau tells us:

> If he does not feel the secret influence of heaven,
> If his natal star has not made him a poet.

Today's existentialist tragedy is that this claimed inner emptiness has led to us losing the meaning of life. Camus was obsessed with this theme: 'I think the most important question is the meaning of life' (*The Myth of Sisyphus*), 'To lose one's life is no great matter; when the time comes I'll have the courage to lose mine. But to see the meaning of life being swept away, to be told that there is no reason for existing, that is what is intolerable' (*Caligula*).

We could rightly wait for astrology to rediscover this essential goodness. More than any other kind of knowledge, it helps to find deeper meaning in life because it holds a range of different ways of satisfying our aspirations, and we can come close to knowing which tendency is uppermost at any given moment or period in life, a tendency that becomes apparent when we discover what it allows us to do. It is about the manifestation of the essence of the being, which colours the expression of the act or the situation in question and with which it is rooted on any inner journey: it is the tone of the process that gives it meaning, a meaning that the act does not have in itself, because all acts that don't have the support of a matching one are meaningless. What gives it flavour and value is the feeling of being at one with the vibration that the person has when they are in harmony with the world order. For the case being judged to start speaking to the interpreter the outer shell of the act has to be cracked open to obtain its hidden meaning. This is where we discover the prime importance of the inherent value of the planetary alphabet with the fundamental nature of its categories, and come back to its array of temperaments (Venusian, Martial, Jovial…), the important signatures that form our interpretive pathway.

Deciphering a map of the sky is an exercise in exploring the inner empire of the human soul, in contacting its profound reality. This unique means of investigation is a journey through our inner space whereby we can reach and reveal the essence of life and are able to illuminate the truth of our matter. A real 'going back to nature', it gives a voice to the strong forces that have their source in the night of the being and are delivered by the pleasure principle, using the reality principle to develop a sense of self. Its path goes from the dream to the most enlightened state of consciousness. It is also a sort of ecological quest, where we can distinguish the history of each tendency, from our inner desires to their exteriorised manifestation, localising the relationship between man-subject and man-object in the being, the quality of the nature-culture connection.

The usefulness of such a probe is obvious … if self-knowledge is felt like a need for food for the mind, it is really because it is intuitively perceived as essential, with instances of narcissistic indulgence or pretension being only like moss on a rock. Certainly, someone with a strong character and a well established sense of what's real does not need an astrological cure, but someone who is still searching has to take care of themselves. Likewise, nobody is interested in forecasts when things are going well, but it is different when the future is shrouded in mist. In any case, as Diderot said, man is no more than a 'mixture of strength and weakness, grandeur and pettiness, light and darkness'.

It mustn't be thought, however, that astrology is only a recourse for people who need support—no more than psychology only helps people who are weak—people who are well established in life can have reversals of fortune and find that they are more complex than they thought when they are conflicted. Such information is naturally more appealing to those who are distressed because they have lost their sense of self, have difficulty finding their identity and in becoming an adult. In coming to know ourselves again, which is like mining the mineral wealth from our inner ground, we can find out what has been lacking, no longer be a stranger to ourselves and realign our deep inner selves with the way we live our lives. Human destiny in its true form is seen by those who emphasise the play of their tendencies, and it is much more obvious when they live passionately with all the force of their character. What they do is in line with the tendency which sends back the purest echo. They know who they are and where they are going. They feel a sense of well-being and are in tune with their environment, with their hearts singing the infinite.

Astrological analysis is useful in so many ways, helping people to better understand their character, their behaviour, their dispositions, their relationships with others and their direction in life. It helps people to seek happiness and success in the way that is most appropriate to them and to turn their backs on their mistakes. It is a way of discovering the unique nature of the individual and of identifying the vocation that is their particular destiny. Furthermore, an astrological analysis can throw light on a given situation and help to distinguish the likely from the unlikely, the possible from the impossible and the real from the imaginary. In short it can point to what is of value and give meaning to the unknown.

Usually people coming to an astrological consultation feel in need of illumination and most commonly they seek help at a time of crisis in their lives, a time of personal growth that requires change. This can happen to anybody, sooner or later, in life, because whatever ground you stand on can give way. In these circumstances, taking account of the person's psychological make-up, the astrologer can make sense of the crisis, assess how big it is and predict how long it will last.

Let's have no preconceptions about the forecast either: living, sleeping, breathing and eating are all ways of foreseeing. It is impossible to do otherwise, impossible not think any further than tomorrow so as to organise our life for its duration, to not picture our future. We do everything with the thought of what comes afterwards and the future belongs to those who plan well because, as the proverb says, 'forewarned is forearmed', like the farmer who fills his barn against times of scarcity.

We can use this way of demarcating time because we know the course of the stars in advance, thus we can get a handle on the future and this allows us to get a grasp of the person for their complete lifespan and to follow them along the thread of time. This dynamic quest is the most fruitful way of gaining knowledge.

The forecasting phenomenon itself is about the coupling of the individual and the cosmos over time and the positions fixed in the natal sky vibrate in unison with the movement of the circulating planets. When a celestial body, X or Y, is touched by a passing planet it vibrates and the natal planet is activated by the encounter or by the aspect made with the planet in the sky. For example, a temporary configuration involving the natal Venus will, for its duration, express the verb 'to love'. The mood will be emotional and may have a quality of joy or sorrow, happiness or heartache, and it may be strong or weak depending on the importance of the flow. If it is a Martian configuration then a climate of aggression or passion will be expressed which can be either constructive or destructive. By sticking to this kind of language, which describes the person's subjective state and their feelings about life, the interpretation becomes part of the fabric of the being and is woven into their evolution. The risk with forecasting is in wanting to go beyond this and to attempt to link this feeling to a situation or a companion event which is supposed to be the cause or the consequence of this inner activity: a whole range of possibilities present themselves to the interpreter, who then has to make a choice and is not usually able to control what happens externally. However, when it comes to information, we have what we need: the configuration is indicative of the event or situation, because it is our interior response that gives meaning to what happens to us, as if it came from the beat of our hearts and even the source of life. The duration of a passing configuration is a time of self-scrutiny when people discover themselves, reinvent themselves, create and realise themselves, in that part of the personality activated by the configuration, but they can, if it is dissonant, fail in the situation presented to them or feel defeated in some way.

For all that we mustn't think that it is the circumstances that make it rain or shine: we make our configurations as much as the configurations make us. The danger, in a case of dissonance, for example, is in balancing the risk we are exposed to, within the area dealt with by the configuration, and this varies a lot according to the person concerned, depending on their temperament, experience and level of evolution. That is not counting the obvious benefits that can be derived from a difficult configuration, and the wise person can take advantage of the effort that is required of them. 'What have you made of your configuration?' is a question we could ask as one situation changes into another. Each of them provides the material for a garment made to fit the person. There is only a basic outline of this material in the birth chart: it is for each of us to cut our cloth in our own best interests. The same conditions can bring about a whole range of endings: as when a cycle ends and is renewed, a transit of Saturn to the Descendant, the place of coupling, can, in an adult, just as well 'bring' an affair if the person is single or bring about the end of an existing union, as well as other alternatives.

How flexible it is when we represent the future as being open and where we achieve wisdom by being more in tune with the universe in which we belong... So a forecast gives us awareness and illumines a time period like an exercise in living, an illumination that is beneficial because it provides structure. To exist is to make ourselves visible. Being able to project ourselves into the future we can see ourselves as a person in the making and can prepare for what is ahead by referring to our own personal system, which has our destiny at its heart and where we find the reason for our existence. Finally, we come back to this perfect basic formula: 'Become what you were made for.' Live with a shining centre in close union with the world.

Chapter 11 - The Four Elements in Painting

This study would not be complete without my providing an understanding of astrology through its practice, that is to say by giving an example of chart interpretation, and in first making a wide application to the general field to which the person having that chart belongs.

I have chosen a painter and painting because the painter projects his or her own microcosm directly on to the canvas, and expresses their interior universe in a creative way that can be interpreted through the rich symbolism generally used in pictorial composition: space, volume, form, matter, texture, drawing, line, colour, light... The subject is ideal because the input is direct, allowing us, the observer, to capture the psyche in a visual way.

To begin with, let's rid ourselves of prejudice. In approaching this pictorial universe with regard to the four elements and the four elementary principles, in accord with Ptolemy's basic astrological classification, we mustn't think for a moment that what we are practising is archaic, and that this doctrine of the elements is but a 'poor pseudo-physics' (Couderc), an idea which Van Helmont has shown to be absurd. Astrology-subject, in operational mode, is what astrology-object makes in the field of operation; its references are not those of the external material world, they are those of our inner being, our 'psychic reality' as Freud used to say.

Let's start with the fundamentals by going back to the four states of matter: liquid, gas, incandescent and solid. These properties have been connected to the quaternary rhythms of nature: the four times of day (midnight, sunrise, culmination and sunset), the four weeks of the month (new Moon, first quarter, full Moon and last quarter), the four seasons of the year (winter, spring, summer, autumn). This was the first way in which people 'naturised' themselves, while they also 'cosmosised' themselves, with a continuity of correspondences (infancy-youth-maturity-old age) which resulted in the temperaments of Hippocrates.

Externally, matter can be perceived in different states in the types of water, river and sea, of atmosphere, of radiation from both the Sun and the ground, and they are replicated internally with our watery, airy, fiery and earthy human types, the fluctuating continuity of the water that surrounds us corresponding to our aquatic interior (lymph, blood, humoral secretions): our copious respiratory exchange makes us at one with the flow of air in the space around us; the warmth of our solar hearth resonates with our temperature, our organic ways of creating energy and our psychic reactions; built from the Earth's crust that is akin to the earthly precipitate of our skeleton. 'All things are (...) more or less earth, more or less water, more or less air, more or less fire, more or less of one kingdom or another (Diderot's *Encyclopaedia* on the 'Elements'). Here, sustainably, we have the fundamental essence of mankind and the world in a unity of man-nature-sky.

By the same token,[93] we have here the source of the vital components of the astral language. Reading it we can immediately decode the material that makes up our inner universe and so penetrate the enigma of human essence. To be born, as Maurice Merleau-Ponty said, 'is to be both born of the world and born into the world', and to be born of the world, is to have received its impression. And yet the stuff of these mother components of the universe is that of the same basic constituents, and the composition of organic substances can be reduced to four simple substances that echo the elements of hydrogen, oxygen, nitrogen and carbon.

This is the reason that, under various neologisms, the traditional theory behind the Hippocratic temperaments periodically rises from the ashes, because if the form becomes outmoded, its underlying basis stays the same and it is modernised and reconstructed through the morphological, physiological, embryological and reflexological data that goes with the changes that have occurred over one and a half centuries.

Thus, for example, the vital processes associated with air have oxygen for their signature and this corresponds with the sanguine humour of the Ancients, the main function of which is to carry air to all parts of the living body through the processes of respiration and circulation of the blood. Sanguine (humid and hot) appertains to the respiratory, atmospheric, nasal and chest type. When their pulmonary bellows are fully ventilated by abundant amounts of oxygen they are literally heated. Thus they become animated, they expand, open, express themselves, become excited, release large amounts of energy with the abundant consumption of animal life. Hippocrates was unaware of the existence of oxygen but, for all that, he established this wonderful archetype![94]

Lymphatic   Sanguine   Bilious   Nervous
(Phlegmatic)   (Choleric)   (Melancholic)

These essentials of life affect our intimate selves, to the point of being recognised as mother components, and it is understandable that a Posidonius would identify the essence of fire in masculinity going as far as to equate orgasm with a spark or a flash, and that a Seneca would depict anger using fire-like colours, in an otherwise perfect physiological and psychological description. This intimate approach has its value. Heat and cold, for example, have a place in many sciences: agronomics, ecology, seismology, epidemiology... The atoms themselves, when heated by a laser beam, move faster, and slow down when cooled. Aren't we in the same boat? Was it so foolish then to determine the human constitution as being hot or cold, humid or dry, and isn't this the essential terrain of human nature?

'My soft complexion' (Montaigne); my 'energetic, ardent and crazy manner' (Diderot); my 'lazy soul (…), and ardent, bilious temperament' (Rousseau); 'I have a fiery temperament' (Stendhal). '(…) thoughts run through my head, like water from a fountain' (Balzac); the 'troubled and bitter waters of the ocean that are in me' (Michelet); 'my brain full of flames' (Baudelaire); 'yes I know from whence I come, like a flame, I burn and am consumed' (Nietzsche); 'my soul was a standing wave, (Poe); my 'great lake of melancholy' (Virginia Woolf); the 'fever' (from a hoard of desires) of Maïakovski... There is no end to the way such concepts are assimilated. Fire can be the stars we see when hit on the head: a fiery character, someone who is heated, a consuming passion, a burning soul, a tongue of flame, an incendiary look, glowing eyes, a burning desire, a fiery kiss, a lightning gesture, being fired up for a cause, even having a sacred flame or burning yourself out, like a flame fading before making its last breath. The converse is cold bloodedness, a cold manner, the frigid woman and an ice-like soul … not to mention a soft nature, a fluid character, which can be compared to a dry character, a cold heart, to dry fruit. The references to elementary language abound.

It would be all too easy to only give anodyne analogies. Some anthropologists are bold enough to describe traditional societies as being 'cold' and relatively stable while they call modern societies that are in movement 'warm'. Their epithets have power because their references are justified by the way that atoms behave when subjected to temperature variations. It is understandable then that the great epistemologist Gaston Bachelard wanted to open up new ways of looking at human knowledge in this field with his idea of going back to original values: 'Those who would dismiss the images produced by these simple metaphors disregard the deeper meaning that they are covering: the prodigious intuition formed by the intimate link between the great forces of nature and human life.' Because as he explains, 'fire is not just an exterior reality: it smoulders in the soul as surely as it does under the ashes and we know that when dreams are about fire an erotic interpretation is usually correct.' (*The Psychoanalysis of Fire* [Gallimard, 1938]). This is where we come back to Posidonius.

> One cannot even say that a metaphor comes near to reality; it is more accurate to say that it is the most direct way of expressing something because it highlights the similarities. Far from the idea of looking for rags in a picture shop to dress up what the person is feeling, it is the world as imagined in human reveries. It is in the secret harmony that has been wakened by a mysterious echo that metaphor, in the form of an image, serves as a reflection of the human soul, joining and matching or moving between the interior universe and the exterior universe.[95]

Before Bachelard, many other creative people had depicted this communion between mankind and the world, the universe being the country of our hearts. Notably there is Victor Hugo:

> The soul, like the sky, contains four breaths; the soul has its poles, the soul has its cardinal points. The great chariot of the Spirit runs on four axles. The soul like you, o winds, sonorous group, has its north, its midday, its sunset and its dawn.[96]

But it was Bachelard who was to perceive that metaphors work to open truth; the 'hormones of the imagination':

> Tell me what is your Phantom?
> Is it a gnome, a salamander, a mermaid or a sylph?
> Tell me what is your infinity, I will know the sense of your universe,
> Is it the infinity of the sea or the sky, is it the infinity of the depths of the earth or that of the pyre?[97]

So this epistemologist undertook the huge task of looking at the symbols used by the creative mind in literature, a work which ended with the discovery that poets belonged to one of four large families, each of which had a specific kind of imagination: poets of fire, poets of water, poets of air and poets of earth. The typical images that belong to a given family of poets are not isolated; they command a real network of images which tend to work together and to echo each other, to group themselves according to the relationships of their subtle but recurring analogies so that the parts that make up the group are in concert and each person's world in miniature is incorporated into the universe. We can see then that a material element like fire can be attached to a kind of reverie which influences the beliefs, passions, ideals and philosophy of life. It makes sense to talk of the aesthetic of fire, of the psychology of fire, and even of the morality of fire.' Bachelard came to link this element 'to a primitive human feeling, to the first organic reality, to a basic dreamy temperament.'

Guy Michaud, professor at the University of Paris X who took up this research, declared 'that the image of water is readily associated with images of plants and therefore with green, and also with the Moon, pallor, reflection, muted colours, while the image of fire generally carries with it visceral images, also bright red, the Sun, the rich sounds of trumpets and horns'. Using the statistical methods of Pierre Abraham, a vast inventory was created of the predominant images found in the entire works of each poet to determine the type of mental structures involved, because in every writer there is 'a life in images' which is a world that is never still. By studying them Bachelard, struck by the contrasts between the categories, started talking about a 'law of the four elements' in the world of the imagination, and he ended by speaking of an aesthetic, a psychology, a morale, a lyricism and a philosophy of water, air, fire and earth... Isn't this a reintroduction to the world of astrology?

So it is natural to think that there must also be four

great families of painters that are related to the four elements. These four pictorial types are present at the level of temperament, the creative word. We have to look beyond the demands of what is outside us, the external causes dear to Taine of race, land, the environment, time... This temperament springs from within, lends itself to a particular quality of expression, and then generates four specific types of style of painting related to the psychological quaternary of the elements.

.

Chapter 12 - The Four Approaches to Painting

Standing in front of their easels, painters exercise their powers; the skills they deploy with their tools (pencil, brush, colours…) are in accord with the nature of the relationship that they have with the world and this results in a given mode of behaviour. Nevertheless, there are predominately four main ways of approaching the canvas.

1. The ability to reproduce nature at the surface level together with the sensory pleasure derived from the beautiful subject matter. These artists have an aptitude for depicting the visible and concrete, the palpable reality, the physical aspect of matter set in space and in an atmosphere that is breathable. They paint in order to document, tell a story, present the picturesque. There is a feeling of extraversion, of being extremely open to seeing the world in a sensitive and immediate way, and this corresponds to the sensualist temperament that is associated with air.

   > I only paint what I see. (Courbet)
   > Painting is essentially a concrete art. (Courbet)
   > I am only an eye. (Monet)

2. The predisposition towards interpreting the outside world. Artists order the objects they observe, organising their relationships and giving importance to the relationships between forms, lines, colours… the idea, the structure or the principle behind it having priority over what is real or immediate (as with the Cubists). This introverted attitude corresponds to a 'conceptive' temperament, associated with earth.

   > I believe neither in what I touch nor what I see. I only believe in what I do not see and solely in what I feel. (Gustave Moreau)
   > Art is an abstraction taken from nature. (Gauguin)

Painting is a mental occupation. (Vinci)

3. *The tendency to accentuate* emotion or to give vent to
    passion when faced with something real, the 'subject
    matter' being the receptacle for the artists' fervour,
    effort, fever, their drama, leading to an exaltation and an
    intensification of expression (like the fauves howling
    their inner state). This expressionist temperament relates
    to the nature of fire.

    It is necessary to be in a fever. (Delacroix)
    I would like to express the terrible passions of
    humanity. (Van Gogh)

4. *The contemplative surrender* to received impressions; being
    receptive to the harmony of things, identifying with the
    ambiance, belonging in a poetic way to the environment,
    creating a comprehensive vision in which the details are
    lost and everything becomes part of a subtle and nuanced
    state of harmony. This is the impressionist temperament
    associated with water.

    Beauty in art is truth bathed in an impression received
    from nature (Corot)
    It is not the objects I paint but the sensations they give
    me (Cezanne).

Like a sphinx, human beings are a synthesis of all these
propensities, each painter being driven by these four basic
tendencies which they have to varying degrees. As with all
typologies, a painter can only be placed in one of the basic
great families when one of the tendencies is more dominant
than the others.

The sensualist temperament (air)

Being predominantly extraverted the painters are mainly

attracted to the realism of material objects, to their appearance, and to their documentary or anecdotal value. These are the narrators who love the figurative with its way of representing things. They love to describe things and they do it with care, distinguishing them and savouring them; they are interested in beautiful materials so they recreate reality in a tactile way (the painting is seen with the hand) with a respect for form, colour, texture, expressions. They have a tendency to imbue objects with a particular feeling that is energetic, robust and sound and which gives their subjects an earthly realism. Captivated by the representation of the sense of touch and exploiting their rich fleshy material, they use their gift for re-enactment to convey the pleasure of carnal possession. Their exuberance sometimes leads to the production of very large paintings showing crowded scenes from real life. This is a comfortable art form that is at risk of ending up as bad taste, prolixity and window dressing.

> Perhaps I have gone too far in the richness and realness of subjects. (Rubens)
> The truth rather than a painting. (Velázquez)
> The truth is what is beautiful in art. (Courbet)

Some great sensualists : Van Eyck, Caravaggio, Rubens, Ribera, Jordaens, Teniers, Le Brun, Boucher, Meissonier, Courbet, Fougeron.

The conceptive temperament (earth)

Predominantly introverted, these painters are drawn to interpreting pattern: their work moves on from the pictorial to become non-figurative. They tend to do intellectual works of art in the studio, where an inner alchemy, which tends to simplify, dematerialises the natural elements in order to emphasise the structure or the idea, and separate out the intrinsic value or spirit of the thing. The image disappears beneath its pictorial expression, like matter beneath its quintessence. They structure or stylise the picture, reducing the forms to simple geometry or a formula and only using colour when essential, in the search for the perfect truth. The opposite of the sensualist's voluptuous attachment to visible reality, they deliberately abstract from external life, following an idea or a feeling from their inner selves, which leads them to the bare essentials within the integrity of pictorial artifice. They are rather fond of the smaller format and lay out the design in an economical way. Their art communicates intellectual pleasure, but there is a risk that by paring down too much the work becomes stiff, dry and impoverished.

> I live with my thoughts (...). Nature for us men has more depth than surface (...). All is, especially in art, a theory developed and applied in contact with nature. (Cézanne)
>
> (...) a painting is, above all, a plane surface, divided into forms and colours assembled in a certain order. (Denis)
>
> I look into myself and not into nature (...). We don't search with our eyes, but with where our mysterious inner thoughts are centred (...). Salvation is only possible through a reasoned and frank return to principle (...). Nature only lets us understand it through symbols. (Gauguin)

Some great conceptive artists : Uccello, Verrocchio, Botticelli, Vinci, Poussin, Ingres, Puvis de Chavannes, Cézanne, Rousseau, Gauguin, Seurat, Matisse, Denis, Léger, Lhote, Modigliani, Dufy, Buffet.

The expressionist temperament (fire)

The inner tension felt by these artists makes them animate, shake up, attack and change the natural appearance of things, under the pressure of their dominant passion, revealed by an accentuation of the strokes (somewhat vertical and towards the right), the contrast between forms (usually in straight lines) the vivid colours (mainly warm tones), and their direct and visible brush strokes. The space is often filled with explosive contrasts. The effect is that of a violent struggle to take hold of life by seizing, tormenting, glorifying, distorting or ferociously torturing the exterior object. Instinctively they simplify to get straight to what is essential, to give it feeling, to make it striking, sometimes even making caricatures of the faces and gestures. They create a frenetic, burning atmosphere that is dramatic but it borders on excess, delirium and an inner whirlwind with the movements destroying the forms...

> The life is in the movement. (Delacroix)
> (...) the Sun makes us mad (...) but I cannot, suffering myself, do without something greater than myself, what is my life: the power to create. (Van Gogh)
> (...) I make a painting which bites. Violence, the clash of cymbals (...) an explosion, a good picture, a picture, what! It should be bristling with razor blades. (Picasso)

Some great expressionists: Giotto, Bosch, Grünewald, Tintoretto, Breughel the Elder, El Greco, Fragonard, Géricault, Delacroix, Toulouse-Lautrec, Van Gogh, Soutine, Picasso, Delaunay.

The impressionist temperament (water)

For the contemplative temperament of these artists the exterior object is a pretext for abandoning themselves to their imaginations, their feelings, personal sensibilities, to dreams and the phantasmagorical. The result is a cohesive vision which is steeped in an intimate atmosphere. The individual parts of the painting lose their separateness so that the whole has a unity created by the harmonious groupings. This temperament that we call impressionist or intimist is sensitive to nuances, to the value of the delicate and indistinct. The movements are calm (mainly horizontal and more towards the left), the dimensions seem to be smaller and the colours and contrasts softened; the forms are also softened, stilled, indeterminate and indistinct, mirroring still water, as if to prolong the effect on the mind receiving the impression. These poets of shadows and mists find pleasure in the ephemeral and transient nature of objects which they bathe in an atmosphere of feeling and they invite the spectator to participate in the dream. Taken to excess, the risk for the intimist is that the forms will dissolve in a composition that is disorderly and lacking in architectural interest.

> I don´t paint with colour, but with feelings. (Chardin).
> When I paint a head, I also look at the feet. (Gros)
> I need to abandon myself to the imaginary. Everything is carried out by passively submitting to whatever comes from the unconscious. (Redon)
> The gods are necessary for our imagination. (Renoir)
> For me art seems to be mostly a state of mind. (Chagall)

Some great impressionists: Giorgione, Raphaël, Rembrandt, Velázquez, Watteau, Vermeer, Chardin, Corot, Fantin-Latour, Monet, Pissarro, Renoir, Redon, Marquet, Bonnard, Vuillard.

The chosen subjects

The pictorial temperament, the expression of the tendency, sets the tone of the work, and is revealed by the artist's interpretation. We will now make a series of detailed comparisons of the ways in which specific temperaments produce different versions of the same subject, the picture just being a way of expressing the tendency.

First, the paintings that have historical subjects: Uccello, Rembrandt, Gros and Picasso have all interpreted military scenes. In his *Cavalcade*, the conceptive painter

Uccello executes, with his magnificent and turbulent representation of soldiers with their weapons, a clever play of line and form that is arranged on the canvas. As for the people in *The Night Watch*, by the impressionist Rembrandt, they advance in the immateriality of a fluorescent dream, going to who knows what incident out there in the world, but the same troop of musketeers could have been represented (by the expressionist Franz Hals, for example) gesticulating and brawling. The sensualist Gros gave his *Plague Victims of Jaffa* the form of a historic document, painting it in an idealised way with the horror of the situation almost forgotten, while *Guernica* by the expressionist Picasso screams with all its might with a cry that pierces the infinite, catapulted forth by the violence of the shapes, the lines and the contrasts. This same subject could have been portrayed by depicting the stillness and silence of death in a place devastated by bombing.

Now landscapes: Auvers-sur-Oise as seen by a painter with an expressionist temperament (fire) looks nothing like the same place as seen by a painter with an impressionist temperament (water); for the tormented Van Gogh, the breath of his delirium fans a tragic fire, while Pissarro, elated, loses himself in his luminous atmosphere which envelops everything in the aura of a peaceful life. Furthermore, while the sensualist Courbet, the Dionysian lover of rustic revelry, paints his *Lake Geneva* on velvet like-material, the conceptive artist Villon with his *Vegetable Garden with Pumpkins* is only interested in the positions of the trees and the colours.

Next let's look at flowers: *The Sunflowers* by the expressionist Van Gogh is frantically animated like a wild animal at bay, the intense brilliance of the chrome yellow loud against the background of Veronese green, while the *Wild Flowers in a Vase* by the impressionist Bonnard melts away secretly in a quiet corner of the studio. The *Vase of Flowers* by the sensualist Jan 'Velvet' Brueghel awakes our sense of smell as much as it captures how the flowers look; it displays the floral diversity and draws attention to the fleshy texture of the flowers as one of them is foraged by a greedy insect; we could imagine that we are in the middle of a field in summer. The *Scents* by the conceptive artist Dufy is just the opposite and is only an idea: there is no volume or depth, the material nature of the flowers only survives by tsubtle relationships between the forms, marks and colours. Now, the subject of animals: the savagery of cruel combat in *Bull and Horse* by Picasso is fully portrayed by only the frenzied movements and convulsed forms; there is no blood, no banderillas, no extras. Next we have *The Two Lovers,* by the impressionist Chagall who charm the painter by flying gently towards the left, in the Moonlight, on a friendly horse. Like a good sensualist, Dürer made his *Hare* look very real with its fur so soft and warm that we want to stroke it, and so true to life that it could illustrate a children's text book. By contrast, in *War* by Rousseau the horse is only a phantom, something secondary, with its black silhouette playing a decorative role along with all the other signs applied to the surface of the picture.

It is the same with the nude: the various Venuses (as with the Nymphs and the Graces) of the sensualist Boucher, drawn from the chords of their voluptuous lyres, with their radiant bodies of pink and pearl and their way of pleasing the eye, arouse a feeling of pleasure and stimulate desire. There is nothing of that kind with *The Model* by the conceptive painter Suzanne Valadon: she delineates her figure with such rigor that the concrete feminine reality is forgotten in order to give life to an arrangement of pure line and colour. The intense animation of the scene in Tintoretto´s *Susanna at her Bath* shows that it is the work of an expressionist: Susanna's legs move like the sails of a windmill, her expressive head turns towards us, her arm reaching out to take hold of something that is behind her, the lively maidservant doing her hair, the animated lust of the old men, and the trembling plants… In *The Bathers* by Renoir, on the other hand, the main figure is still, its outline diluted by artistic feeling and looking as if it is saturated in the aquatic element.

Even a subject like that of Christ will have various versions according to temperament: El Greco, Rembrandt, Rubens and Matisse, inspired by the Crucifixion, treated this subject according to their respective temperaments. The first, an expressionist, treats it by elongating and wonderfully animating the gestures and expressions, making his Christ a vibrant hero. The second, an impressionist, treats it by creating a mystical atmosphere where, in the shadows of a palpable mystery, his martyr, overcome by the situation, lies abandoned, a Jesus who already belongs to another world. The third, a sensualist, gives a naturalistic rendition of the subject with an exuberant, raucous theatrical scene, with a Christ who is present among us, a carnal physical creature, having descended from a bulky Cross made out of wooden beams. Matisse, a conceptive artist, treats it to a stylised rendering of a pared down Christ on the road to the Cross, retaining only the idea of the Passion, the person being disembodied.

The same temperament can be found in a great diversity of subject matter, the subject being only a pretext for its expression. We can confirm this by looking at it from the other point of view.

Thus when Hubert Robert sets out to paint the *Pont du Gard,* a meticulously exact architectural structure that has withstood the centuries, he observes it in a sensualist way and only sees the way the stones are fleetingly gilded when lit by the setting Sun; how far is this spontaneous free expression, this fantasy, from the geometric thoughts that laid the plans for this impeccable alignment of arches, a subject more suited to the conceptives. In the same way, when Picasso paints *Maternity,* he does it with the same wild energy of his inner fire and his toddler has none of the allure of a cherub but looks rather like a little boxer standing up to a mother dragon, whereas such a subject has more affinity with the intimists like Berthe Morisot or Carrière. The same could be said of his flowers with their fangs and his bouquets with claws for pistils and, indeed, his female faces.

The bi-types

As the four specific tendencies exist inside us, each personal temperament is expressed according to the order of a particular classification which goes from the most important to the least consequential. It not being possible to cover all the possible manifestations, I will give just a brief explanation of the bi-types who are representative of those who have two dominant components.

- Sensualist-expressionist: the representation of physical reality is intensified by animating the expression. It is applied to the spectacular, the theatrical, the ode or the epic saga (Caravaggio, Rubens, Ribera, Jordaens, Decamps, Gavarni, Boldini).

- Sensualist-conceptive: this time physical reality is represented in minute detail or treated in a stylised way (Holbein, Durer, the Le Nain brothers, Isabey, Chassériau, Rosa Bonheur, Foujita, Fougeron).

- Sensualist-intimist : there is the same attraction for what is real and external but the different subjects are swathed in a dream like atmosphere or in poetic feeling (Velvet Breughel, Rigaud, Nattier, Hogarth, Vernet father and son, Greuze, Boucher, Vigée-Lebrun, Isabey, Gros, Meissonier, Bouguereau, Carolus-Duran, Sisley, Chapelain-Midy).

- Expressionist-sensualist: the intensity of expression is applied mainly to a realistic representation of things. This may lean towards the epic, the colossal, and grandiloquence (Giotto, Michelangelo, Tintoreto, Fragonard, Van Gogh, Toulouse-Lautrec, Vlaminck, Van Dongen, Lurçat, Lorjou, Gruber, Dubout).

- Expressionist-conceptive: this time the intensity of expression is paired with an art that is rigorously organised and very formal (Piero della Francesca, Hieronymus Bosch, Grünewald, Breughel the Elder, El Greco, Picasso, Delaunay, Pignon).

- Expressionist-intimist: the intensity of expression animates a poetic and profound impression which is like the exaltation of a song from the soul or the forces of the subconscious (Angelico, Brouwer, Constable, Delacroix, Daumier, Doré, Rouault, Permeke, Soutine).

- Conceptive-sensualist: the way the picture is organised or stylised enhances the realism of the objects (Botticelli, Cranach the Elder, Poussin, David, Ingres, Puvis de Chavannes, Suzanne Valadon, Lhote, Gris, Gromaire).

- Conceptive-expressionist: the artistic composition is intensified by interior or exterior animation (Uccello, Signorelli, Léger, Gleizes, Modigliani, Buffet).

- Conceptive-intimist: the artistry of the painting is in harmony with their poetic feeling and imagination (Leonardo da Vinci, Georges de La Tour, Zurbarán, Cézanne, Gauguin, Rousseau, Matisse, Denis, Seurat, Dufy, Braque ('I like the rules that temper feeling').

- Intimist-sensualist : a poetic approach to feeling enriches the representation of the theme making it a sensual poem (Memling, Titian, Giorgione, Watteau, Chardin, Reynolds, Prud'hon, Millet, Jongkind, Boudin, Moreau, Henner, Pissarro, Degas, Whistler, Fantin-Latour, Monet, Renoir, Carrière, Signac, Bonnard, Utrillo).

- Intimist-expressionist: a tremulous poetic sensibility, in a state of intensity, the dream may tend towards lyricism or even the fantastic (Turner, Monticelli, Ensor, Chagall).

- Intimist-conceptive: the soul expressed through art (Raphaël, Velázquez, Rembrandt, Vermeer, Goya, Corot,

Manet, Redon, Vuillard, Marquet, Klee, Miró).

The compass rose of the temperaments

We can now show the painters, who are the most representative of their group, distributed around a circle that is divided into temperamental categories: each painter is in a quarter of the circle that represents a temperament, and how near they are to a neighbouring quarter corresponds to how strongly they express the second temperament.

This distribution, which of course is only approximate and which does not always correspond to a fixed evaluation,

certain painters (like Velázquez) having many periods in different styles, has the advantage of incorporating the elements, the elementary principles, into the axes.

So, on the left are the 'dry' painters whose art is differentiated, detached, clear, pure, contrasted, lean, hard or tight, and opposite, on the right, are the 'wet' painters whose art is modulated, pleasant, soft, fluid and enveloped in an atmosphere where everything has been blended together: Buffet is opposite Renoir (except for his 'dry period'). Similarly, at the top are the 'hot painters', the painters 'on the surface of the canvas', who depict the superficial, life as it appears in space, in movement, forms and brilliant light. At the top, Rubens, of whom Fromentin said that he was a 'man ... totally of the outer, marvellously but exclusively, made to grasp the exterior of things'. Opposite, below, the 'cold' painters, the painters of what is within, who go inside themselves to express interior life, the depths of the mind, the world of silence and the invisible, an evanescence of tangible reality, the ecstatic perception of the mysterious and the subtle relationships between things. They abandon themselves to the dark world of the subconscious from whence comes the voice of the soul. They are introverted idealists as well as being dark, delivering themselves up to their fantasies, their obsessions, their nightmares or their inner monsters. In the fore is Rembrandt, visionary of the mysteries of the soul.

Naturally, each painter personalises their temperament, giving it their own particular quality, because the type itself is only a template: a gallery of portraits which shows all the typologies provides a basis for identifying the types from among the heterogeneous mass of countless humans, and then we can proceed to comparing and classifying in order to find and understand the human families that we see most frequently. When we recognise a type it means that the subject-case has already left the anonymous and excessive mass where it was living, and even if we don't yet have an exceptional individual at least we can place it in a category on some great determining axis of human beings, an approach which helps us to understand it as a member of a family with essential characteristics or even a comprehensive description.

The choice of subject

There is a direct relationship between temperament and style: with artists temperament is expressed pictorially. However, there is no direct relationship between temperament and the subject chosen as this is just down to preference and taste.

Now we move on from how the tendency is expressed to its object, and this brings us back to Bachelard, who dedicated himself to finding the relationship between the objects of elements and a writer's imagination. René Huyghe tried a similar approach with painting, showing that the pictorial styles of Poussin and Courbet had particular affinity with earth, that of El Greco and Van Gogh with fire and that of Turner with water... This research deserves to be systematically followed up.

The necessities of life can prevent the painter from satisfying their tastes (customer orders, fashion, religious or political demands), nevertheless we cannot separate Rembrandt from his contemplation, Rubens from his spectacular displays, Le Nain and Millet from their peasants, El Greco from his mystical subjects, Chardin from his domestic utensils, Corot from his ponds, Watteau from his parks, Goya from his nightmares. It is impossible to imagine: Corot or Renoir spending the whole day painting scenes of carnage or bloody battles like Callot or Fra Angelico, depicting hell like Bosch, Watteau painting peasants like Courbet, or Michelangelo detailing miniatures like Isabey.

When we start to analyse the subjects treated, we find that a theme will have an affinity with one of the temperaments. Thus, the sensualists are especially fond of the richness of nature, its opulence, its beautiful subject matter and its physical pleasures: pagan scenes, festivals, love, drink, feasting, nudes, animals, fabrics, flowers, fruit, landscapes and portraits usually of people in a setting... The expressionists feel an affinity with dramatic scenes, in particular those that involve heroes, knights, combat, fighting or massacres, even monsters but also with scenes that are idealistic, mythological or religious. Conceptives prefer to work with subjects in the studio, with still life and abstract designs, while impressionist-intimists have a preference for interiors, people in repose, motherhood, children, self-portraits, water scenes.

We can also distinguish the temperaments by the different techniques used to create the picture: the drawing, colour, pattern, processes and techniques, creative rhythm, styles and schools, countries and eras... Whatever the diversity of creative originality a comparison through the centuries of the pictures of painters who have the same temperament reveals that despite changes in fashion, that temperament remains the same: the form may vary but the underlying basis does not alter.

Astrological verification

Michel Gauquelin in *La Cosmopsychologie*[98] (Cosmo-psychology) made the rather crude statement that 'Jean-Louis Barrault was successful in theatre as a sportsman, Jean Vilar as a scientist, Gustave Nadaud as a poet and Marcel Achard a man of the theatre', but he was justifying the comparison after having stated that the first was born with Mars rising, the second with Saturn culminating, the third with the Moon rising and the last with Jupiter culminating. With the prominence of these four planets our statistician had again found the four temperamental types and applied them to the theatre.

For us, astrologers, the correlation of these types with the astrological indices is much larger and more complex: the order of the planets, the zodiac and topocentric movement are also involved. All the planets are involved in delineating the different aspects of temperament. Thus sensualism is certainly Jupiterian but it is also Venusian; expressionism is Martian, but also solar and Uranian; impressionism is lunar but also Neptunian. Conceptivism, for example, is very different because it may have a dominant Mercury as seen with Dufy, in his lively writing, cursive style, brisk sketches and spiritual references, or a dominant Saturn-like Cezanne who was orientated towards the rigour of geometric form, compositions that are architectural and balanced, the solid organisation of forms and three-dimensional structures and no interest in what is perishable but rather in what is permanent.

Huge efforts have been made to collect the birth data for the great painters of the past by researching in libraries. Unfortunately we don´t know the day and often even the year of birth for many of them (Botticelli, Cranach, Dominiquin, Holbein, El Greco, Lorrain, Primaticcio, Tintoretto, Titian...), and the time of birth is unknown for many others. We have only been able to use other painters, the ones for whom we have birth data, for verification but the results obtained are largely conclusive. Just looking at angularity, for example, we see that the Moon is angular for the impressionist-intimists (Reynolds, Turner, Corot, Monticelli, Millet, Marquet), Venus or Jupiter angular for the sensualists (Dürer, Courbet, Bombois, Fougeron), Mars angular for the expressionists (Gavarni, Van Gogh, Vlaminck, Picasso, Derain, Friesz, Waroquier, Carra, Ensor, Permeke, Gruber, Lorjou), Saturn angular for the conceptives (Da Vinci, Puvis de Chavannes, Severini, Gleizes...). Stating that, in other cases, the angularity of planets corresponds to the second type of pictorial style.

Beyond this...

This classification is not the only way that the different types can be investigated on an astrological basis. There are many interesting ways of dividing the types: for example by having optimism and pessimism on the axis, the painters could be placed, in each of the four temperaments, going from happy (Rubens, Fragonard, Dufy, Renoir...) to sad (Durer, Soutine, Modigliani, Watteau...).

But we can slip easily from the four elements to the ten planetary types and, rather than a 'painter of water', we allude to the more familiar 'lunar' painter, which is how

Chagall considered himself, or to a Saturnian painter like Utrillo, brother of the cursed poets, addicted to misery, solitude, melancholy, spleen, suffering, illness and fatality, even tragedy, the Saturnian song being more like a voice from beyond the grave than the self-satisfied intoning of a stout tenor in Jovian mode.

Let's not forget the zodiac with its keyboard of twelve signs each with their specific characteristics. A judgement can be made by referring to the books in our 'Zodiaque' collection, from the Aries Van Gogh to the Pisces Renoir; with Delacroix and Courbet both being Taurus; Dufy Gemini; Rembrandt, Corot, Modigliani and Dali all Cancer; Leos Rubens and David; Virgos Ingres, Greuze and Millet; Libras Boucher and Watteau; Scorpio Picasso; Sagittarius Toulouse-Lautrec; Capricorns Cézanne and Utrillo; and Aquarius Manet; and remember also that painters, musicians and writers are placed side by side in each of the signs.

Finally, there is the way a painter expresses their affinity for the seasons and times of the day, depending on the colours on the palette and the variations in their intensity. Fresh light tones for morning and for spring; the intense vibrant tones of high noon and summer; the copper-coloured tones, deep rich reds, faded yellows and the blues which are associated with the cold, characterising the spent tones of autumn and dusk; for winter and the evening the colours fade and become icy in the chromatic register of the hours and year. René Huyghe has pointed to the relationship between Botticelli and spring mornings, Rubens and the height of the day in summer, Watteau and evenings and the autumn, Rembrandt and night. We do not, alas, know the date of birth for Botticelli or the birth times for the other three painters but at least we know that Rubens' planets are in summer signs and those for Watteau are in autumn signs.

There is, said Elie Faure, 'a great interdependence between nature's elements which unites the movement of the stars with the succession of the seasons and the beat of our hearts.[99] We are only just beginning to understand human beings in this universal way.

Chapter 13 - Pablo Picasso's Stars

According to the civil records in the town of his birth, Malaga, Pablo Picasso was born there on 25 October 1881 at 11.15 p.m. What was the alignment of the stars for this first event in the life of this celebrated painter?

Let's look at his birth chart shown below. The newborn Picasso is in the centre on the plane of the horizon (the line drawn horizontally), above is the visible hemisphere of the sky, and the vertical line represents the plane of the upper meridian. In terms of the zodiac, the point where the planets rise over the horizon is at 5 degrees Leo: this is the Ascendant (AS). Opposite is the Descendant, or where the planets set, at 5 degrees Aquarius. Culmination is at 25 degrees Aries: this is the Midheaven (MC). Opposite is the inferior meridian at the lowest point in the sky (IC).

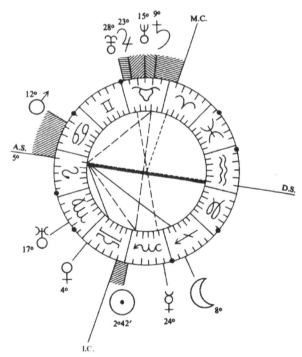

Pablo Picasso's birth chart

Approaching this line at 11.15 pm, local time is the Sun. At that time on 25 October the Sun is on the second degree of Scorpio. Moving on, in the topocentric direction, from this Sun as it approaches midnight we meet Venus at 4 degrees Libra and Uranus at 17 degrees Virgo, both under the horizon. Above the Ascendant appears Mars at 12 degrees Cancer, then a group of planets, Pluto, Jupiter, Neptune and Saturn, at 28, 23, 15, and 9 degrees Taurus respectively approaching culmination. From there we come to the Moon, at 8 degrees Sagittarius, and to Mercury at 24 degrees Scorpio, both under the horizon going towards their midnight.

Between these points in the sky is the criss-cross of aspects, of which the most important are the links between the Ascendant and the Sun, its ruler (Sun-Leo relationship), the Moon, Saturn and Venus, together with the oppositions formed between the two stars in Scorpio and the four others in Taurus.

Among these, three astrological phenomena stand out: the proximity of the Sun to midnight, the proximity of Saturn to culmination and the fact that Mars has just risen. There is also a triangle joining the Leo Ascendant to the Sun in Scorpio which is close to the meridian and at the base of the opposition with Saturn in Taurus.

Let's begin by clearing away the illusions created by poor astrological practice: this group of configurations does not show that Picasso is a painter, nor that he became a multi-millionaire, or that he received exceptional recognition in his genre, or even the simple fact that he lived for ninety years.

As disappointing as this preamble is, highlighting as it does, in his personal case, the limits of astral determinism to the point where you could ask 'So, what's left?', at least it has the merit of making a clean sweep when it comes to the reality and to what is knowable.

Let's leave longevity on one side, since life expectancy is not a factor that is determined at birth: in fact it is only partially linked to the vital potential of the individual, which is the only indicator provided (and which is here undeniably and even exceptionally high). With celebrity, it is just conceivable that we would suspect it or believe it to be possible, because there is a very marked 'vocational' element, a direct catalyst for fame. As for painting, there is nothing to indicate it, especially as, in itself, an aptitude for painting or a 'gift for painting' does not exist in astrology.

There is however, from the very beginning, a crucial psychological situation which puts us on the path leading to this exceptional destiny. Picasso was born under a major solar dominant: the star is on the meridian at the same time as it reigns on the horizon, being ruler of the Ascendant (in its sign, Leo) and forming a square aspect (90 degree) to it. Such a Sun is a primary indicator of the powerful effect the father has in the formation of the personality, especially as this Sun is placed, as midnight approaches, in House IV which deals with the family and its influence. Furthermore, the four planets in House X, which are approaching culmination, making the house especially occupied (four astral positions out of ten), give some importance to this area which affects our situation in life, our career. So, with this concentration on both the solar indicator and House X, we have the conditions for destiny in which the vocation (the overriding state of someone totally dedicated to their central passion, exclusive and sovereign) will be rooted in the paternal model. Having already formulated this interpretation, it is interesting that it can be confirmed: Pablo's father, José Ruiz Blasco, was an art teacher.

It is on the original paternal identification that everything begins and on which the architecture of this individual is structured. From an early age, Pablo showed a gift for drawing and painting which his father encouraged: he will be like his father, better and more than him, dogged by an idea of himself that will never leave him. At sixteen, his first exhibition; at twenty, Paris... a paintbrush in his hand almost every day for an entire Uranian revolution (Uranus goes round the zodiac once in eighty-four years)!

It is not important that the main reason for Picasso becoming a painter was that his father was a draughtsman and he had a great thirst for paternal introjection (the Sun opposite Saturn in Taurus); what counts is what he did with it. Yet already, this identification in itself has a psychological impact because he is deeply engrained with masculine adult values especially those of superiority, grandeur, light and brilliance, perfection and the absolute: to live at the solar level is to identify with our ideal, to fall in love with our own idealised self and to keep climbing in order to reach the summit and excel. Before examining Picasso's Sun more closely, it is tempting to return to the myth that links this star of the daytime to the father and to the eye. Wasn't the eye a complete project for him? The eye of the painter, naturally, but also the fixity of his dark gaze (of Scorpio), of his jet black eyes, sharp and piercing, big owl eyes shining with rapacious intensity, devouring everything, eyes which, according to André Malraux, 'played such a role in his face that, when they were lowered, nearly closed, it no longer looked like him.' So there is the importance of eyes in his pictures, expressing this vital function: to see, to see in order to have a hold over things, to conquer, to possess, the myth, associating the Sun, father, eye, and phallus.[100]

Yet this Sun is in Scorpio (with Mercury, which emphasises the values of the mind), inseparable from a rising Mars which is the ruler of this sign. Therefore we have to take the whole complex into consideration: Sun-Leo-Mars-Scorpio, which make up the keyboard of the dominant features in Picasso's chart, without counting Saturn in Taurus, along with three other planets in this sign, which are culminating and which make a second pole of his personality.

With these two fiery stars in the two strongest signs in the zodiac, we already have a picture of Picasso, with his high-powered animal nature and strong sex drive as the basis of his character, along with his instinctive vitality, his vigorous love of life, intense presence, strong impulse to conquer, his willpower and his character of iron. And behind this Sun-Mars duo, the Moon - as ruler of Mars in Cancer, a Sagittarius Moon linked to the Ascendant and the Midheaven! – comes to play the role of a sounding board for this highly strung temperament, giving him the maximum amplitude by way of fertility, luxuriance, blossoming, colourfulness, breath, freedom.

This astral trio Sun-Mars-Moon (Scorpio-Cancer-Sagittarius) with its links to the Ascendant and the Mid-heaven gives us, symbolically, the complete picture of the man who became this unique sacred monster of painting, who, like a true monarch, placed the entire world under the power of his sorcerer's game for three quarters of a century! Apollinaire was correct in his judgement of this Scorpio-eagle when he wrote: 'Picasso is one of those of whom Michelangelo said that merit the name of eagle because they surpass all the others and soar through the clouds into the sunlight.' In fact, he was the most extraordinary creative force in the history of painting for several centuries. His prodigious vitality resulted in a perpetual outpouring with his inspiration always changing and his creative instinct unconstrained. He belonged to no school, theory or movement and there was no brake on his free spontaneity. He often finished a canvas in a few hours; tirelessly providing for the uninterrupted inner flow of frenetic creativity which never left him throughout his long life. He accumulated a monumental oeuvre without compare! In addition, his work was ceaselessly reborn by the challenge of a great new venture, except for in his advanced old age, when he became banal and maybe starts to ramble with his paintbrush. However, he never stopped, never rested; he also never hesitated or went back: 'I don't seek, I find.' In fact if it is excessive to think of the 'big shot Picasso' painting with a brush that is a phallic substitute, it is no exaggeration to maintain that, with him, there is a direct link between the genitals and the eye, his eye being sexualised,[101] so completely that all his immense creative power is sexual and his entire work is the product of his animal nature, his earthiness, his sexual magnetism.

This interpretation came to be supported by André Malraux in his study of Picasso[102] that provided quotes that were characteristic of the painter.

His ideas about painters, and consequently about himself: 'Painters are likely to be reincarnated as painters. They are a breed. Like cats. More than cats...'

There is a special association, which is repeated: 'painting, death, life'

Also this angry male sentence: 'Nature has to exist, in order to rape it!'

How many times did he say, says Malraux, sometimes joyfully, sometimes angrily, sometimes with surprise, as if talking about a mistress: 'Painting makes me do what it wants...'

And then there is this other expression, which is just as eloquent: 'There are canvases on which one makes children...'

The 'mystery of Picasso' is, to begin with: his creative eroticism, the use of his creative power and sexual magic, a true sorcerer's art, used to carve out a vast empire of pictures.

But just as important is the culmination of Saturn in Taurus, the sign of the zodiac which it shares with three other planets. And as this planet is in opposition to the Sun, it provides a second component, or second pole of the personality, opposite the first which was symbolised by the Sun.

This Saturn-Sun duality near the meridian thus represents a sort of 'Homo duplex', a bipolar personality, a Janus.

Saturn in Taurus has a strong oral component (as with the Freudian oral stage) which basically expresses itself as immense greed and the desire to possess, a rapacious nature. Also as much as the solar pole carries with it the intense joy of existence, equally the Saturnian pole negates this satisfaction in awakening a profound sense of frustration: his Janus, it is the dialectic between the liberating orgasm and an unsatisfied hunger.

Picasso is mostly Saturnian in his own life. We have already mentioned the contrast between the violence of his work (Sun pole) and the parsimonious tranquillity of his life (Saturn pole). We find a dialectic within his Saturnian condition. This taciturn Spaniard, who became a solitary majestic figure behind his legendary popularity, had a sort of taste for poverty which also influenced his art: the sadness or the despair shown in the themes and the figures of his early periods (acrobats, down and outs, Harlequin), like making of his strongest sculptures not in marble or bronze, but with dry bread, outmoded objects, bits and pieces, scrap; he himself lived like an ascetic, drinking only water and dressed like a down and out... but behind this face of Saturn, the symbol of rejection, there is another face of Saturn the bulimic, starving and devouring and this is what is dominant and that he has to throw light on.

It wasn't just because he was hyperactive, headstrong and impulsive that Picasso never stopped painting, to the point of giving the history of painting a new term, or turning out etchings, sculptures and ceramics, it was also because he was secretly driven by a feeling of discontent, something to which we owe the gigantic production of all painters, for him the joy of creating something was short-lived and was always accompanied by a pressing need to remake or start something new. This state, which is similar to the kind of sadness experienced after orgasm, is expressed in his own words: 'When a man knows how to do something, he ceases to be a man when he does not do it.' When a culminating Saturn does not allot its negative meaning of a gift that is unexploited, unrealised ambition or a lack of social responsibility, it leads to social hyper-achievement: a voracious engagement with a career, pushed by a relentless vocation, ferocious ambition.

His own Chronos never stopped devouring him, and he submitted to it as he would to the tyranny of a superego. His craving is not to be satisfied by the personal glory that he monopolised in the world of art, the stardom with all its narcissistic inflation of the self nor on another level by accumulating an astonishing knowledge of art history on a par with that of competent art historian. To be becomes to have and encompasses the objects that he does not know how to throw away, that he does not want to let go, these objects that accumulate around him until he's overloaded with them.

His inventive nature wanted to exploit everything, and his wife, Jacqueline, was prompted to say: 'I cannot leave a piece of string lying around without him making something.' This Saturnian impulse made Picasso a manic collector; he collected a bit of everything: hats, masks, African sculptures, pottery, engravings, lithographs, drawings and pictures.

For half a century, he accumulated innumerable piles of canvases painted by his contemporaries but he mainly collected his own work and was happy to live surrounded by his best pictures, illustrated books and sculptures, so that his home came to resemble a rich international museum!

Opposite this Saturn above, there is life as expressed by the Sun below (in House IV), which represents the private Picasso, his home life, his successive families and the properties in which he enclosed himself: his villa in one hectare of land in Cannes, 'La Californie', with its nine bedrooms and four living rooms; his residence in Mougins which had thirty-two rooms and, especially, his Vauvenargues chateau, at the foot of Mount Sainte-Victoire, with its thousand hectares and its forty bedrooms.

As for the work itself, it is obviously the supreme representation of his projected personality. Expressionist, conceptivist, intimist and sensualist, these are his four modes of expression in their order of importance: fire is predominant, with the grouping Sun-Mars-Leo-Scorpio, then comes earth, with Saturn, and water, with the Moon, air is lacking. In fact, engaging with the real world was the last of Picasso's concerns: even the pictorial world that he creates has no connection to reality, its subjects obliged to surrender completely to his artistic demands and so removed from nature as to be no more than an astonishing linear and chromatic counterpoint (he does not have to paint landscapes). The aquatic element is especially noticeable in the work of his Blue and Pink Periods. In fact, fire and earth are the sovereign rulers, in the type of bipolarity symbolised by the Sun-Saturn opposition. Sometimes he leant towards the solar pole, the expressionist-conceptivist, nourishing a rigorously elaborated passion, sometimes the Saturnian pole took priority and he became (less often) the conceptivist-expressionist creating artistic violently expressed constructs.

The painter Bernard Di Sciullo gave a wonderful reading of Picasso's duality, of the Sun-Saturn opposition which cuts his sky in two:

> ...the planet which is culminating in his sky, Saturn. This is well known as a symbol of tradition, of archaeology, of treasures from the past, the immense superimposed strata, deposited by our memory of old civilisations, our libraries, our archives, our museums, our cellars, etc. When Saturn is in Taurus the meanings of this earthy symbol are reinforced; greed, a tendency to hoard, jealous appropriation, stubbornness, faithfulness, the putting down of roots. Saturn is followed by some other heavy planets which lend yet more weight to the already heavy sign of Taurus. There is a huge amount of learning to move, lift and shift. But this is where we get the intervention of an essential, fundamental contradiction: the opposition of the Sun in Scorpio, as it approaches midnight, changes everything. We know that he took 'the bull by the horns' and that he directly attacked the grand masters from the past with his series of deliberate plagiarisms. He began to simply copy some celebrated works whose titles were already genres; Manet's *Déjeuner sur L'herbe*, *Las Meninas* by Velázquez, the *Women of Algiers* by Delacroix, etc. But he worked on them until they were no longer Manet, Velázquez or Delacroix but became Picasso.[103]

This was an original way of expressing his two opposing natures at the same time. Usually Picasso leaves them to speak alternately, first one and then the other, always watched by its opposite number, which resulted in an about face and constant abrupt changes of style. This became a dialogue between the traditional and the experimental which punctuated all his work, the oscillation between classicism of a pure mental construction which would crop up from time to time and a kind of baroquism, fiery poem of great dramatic intensity taken to the point of disintegration, the most infuriating and most explosive of artistic structures.

His principal Saturnian period is surely around 1910 with the Cubist revolution, of which he was the father (Sun), with Braque being 'his wife'. Cubism was a time of polyhedral crystallisations, a severe architecture of the elementary and monochromatic, elaborated combinations of planes, angles, curves, crystals… we couldn't find a purer astral signature! There was another Saturnian period in the 1920s, when he led (Sun) a movement interested in antiquity, the neoclassical period from past Mediterranean civilisations. Among the principal solar periods are the Surrealist period, when he gave a free reign to his museum of an imagination, the period of his monsters, then that of the Spanish Civil War and the world war. Here in contrast Picasso abandoned himself to wild lyricism, to the bravery of his fiery nature, speaking up, thundering, and covering current affairs with the shocking energy of his own violence.

In fact, the two halves of his being supported each other and his pictorial personality was unified by the coming together of the objectivity of classicism (Saturnian) and baroque self-expression (solar): by reviving antiquity, ancient and primitive art, from prehistory to the fetishes of Africa and Oceania, getting hold of a Saturnian past that goes back to the Stone Age, finding the treasure trove of myths and the age-old symbols to which he applied all his freedom of expression, his work went from the tragic to Rabelaisian laughter via derision, the grotesque and the comical.

If now one leans towards the solar pole, one realises that the lyricism of fire in Picasso has the nature of the anal-sadistic stage which corresponds so well to Scorpio-Mars (made dynamic by the Sun): it is at base essentially violent, aggressive and destructive, the dark power of death.

Because of the dynamic of these tendencies, the basis of his character is a fierce individualism based on negation and rebellion: if the feeling of living out his Saturnian pole goes from doubt to a melancholic dissatisfaction; that of his solar pole has the nature of a mutiny. His work is first and foremost a negation: it says no and offends common sense, in rejecting familiar things, in refusing to belong to anything except the ego of the creator.

It has been said that he was born in order for painting to die. When scandalised visitors protested in front of Cubist canvases, Picasso responded with: 'A picture used to be a sum of additions; with me it is the sum of the destructions.' Besides, Cubism was a way of going back to principles, to the vital minimum, of starting again from nothing. But beneath the new terminology, the new syntax invented by this genial virtuoso, can be seen 'a devilish desire to only interest himself in creation in order to destroy it, in its present form, and remake it, as it could be conceived, in the interests of artistic research.'[104] There was a 'desire to create so savage that it cut the creation off short,'[105] from whence the violent and tragic stamp of his work, which could be especially cruel, from his expressionism to his angular graphic writing that was almost sharp, like a claw, even to the point of curving like a fang or a scorpion's sting. Under his savage brush reality was horribly tortured and put through the machinery of distortion, degradation and monstrous annihilation. The human face itself – an object of moral and aesthetic respect – was steeped in these insulting and horrible metamorphoses, in forms that were injured, dislocated, with vehement and terrifying expressions: these 'faces' with noses seen from two sides or two noses with the eyes on top of each other... this aesthetic of ugliness produces monsters, even if, ultimately, great is the artist and aristocratic is his hermetic art.

When familiar with the symbolism of the sign of Scorpio, it is impossible not to see him by way of the very particular special features of this zodiacal type. The basic psychology of Scorpio is represented by the union of Eros and Thanatos. However with our painter (of whom Malraux said that he loved bats and collected scorpions and owls), in the utmost depths of his being and his work, sex and death are intertwined. We saw him being for death, under all its aspects and nuances – also we must add that it is not sure that the successive metamorphoses of this sorcerer, while faithful to his rebellion, are not ways of dying in order to be reborn[106], - but what about sex? Centaurs, fauns and minotaurs, even the bulls facing the matadors with their skull and crossbones, show the artist's taste for representing himself in his work using the most characteristic attributes of Dionysian animalism: the sad and sorry young Harlequin from the Saturnian pole of the Blue Period is answered by the obscene old satyr pole from the Sun in Scorpio at the end. Except for *Guernica*, where the tragic devastation caused by a military atrocity was a pretext for his fiery temperament to launch a sublime cry of anger and horror, and some other, very few, opportunities, Picasso's work shows that, despite the thousands of canvases, he is always painting himself: 'I want to see my branches grow. That is why I started to paint trees; but I never paint after nature. My trees are me.'

An ego that was in truth very dark, confounded by questions, inhabited by the heaviness of an impenetrable mystery, exhausting itself with vain questions: 'With the pictures, one never knows how that lives or how that dies'; 'Like you, I think that all is unknown, is hostile'… Behind the unforgettable celebration and the magnificent depictions was an egocentricity that was condemned by his own nihilism, the Sun neutralised by Saturn.

This is what his chart has to say about Picasso. At the beginning of our analysis we had to give up the idea that it could show that he was a painter, an internationally famous star, a wealthy seigneur or almost a centenarian, but surely we made up for it along the way? Haven't we, in a more subtle and profound way, fixed and ordered what is known about him, configured his elements into related groups and given a true picture of the person living his destiny?

Chapter 14 A Sign of the Times

It is foreseeable that astrology will be gradually reinstated in balance with the gradual way it was dismissed. When referring to its occultation during the 17th century, Pierre Larousse[107] just said, 'it is gradually vanishing like a chimera in front of the growing light of scientific certainty'. Pierre Thuillier pointed out that it was not the victim of a qualified epistemological condemnation but just a 'simple change in fashion', and he adds that 'the reason that astrology became marginalised is not because it is false, but rather because most of the historic players had decided to commit themselves elsewhere and had no special need for it.[108] Certainly, at that time, it was more exciting to look at Earth's satellite through the lens of the newly created refracting telescope than to speculate on lunar aspects.

A change in fashion; more profoundly, we could say that there are collective moods that influence the human mind and which at this time pushed it towards a practical, simplistic rationale. This led Thuillier to ask the question: 'Why did western society no longer feel the need to consult astrologers from the 17th century onwards? This fall in demand needs to be explained.'

Helpful to us now, the pendulum of the collective unconscious has received a push in the opposite direction and the question is again on the agenda. Now, the 'return' of astrology, with the renaissance of its anthropo-cosmological ideas, shows that the public needs to ask some very important questions, even if, when the answers are found, the result is an epistemological upheaval and the generation of a completely new kind of knowledge.

> Astrology is not residual folklore that will soon disappear in a modern society. Although marginalised in the history of western culture, it did not remain impervious to that history, unchanged since its origins. Astrology has developed in a distinctly modern way.[109]

Having vanished like a chimera when the outer world was illuminated by enlightened minds, the reason for its return is that our inner world is still in the dark and needs some light of its own. It is as though, from being a kind of generic scientific knowledge that applied to all things natural, a mutation has caused it to become individualised, allowing us access to a person's individuality, a lighted pathway in the quest for the self where the experiences of the subjective being are to be found lit by the world, a step which at the same time restores mankind to its universal dimension.

We are no longer in a time when its prodigious conception of the unity of the world and all that converges into one is thought shocking and offensive. We now accept that mankind is made of the same space-time material as the universe and every sphere of knowledge makes increasing use of the idea of synthesis that treats the object as part of the universe. The increasing acceptance of its founding principle means that we have to take into account the now incontrovertible statistical assessment, and all that remains is the debate about its existential nature, which is naturally always open to criticism.

We are in the grip of popular astrology which is obsessed by zodiacal decans of birth, still giving anodyne horoscopic announcements for that day's health, business and romances that thousands of people read at the same time and which would concern millions! This is a low point in public delusion.

We know that we are now far from what André Breton[110] called 'the great lady' of tradition and of whom he said 'that today – at least for the vulgar – she has been replaced by a prostitute'. How are we to understand the blot of this prostitute's reign and also the fact that, more widely, under its divers and many aspects, astrology has developed considerably over half a century? The explanation for this renewal is the relationship between the symbolism used by astrology and the value system of the contemporary world.

In our modern society, people live increasingly in an intellectual space governed by the daily concerns of the mind: reason, logic, knowledge, concepts, quantitative values and material reality, among others, hold sway at the heart of the human being who has become man-object, in a social cultural context where notions of usefulness, productivity and functionality dominate. In this world technology can triumph and the technocracy is overwhelming. Aligned with this is the scientific world with its icy objectivity, hopelessly dehumanising and offering no better image than a man-Harlequin divided by specialisation, lost in the extragalactic abyss of a universe that has become incomprehensible, alienating and devoid of meaning which arouses a widespread underlying feeling that our society, and even our civilisation, is sick, noxious, and already severely affected by pollution and the nuisances caused by mankind.

This 'one-dimensional' (Marcuse), contemporary human being, unbalanced, who has become a functional object, depersonalised, robotised, with needs and personal desires which have substituted the need for a social life, contains within himself a whole repressive system which works against the imaginary, the primitive, the sensitive, the inner nature, that is to say against a mankind as subject, a system that serves a collective superego erected by the conscious like a barrier against life.

Under the anxiety-making pressure of this repressive system, people defend themselves by turning their backs on the values established by this society and remaking their natural state as if returning to a lost golden age. This regression towards interior sources consists in making a return to the other world, that of the magical values which arise from the unconscious.

It is in making such a return, which is quasi self-therapeutic, that people today find and recover, by way of the sensitive and thoughtful system which is astrology, the state of belief of a popular astrology that seeks to satisfy the need to feel connected to the world we live in.

In an astrological representation, the individual IS and he or she participates in the WHOLE. Such is our human condition at the level of this unconscious that we now know to be at the origin of the animation of the astrological cosmos. Not only is the human person valued qualitatively as an individual unit, but they are at the centre with everything arranged around them: the native, don't forget, is at the centre of their birth chart, coextensive with the whole celestial representation.

This brings us back to the principle theme of mythology, the *imago mundi* and the *axis mundi*. In this astrological dimension, the individual feels, and is, re-centred and restored, given a specific and original individuality and incorporated as a member of mankind. This is a real recovery of the nocturnal values of the soul (this soul that is sick due to the distortions and simplifications of analysis, and which emigrates there where there is no unity) which operates by satisfying this primitive need to be centred, as well as bringing back a global and overall vision of the person and the world. Thus we have the renaissance of mankind as subject (or, more preferably, of the interior being, even the psychic reality of Freud), as a reaction to the system which leads to the person being rejected.

Mankind does not live for bread and liberty alone: we only have our health and equilibrium on condition that our personal universe, which is completely interior and subjective, is realised, any hindrance resulting in more or less serious psychological problems. And it is the person as subject who looks to astrology because it is to them that it reveals itself, because in it or through it they see themselves and take part in the development of their own life story. Their need is great, and it is not difficult to explain the success of modern psychology which insists on the existence of human nature, the foundation of the person, and of the necessity of being truly oneself, discovering one's own system of values, living an interior experience that is whole, in order to become authentic and fully accept ourselves.

At the end of the day, if one analyses the obvious symptoms of malaise of the being in the world that

represents this astrological renaissance, one discovers that
this enthusiasm expresses an instinctive protestation against
a scientism which only accepts head thinking in the human
to the detriment of vital indispensable functions, reinstated
reaction vis- à -vis a schizoid soul destroying rationalism,
which dehumanises knowledge and separates the human
being from the universe as from himself; condemning him to
a spiritual decline. I'm not afraid to say that this unfortunate
trend in popular astrology expresses the revenge of a deep
psychic life which is too repressed and which has burst the
dyke of a society which happiness has forsaken, and which,
distinctly, lacks the values of the soul. From this essential
psychological angle, one can see how it is a mistake to take
astrology for something that is still hanging around, old
fashioned, obsolete or from another era. In the crisis of
questioning which has shaken the world for some time it is,
on the contrary, on the side of revolutionary truth. It is
heading towards the liberation of the soul.

Equally we cannot go on with this silly popular
astrology, or leave serious astrology in the hands of naive
amateurs, because, under the pressure applied by the
current repressive intellectual system, the Art of Urania is
excluded from the field of reasonable and legitimate
knowledge, and cast off into the darkness of occultism,
magic and the macabre. It is a suppressed product which
society only tolerates in the framework of dreams, games,
poetry or the imagination. Nevertheless, the more repressive
the system, the more one-dimensional mankind encourages
people to be childish.

Yet, it is not only the imagination or the inner being
that can be childish or unhealthy: it is also true of the
repressed. While astrology is in this state it is inevitable that
archaic and childish elements will flower in its fields, but we
must not confuse the seed with the land it is on.

I have been saying for a long time that we must get
astrology out of its ghetto. That is the only way to silence the
chattering of the ignorant, the stupid, the phoneys and the
charlatans, and to reduce the unhealthy inflation inflicted on

it by popular use, because falsely to declare that astrology is wrong, in the way that those who would like to see it repressed trot out periodically, can only make the results of that repression worse. Powerless and **futile** in their intention to destroy it definitively, these critics block its evolution towards maturity and high achievement, making themselves unwilling accomplices in its inferior, errant and fraudulent expression; in this way, this 'anti-astrology' is just a parasite of the mind. Besides, the truth will not be found by trickery, fooling about or scorn.

The only solution is to take charge of it, with the same means that are at the disposal of official fields of knowledge, in order to sort out what is true and what is false; retain what merits retaining and reject the rest. What we should think of it no longer being left to the foolishness of the public, but given to some relevant body which contributes by giving public information.

Then, and only then, will astrology be able to achieve its mission: to enlighten human beings about themselves, to help them to improve in accordance with the eternal rules, which are themselves active , so that the structures they have in common with nature can blossom. Our mission to serve human happiness allows us to allude with feeling, as Kant did, to 'The starry sky above me and the moral law within me', reuniting them like the two halves of a whole.

.

Bibliography

Martine BARBAULT *Méthode d'interprétation astrologique* (Methods of Astrological Interpretation), Bussière, 1997.

Bernard BLANCHET *L'Homme astrologique* (The Astrological Man), Guy Trédaniel 1994.

Ferdinand DAVID *Les Planètes* (The Planets), Bussière, 1996.

Roseline D'ORMESSON *Vos premiers pas dans le cosmos* (Your First Steps in the Cosmos) Éditions traditionnelles, 2000.

Suzel FUZEAU-BRAESCH *Pour l'astrologie* (In Favour of Astrology), Albin Michel, 1996.

Michel GAUQUELIN *La Vérité sur l'astrologie* (The Truth about Astrology), Le Rocher, 1985.

Robert and Francine GOUIRAN *L'Astrologie des trajectoires de vie* (The Astrology of Life Trajectories), Le Rocher, 1998.

Yves HAUMONT *La Langue astrologique* (Astrological Language), Bussière, 1988.

Roger Benoît JOURLIN *Déterminisme universel et liberté humaine* (Universal Determinism and Human Liberty), Dervy, 2005.

Wilhelm KNAPPICH *Histoire de l'astrologie* (A History of Astrology), Vernal-Philippe Lebaud, 1986.

Emmanuel LE BRET *Uranus et l'éveil spirituel* (Uranus and the Spiritual Awakening), Dervy, 1999.

Yves LENOBLE *Initiation à la pratique des cycles planétaires* (Introduction to the Practice of Planetary Cycles), ARRC, 1994.

Solange DE MAILLY NESLE *Le Thème astral* (The Astral Chart), Nathan, 1989.

PTOLEMY *Le Livre unique de l'astrologie* (The Unique Book of Astrology), translated by Pascal Charvet, Nil Éditions, 2000.

Dane RUDHYAR, *Les Aspects astrologiques* ,Le Rocher, 1985 (*Astrological Aspects* Aurora Press1980)

Alexander RUPERTI and Marief CAVAIGNAC, *La Géométrie du ciel* (The Geometry of the Sky], Le Rocher, 1985.

Pierre SAINTYVES *L'Astrologie populaire* (Popular Astrology], Le Rocher, 1990.

Daniel VERNEY *L'Astrologie et la Science future du psychisme* (Astrology and the Future Science of the Psyche], Le Rocher, 1988.

François VILLÉE *Astrologie des Profondeurs ou des motivations* (Astrology of the Depths], Éditions traditionnelles, 1986.

Notes

Chapter 1 The Art of Urania

[1] French days of the week are based on Roman names for planets, whereas the names for the English days come from the corresponding Norse gods.

[2] For example, the original document pointed out that Petiot's fate would have been shaped by one or several deaths, and that 'these would have played an important role in his lifetime' which (all the same...) should have been mentioned in the conclusions of the enquiry.

[3] From the preface of *La Science devant l'étrange* (Science Facing the Unusual)

Chapter 2 Very Early Sources

[4] Cf. René Berthelot, *La pensée de l'Asie et l'Astrobiologie* (Asian Thought and Astrobiology), Payot, 1972

[5] Cf. M. David, *Les Dieux et le Destin en Babylon* (The Gods and Destiny in Babylon), PUF 1949

Chapter 3 Grandeur, Decadence and Renaissance

[6] *Ciel astral* (The Astral Sky), number 1, 1950

[7] *Lettres* (Letters), t. II, letter number 67; Baillet, t. I, p. 234

[8] *Exposition du système du monde* (Expounding of the System of the World), second edition, year 7 (1798-1799)

[9] A special mention has to be made of Great Britain which did not have the same interruption to astrology as the continent. Even in the Victorian age there was a resurgence illustrated by Raphaël, Zadkiel, Simmonite, Pearce, followed by Alan Leo, Sepharial...Then in the last quarter of the century there was a spiritual wave of oriental esotericism led by Helena Blavatsky. Theosophically inspired astrology conquered the United States (Max Heindel, Alice Bailey) and brought Dane Rudhyar to prominence with humanist astrology. Even so this noble contribution would have been better served by adopting the classical interpretive technique highly recommended since Jean-Baptiste Morin, the art to be based on mastery of the material used; something western karmic astrology tends to lose sight of.

Chapter 4 The Scholarly Tradition

[10] Some meaning will be lost if Ptolemy is translated via the French to English. So, for all extracts from the *Tetrabiblos* we are using English translations by or recommended by Dr Dorian Greenbaum that are directly from the original; our thanks to her for this kind help and permission.

[11] Ibid

[12] Ibid

[13] Ibid

[14] Ibid

[15] Ibid

[16] The Latin word signifying 'individual' can only be translated into Greek by the word 'atom'; both mean indivisibility, totality, unity.

[17] See note 10

[18] *L'Astrologue* (The Astrologer), number 19

[19] Morin de Villefranche, *La Théorie des déterminations astrologiques* (Theory of Astronomical Determinations), translated by Henri Selva, Bodin, 1902, re-published by Éditions traditionnelles.

[20] As we will see in the case of Picasso' birthchart.

[21] First finding what it means, astrologers make their own star studded robes from the biddable material of astrology; it is only after long experimentation that they come to distinguish it from themselves and accept its own reality.

[22] L'Influence astrale (The Astral Influence), Chacornac, January 1913.

[23] K. E. Krafft, *Traité d'Astro-biologie* (Treatise of Astro Biology), Legrand, 1939. .

[24] *Langage astral* (Astral Language), Chacornac, 1921.

[25] *L'Astrologue* (The Astrologer), number 9, 1970

Chapter 5 The Astrological Sky

[26] P. Saintyves (a.k.a. Émile Nourry), *L'Astrologie populaire* (Popular Astrology), 1937; Le Rocher.

[27] Ibid.

[28] Scientism (n.), scientistic (adj.): a fundamentalist linear

mechanical view of scientific reality.

[29] The zodiac has been the object of repeated criticism on the part of astronomers, linked to the movement of the precession of the equinoxes, which shifts the signs and constellations, relative to each other, by one degree every seventy-two years. At the time of Ptolemy the sign and the constellation of the same name were aligned. Today, everything is out of place due to the extent of the movement: for example, the constellation of Cancer is now in the sign of Leo! Thus, everything should be questioned, assuming that the constellations - which are no more at the same place – have any influence. This criticism calls for several replies. First of all, since Ptolemy, no confusion has ever existed by astrologers between the sidereal zodiac of constellations and the tropical zodiac related to the rhythm of the seasons, which is the one they always referred to.

Next, Ptolemy himself stated that the names attributed to the signs came not from the constellations themselves but from their own condition: the seventh, Libra, because 'the space given to day and night is equal everywhere on Earth' at the autumn equinox; the Crayfish (Cancer) fourth sign, 'because the Sun, entering this sign, turns back, bending its course towards a reverse latitude (...) the Crayfish (Cancer), "causing" the summer (...)the general virtue of the signs being in harmony with their time'. In fact, it is clear that the zodiacal months, the first calendar connecting the sky with the Earth, take their names and their significations from the natural phenomena of the seasons and not from the constellations whose starry assemblages look nothing like their zodiacal designations.

Finally, the processional shifts have always been calculated by astronomer/astrologers (by Tycho Brahe for the year 1630 for example), and whenever interpreters have dealt with the stars and the constellations they have taken it into account. That astronomers continue to rehash this processional nonsense is proof of complete ignorance of the subject that they purport to criticise.

[30] Uniqueness does not mean exclusivity. So when in 1967 France celebrated its fifty millionth citizen, a child was being born every 37 seconds, and 2,300 were born in a day.

[31] François Jacob, *La Logique du vivant* (The Logic of the Living), Gallimard, 1970

[32] Ibid.

[33] Some biological clock specialists who try to claim that these

have nothing to do with astrology, call this tasty caprice: 'Give me your watch and I'll give you the time.'

[34] Luigi Gedda and Gianni Brenci, *Chronogénétique* (Chronogenetics), Hermann, 1975.

[35] *L'homme et le cosmos* (Man and the cosmos), Planète, number 6.

[36] Bernard d'Espagnat, *À la recherche du réel* (In Search of the Real), Gauthier-Villars, 1980.

Chapter 6 The Statistical Assessment

[37] Paul Couderc, *L'astrologie* (Astrology), « Que sais-je ?», PUF 1951.

[38] *L'Astrologue* (The Astrologer), Number 15, 197.

[39] *Les Hommes et les Astres* (Men and Stars), Denoël, 1960

[40] Others closed their eyes. Jean-Claude Pecker, astrophysicist of the College de France said, with a straight face, that these statistics 'are biased and have no value' (*Bulletin de la Société astronomique de France* (Bulletin of the Astronomical Society of France), July/August 1974).

[41] Book 4, chapter 4, 'The Quality of Employment' Vol 40 Page 97.

[42] Book 4, chapter 3, 'The Fortune of Rank'

[43] Michel and Françoise Gauquelin, *Confirmation de l'effet planétaire en hérédité* (Confirmation of the Planetary Effect in Heredity), Laboratory for the study of the relationship between cosmic and psycho-physiological rhythms, 1977. The number 171,695 is that of the verified positions for the five stars observed: Moon, Venus, Mars, Jupiter and Saturn.

[44] Paul Choisnard, *L'Influence astrale et les Probabilités* (Astral Influence and probabilities), Alcan, 1924.

[45] Michel Gauquelin, *Le Dossier des influences cosmiques* (The Cosmic Influences File), J'ai lu, 1970.

[46] Paul Flambart, *L'Astrologie et la Logique* (Astrology and Logic), Chacornac, 1922.

[47] Ibid

[48] Plotinus, *Ennead*, Les Belles Lettres, 1972

[49] Paracelsus, *La Grande Astronomie ou la philosophie des vrais sages* (Great Astronomy or the Philosophy of the Wise), Philosophia Sagax, 2000.

[50] Michel Gauquelin, *Le Dossier des influences cosmiques* (The Cosmic Influences File), J'ai lu, 1970.

[51] Ibid

[52] See each of the twelve books in our collection *Le Zodiaque* (The Zodiac), Éditions du Seuil.

[53] Die Akte Astrologie, Goldmann Verlag, 1997 ; The Astrology File, Orion, 1998, *Le Dossier astrologie*, Michel Lafon, 2000.

[54] *Les Cahiers du RAMS* Number 8 (March 2000).

[55] Georges Charpak said in speaking of astrology that it's 'a fairy tale that doesn't require any scientific analysis.' (Suzel Fuzeau-Braesch *Pour l'Astrologie* (In Favour of Astrology) Albin Michel, 1996).

[56] On this subject, the reader can consult our site *'Astralités de Napoléon'* (Napolean's Chart), as well as *Les fondateurs de l'astronomie moderne* (The Founders of Modern Astronomy) on http://www.Andrébarbault.com/.

[57] *L'Histoire* (History), Number 55, April 1983.

Chapter 7 Astrological Forecasting; the Facts

[58] Club de l'OBS, Notebook number 3, 1971.

[59] *L'existentialisme est un humanisme* (Existentialism and humanism), Nagel, 1968.

[60] 'In his review *L'Avenir du monde* (The Future of the World) of October 1938, eighteen months prior, Armand Barbault, using Hitler's birth chart, highlighted the following: 'The most critical time will be between the 9 and the 11 of April 1940'

[61] Darlan was representing the French Vichy government.

[62] 'All the Japanese armies independently surrendered in the days that followed. There was only sporadic fighting in small isolated groups.' (J B Duroselle *Histoire diplomatique de 1919 à nos jours* (Diplomatic History from 1919 to the Present Day) Dalloz 1962).

[63] *Les Astres et l'Histoire* (The Stars and History), Jean-Jacques Pauvert Editions, 1967.

[64] FLN; the initials for the Front de Liberation Nationale (National Liberation Front), who fought for and won the independence of Algeria.

[65] CNRA National Council of Algerian Revolution.

[66] OAS (*Organisation armée secrete*), (Secret Army Organisation), a clandestine group fighting for Algeria to remain French.

[67] The review *L'Astrologue* was founded by André Barbault in 1968. He has been the editor for 40 years and one of its most prolific authors. *L'Astrologue* is still being published.

[68] Payot, 1973.

[69] André Barbault, *L'Astrologie* (Astrology), Pierre Horay, 1978.

[70] Bernard Grasset editions 1955

[71] Published by Payot in 1973

[72] Faya 1979 Republished by Éditions du Rocher in 2004 under the title *Introduction à l'astrologie mondiale* (Introduction to Mundane Astrology).

[73] For verification, the reader can refer to my three predictive books: *La Crise mondiale de 1965* (World Crisis in 1965), Albin Michel, 1963, *L'Avenir du monde selon l'astrologie* (The Future of the World according to Astrology), Éditions du Félin, 1993, and *Prévisions astrologiques pour le nouveau millénaire* (Astrological Forecasts for the New Millennium), Dangles, 1998, as well as my irregular contributions to the review *L'astrologue* (The Astrologer)

Chapter 8 The Psychoanalytical Key

[74] Introduction to *Analogies de la dialectique Uranus-Neptune* (Analogies of the Uranus-Neptune Dialectic) by Jean Carteret and André Barbault, published by Centre international d'astrologie, Éditions Traditionnelles, 1950.

[75] by Introduction to *Typologie astrologique: Jupiter et Saturne* (Astrological typology: Jupiter and Saturn), 1951

[76] *La logique du vivant* (The Logic of Living), François Jacob, Gallimard, 1970.

[77] *Traité d'astrologie sphérique et judiciaire* (Treatise of Spherical and Judicial Astrology), Vigot Frères, 1897.

[78] In French, and in several other languages as well, there is a common etymology between the words 'astre' (celestial body) and 'être' (to be) ; the three consonants 'str' are present in the first one and in the root of the second.

[79] Fayard, 1947.

[80] Carl Gustav Jung, *Les Racines de la conscience* (The Roots of Consciousness), Buchet-Chastel, 1971

[81] One of the leading figures in psychoanalysis, Doctor René Allendy, advised this route, which was first explored by Jean Carteret, Roger Knabe and myself, at the end of the last war in France. But C.G. Jung who, with Ferenczi, was interested in astrology in the psychoanalytical milieu , saw the same analogies, and this inspired Dane Rudhyar in the United States.

[82] The spirit of this astral language has been explained in *De la psychanalyse à l'astrologie* (From Psychoanalysis to Astrology), Seuil editions, 1961, which provides a basic terminology for astrological interpretation.

[83] *À la recherche du réel; le regard d'un physicien* (The Search for What is Real; from a Physicists Perspective) Dunod, 1981.

[84] Hubert Reeves.

[85] *L'Astrologue* (The Astrologer) dedicated the issue number 52 to Kepler, in 1980.

[86] The scholarly thesis on Kepler written by Gérard Simon, a professor at the University of Lille, *Kepler astronome astrologue* (Kepler the Astronomer and Astrologer) (Gallimard, 1979), came to the conclusion that it wasn't in spite of the spiritual universe which supported him that Kepler became an astrologer but thanks to it that Kepler the astronomer was able to develop the talent that made him great.

Chapter 9 Determinism and Free Will

[87] 'The stars incline, they do not compel.'

[88] An agonizing dilemma is a term used in French literature, involving the notion of an impossible choice between two equally important values.

[89] Carl Gustav Jung, *Psychologie et religion* (Psychology and Religion), Buchet-Chastel, 1972.

[90] Research will have to be carried out in the systematic manner not only at the level of identical and non-identical twins, where many scholars have already discovered some parallel rhythms with regard to biological clocks, but also and above all with 'twins according to the stars', that is to say individuals with different parents who were born at the same time, and even not far from one another. One often observes parallels and we need to know whether they are due to chance or not. For example, looking at the politics of the last century one sees that the birth of Hitler was

separated by a week from those of Salazar, Prime Minister of Portugal, and Flandin, one of the ministers in the Vichy Regime, and by one day from that of Manuel Prado, President of the Republic of Peru. There is one day's difference between the birth of the American President Coolidge and that of the French president Édouard Herriot. Two ministers of the Third Reich, Goering and Rosenberg, were born on the same day and died on the same day. In the same era, two of Pétain's ministers at Vichy were born on the same day: Paul Marion and Pierre Pucheu. Konrad Adenauer and Wilhelm Pieck, both holding the highest office of state in their countries but on different sides of the Iron Curtain, were born two days apart. President Nixon and the Czechoslovakian Gustav Husak were born one day apart... Should this just be put in the museum of curiosities?

[91] Carl Gustav Jung, *Dialectique du moi et de l'inconscient* (Dialectic of Self and the Unconscious), Gallimard, 1964.

[92] 'All actors peak when they are asked to portray a person who resembles them like a brother' (Frank Capra)

Chapter 11 The Four Elements in Painting

[93] Nothing stops us looking at other combinations to establish the relationship between the stars and mankind. New 'modern' ways have been tried, but they don't have the enduring nature of the initial correlation. The original material is sufficient in itself, but new findings can only enrich the interpretation.

[94] If modern medicine disregards human temperament, it is because it is more interested in the illness than in the person who is ill. Because these temperaments exist and they are important as we will see later, when we come to personal medicine!

[95] Gaston Bachelard, *L'Eau et les Rêves*, (Water and Dreams), José Corti, 1942.

[96] Victor Hugo, *Les Quatre Vents de l'Esprit* (The Four Winds of Spirit).

[97] Gaston Bachelard, *L'Air et les Songes* (Air and Dreams) José Corti, 1943.

Chapter 12 The Four Approaches to Painting

[98] CEPL Library 1974

[99] L'Esprit des formes, Jean-Jacques Pauvert, 1964.

Chapter 13 Pablo Picasso's Stars

[100] 'In dreams, myths, etc., the image of the Sun generally symbolises the eye, the father or the phallus' (Ernest Jones, *Traité théorique et pratique de psychanalyse* (Treatise on the Theory and Practice of Psychoanalysis), Payot, 1925).

[101] His case is close to but different from that of the jupiterian sensualist Renoir who proclaimed bluntly that he made 'love with his paint brush', his fleshy paintings in warm tones said enough about his craving for the female body. The energy of his Jupiter is horizontal while his Sun's energy is vertical: with Picasso, it is not a simple diversion, but pure sublimation which makes Eros into a power, a power which is liberated by the creative act.

[102] André Malraux, *La Tête d'obsidienne* (The Obsidian Head) Gallimard, 1974.

[103] *L'Astrologue* (The Astrologer), Number 23 1973.

[104] René Huyghe, L'Art et l' Âme,Flammarion, 1960

[105] André Maraux, *La Tête d'Obsidienne*, Gallimard 1974

[106] As in his private life with his successive partnerships, at sixty-two he met a woman of twenty who married him and gave him two children, and he didn't stop there... But I deliberately left his private life out of this study, just as I left out an analysis of the way his life evolved chronologically.

Chapter 14 A Sign of the Times

[107] Pierre Larousse is a 19th century publisher well known for his French dictionary that is still very famous today

[108] *Le temps des astrologues* (The time of astrologers), L'Histoire, number 55, April 1983.

[109] Edgar Morin, *Le Retour des astrologues* (The Return of Astrologers), Le Nouvel Observateur, 1971.

[110] André Breton was the leader of the Surrealist Movement

Lightning Source UK Ltd.
Milton Keynes UK
UKOW06f1247010515

250746UK00001B/11/P